BONDAGERS

BONDAGERS

The History of Women Farmworkers in Northumberland and South-East Scotland

Dinah Iredale

First published 2008

Published in the United Kingdom by:

Glendale Local History Society

PO Box 100

Wooler

Northumberland

NE66 9BA

Printed and bound in the United Kingdom by

Martins the Printers Ltd

Sea View Works, Spittal

Berwick-upon-Tweed

TD15 1RS

ISBN 0-955-91320-9

To my husband Alec for his support, encouragement and interest in this book, and for his patience when neglected and deserted because of The Bondagers.

CONTENTS

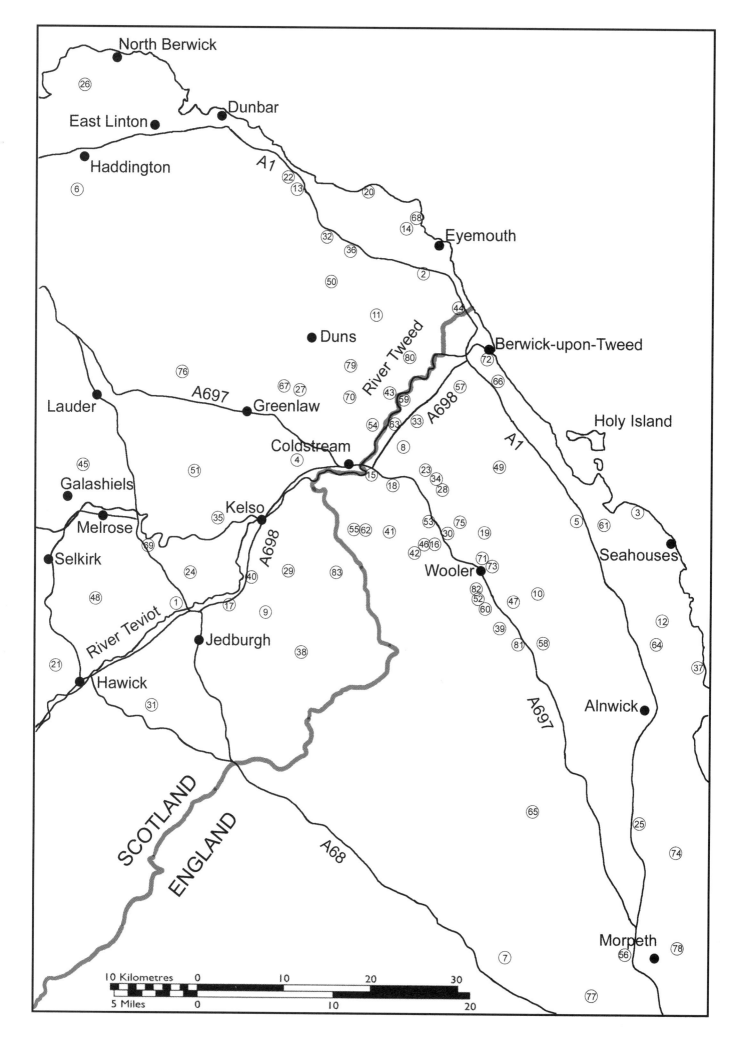

Map of Northumberland and South-East Scotland Showing Principal Towns and Roads and a Selection of Places Mentioned in the Text

Key to Locations Numbered on Map			
1	Ancrum	43	Ladykirk
2	Ayton	44	Lamberton
3	Bamburgh	45	Langshaw
4	Bartlehill	46	Lanton
5	Belford	47	Lilburn Grange
6	Bolton	48	Lilliesleaf
7	Cambo	49	Lowick
8	Castle Heaton	50	Marygold
9	Cessford	51	Mellerstain
10	Chillingham Castle	52	Middleton Hall
11	Chirnside	53	Milfield
12	Christon Bank	54	Milne Graden West
13	Cockburnspath	55	Mindrum
14	Coldingham	56	Mitford
15	Cornhill	57	Murton
16	Coupland Castle	58	New Bewick
17	Crailinghall	59	Norham
18	Crookham Westfield	60	North Middleton
19	Doddington	61	Outchester
20	Dowlaw	62	Pawston
21	Drinkstone	63	Riffington
22	Dunglass	64	Rock
23	Etal	65	Rothbury
24	Fairnington	66	Scremerston
25	Felton	67	Sisterpath
26	Fenton Barns	68	St Abbs
27	Fogorig	69	St Boswells
28	Ford	70	Swinton
29	Frogden	71	Turvelaws
30	Galewood	72	Tweedmouth
31	Gatehousecote	73	Way-to-Wooler
32	Grantshouse	74	West Chevington
33	Grindon	75	West Fenton
34	Hay Farm	76	Westruther
35	Haymount	77	Whalton
36	Houndwood	78	Whitefield
37	Howick	79	Whitsome Laws
38	Hownam	80	Winfield
39	Ilderton	81	Wooperton
40	Kalemouth	82	Yearle
41	Kilham	83	Yetholm
42	Kirknewton		

List of Figures

1. Introduction

Bondagers were first brought to my notice by Mr. and Mrs. Turnbull, Bill and Daline, of Coldingham. They very kindly, and at short notice, provided me with accommodation when I took up my first teaching post at Coldingham Primary School in 1972. Knowing that I was brought up on a small farm in Yorkshire, they talked about their own lives in farming, and mentioned the women workers and their unusual name of "bondager". They also described the costume worn by these women and Bill remarked on the 'muckle hat' which was particularly memorable.

Figure 1. Workers hoeing. Illustration by A.L. Collins in 1912. [Bradley 1912]

Later in 1976 I began some research to find out more about these bondagers and their fascinating costume. The Museum of Antiquities in Edinburgh, the Tithe Byre in East Saltoun and the Gladstone Court Museum in Biggar enabled me to collect information and photographs. This, together with the memories of ex-bondagers, ex-Land Army girls and ex-farm workers who kindly talked to me about their lives, formed the basis for this early piece of work.

Subsequently, I collected information in a casual way as I came across it and in this way amassed many books and newspaper cuttings. Moving to north Northumberland in 1995 re-awakened my interest in the bondagers and I began researching again.

This research enabled me to establish that female agricultural workers in the 18th, 19th and early 20th centuries in Northumberland and the south-eastern area of Scotland were known as bondagers. I was also delighted to find that in living memory women dressed as bondagers were employed on farms in Northumberland, the Scottish Borders (Berwickshire, Roxburghshire and Selkirkshire), and also East Lothian, West Lothian, and Mid Lothian. The following are a few examples of these memories. Mrs. Nancy Taylor of Wooler remembers seeing two bondagers working on North Middleton Farm near Wooler when she was a schoolgirl in about 1942. Alan Scott recalled working alongside a bondager at Castle Heaton as late as 1955. He thought she would certainly be one of the last workers to dress in the bondager costume. She, like him, was part of a gang of workers who moved from farm to farm to do the labour-intensive work of singling (thinning out a row of plants), haymaking, harvesting, and potato gathering.

Also Annie Smith is remembered in the 1960s wearing a bondager hat when she fed the hens at Way-to-Wooler Farm. She was an elderly lady then, and wore the hat with a scarf tied over the top. She had worked for Mr. Dryden and stayed on and worked for Mr. and Mrs. George Logan. Mrs. Logan remembers her as *'Our beloved Annie'*, loved by all the family, particularly the two young sons.

A much earlier eyewitness account of bondagers appeared in a survey of Yorkshire and Northumberland by Sir F. H. Doyle in 1843. At this time the bondagers were very numerous and he remarks that the bondagers are a very *'important part of the Northumberland system of agriculture'*. He reported in detail from various parts of Northumberland - Dilston near Hexham, Netherton near Morpeth and West Horton near Wooler - and pointed out that *'conditions of this engagement vary slightly in different parts of the county, but a woman to be found by the hind as bondager is universally one of them'*. [Doyle 1843].

Cuthbert Bede also noticed the bondagers and includes them in his novel, The Adventures of Mr. Verdant Green, which he wrote in the 1850s. He describes the bondagers as *'great strapping damsels of three or four-women-power, whose occupation it was to draw water, and perform some of the rougher duties attendant upon agricultural pursuits. The sturdy legs of these young ladies were equipped in greaves of leather, which protected them from the cutting attacks of stubble, thistles, and all other lacerating specimens of botany, and their exuberant figures were clad in buskins, and many-coloured garments, that were not long enough to conceal their greaves and clod-hopping boots. Altogether, these young women, when not engaged at their ordinary avocations by the side of a spring, formed no unpicturesque subject for the sketcher's pencil, and might have been advantageously transferred to canvas by many an artist who travels to greater distances in search of lesser novelties.'* [Bede 1877].

Figure 2. Bondagers – 'great strapping damsels of three or four-women-power whose occupation it was to draw water, and perform some of the rougher duties attendant upon agricultural pursuits'. Cuthbert Bede. 1850s. [Bede 1877].

These fieldworkers sometimes called outworkers, when dressed in their decorative costume looked old-fashioned by the 20th century. This led Donald Scott of Caistron to comment, in 1939, that *'the visitor to the farms of Glendale and Tweedside may yet see the 'bondager' busy in the field, clad in what may be described as the last remaining peasant costume in England!'*

Inevitably, because of the position of women in society, historical records that mention bondagers or record happenings that would impinge on the bondager's life are written by men. It is not until the second half of the 19th century that small amounts of information come directly from the women themselves. By this time the system was declining and women workers who dressed as bondagers and called themselves bondagers were often no longer bondagers in the original sense.

The aim of this book is to give a comprehensive picture of these women workers, the bondage system and the farming world in which they lived.

2.   The Bondage System

The Origins

The exact beginning of the bondage system seems to have been lost, but there are many clues to the origin of the name, and to the work expected from these women called bondagers.

Ian Levitt and Christopher Smout [Levitt 1984] suggest that the system is of *'very ancient origin, perhaps even from the seventh century when a single Anglian kingdom of Northumbria stretched from the Humber to the Forth'.* The language spoken originally would have been Old English, sometimes referred to as Anglo Saxon.

Dictionary definitions also underline the ancient origin of the word bondage. The Scots Dictionary lists Bondage and bonnage as service due from a tenant to his superior or from a farm worker to a farmer. The Chambers Twentieth Century Dictionary goes into more detail giving the 'modern' definition of a bondager as a female outworker in the Borders and North of England whom the hind or married cottar was bound to provide for farm work. In addition it also looks at the Old English or Anglo Saxon bonda or boor which was the name for a countryman, peasant or householder. Finally it lists the Old Norse bondi and buandi which was the name for a tiller of the land or a husbandman. Bua means to till. It notes that the old English buan means affected by association with a bond. Old English or Anglo Saxon was the language until 1100 to 1150 AD.

Mark Bailey [Bailey 2002] sets out the various tenures which carried with them obligations to the lord of the manor. He details these categories and obligations in the following way: *'Like some freeholdings, unfree tenures owed seasonal (boon) works at the harvest, for which their workers were often rewarded with the provision of food by the lord. They habitually owed other seasonal works too, such as ploughing and spreading muck in winter, and mowing hay in the early summer, and could also be liable to carry goods on behalf of the lord at specified times. However, their main burden – and distinguishing feature – was the week work, which required an unfree tenant to perform a number of labour services each week outside the harvest period on the lord's demesne. In some places, extensive labour services formed the main 'rent' component of the holding and no cash rents were levied.'* He admits that the situation is complex and says there is *'a bewildering variety of categories'* of unfree landholders; for example, *'customars, customary tenants, tenants in villeinage, villains, bondsmen or cottars (custumarii, custumarii tenantes, tenentes in villenagio, villain, bovarii, bondi, cotarii).'* From this we can see the terms cottars, husbandman and bondsmen are terms that have remained in use through the centuries.

The various obligations owed by tenants to their lord of the manor also continued and are similar to the conditions of service agreed between hind and farmer. For example, the labour services in lieu of rent and the work rewarded by the provision of food.

In the papers referring to the village of Barrasford, north of Hexham and west of Chollerton, there is a plan of the village and list of tenants who are given the name bondagers. The date for this plan is most probably 1813.

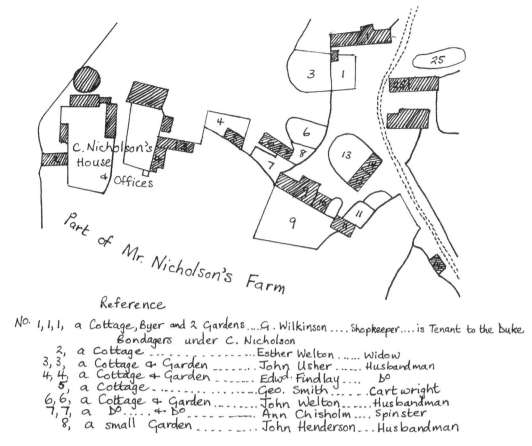

Reference

No. 1, 1, 1, a Cottage, Byer and 2 Gardens....G. Wilkinson....Shopkeeper....is Tenant to the Duke
              Bondagers under C. Nicholson
    2, a Cottage.........................Esther Welton......widow
  3, 3, a Cottage & Garden..........John Usher......Husbandman
  4, 4, a Cottage & Garden..........Edwd. Findlay....Do
    5, a Cottage.....................Geo. Smith......Cartwright
  6, 6, a Cottage & Garden..........John Welton......Husbandman
  7, 7, a Do.....+ Do.............Ann Chisholm....Spinster
    8, a small Garden............John Henderson...Husbandman

Figure 3. Barrasford Village – Map and list of tenants. Notice the use of the term bondager. This is only a small section of the map and list. (Sketch by Dinah Iredale from original dated approx. 1813).

In Figure 3, the tenants are listed as bondagers under C. Nicholson, Mrs Dodd and R. Elliott. These bondagers are male and female, and are categorised as holders of a cottage, cottage and garden, cottage, garden and byre, cottage, garden and blacksmith's shop and cottage, garden and weaver's shop. Their occupation or situation in life is also noted such as widow, spinster, husbandman, Cartwright, tinker, blacksmith, weaver, clogger and shepherd. There are 9 Husbandmen, 2 Cartwrights, 1 Tinker, 1 Blacksmith, 2 Weavers, 1 Clogger, 2 Shoemakers, 2 Shepherds, 2 Labourers, 2 Slaters, 1 Tailor, 1 Shopkeeper, 2 Widows and 3 Spinsters. Some of these people were housed outside the village at Reaver Crag, Elliott's Moor, Coulson's Moor, Nicholson's Moor and Catheugh or Black Dub.

It is interesting that the term bondager was in use at this time when referring to tenants or householders. This is a link back through history to the Old English, bonda which denoted a countryman, peasant or householder. The occupation noted as husbandman links this back to the Old Norse bondi and buandi and the role of tilling the land.

Adrian Ions in 'As She is Spoke' [Ions 2006] also includes 'Bondager' and notes that this name denotes *'a cottager, or servant in husbandry, who has a house for the year, at an under rent, and is entitled to the produce of a certain quantity of potatoes. For these advantages he is bound to work, or to find a substitute, when called on, at a fixed rate of wages, lower than usual in the country.'* He also notes *'Swed. – bonddrang, a farmer's man, a young peasant.'* Finally he expresses his opinion that *'the bondage service, the expediency of which economists have doubted, may be preferred to the villenage tenure of a more barbarous period.'*

The System Emerges

Alexander Fenton [Fenton 1975] notes: *'The fullest early account of conditions of farm service dates from 1656. It is an Assessment of Wages by the Justices of the Peace for Midlothian, in which wages are fixed at maximum, not minimum rates. Servants lived either in 'cot-houses' or the farm-house. Those with cot-houses were the 'whole hind', the 'half-hind', the shepherd and, on the bigger Mains farms, the man who threshed the grain with the flail and who was variously known as the 'barnman', 'tasker' and 'lotman'. The 'whole hind' was so called because he had to maintain a fellow servant to help in carrying on the full work of a plough. In those days, there was a heavy type of plough dragged by from four to twelve oxen or horses and requiring two men, one between the stilts and one, the 'gadsman', urging on the animals with his pointed goad'.* This shows the tradition of one worker having to supply and support another worker in order to carry out his job.

Alexander Fenton goes on to say how the wages were paid in kind and in a further paragraph details the work of the wife: *'The rent of the servants' cot-houses was paid for by the work of their wives. This 1656 document states they "are to shear dayly in Harvest, while (until) their Masters Corn be cut down. They are also to be assisting with their husbands in winning their Master's Hay and Peats, setting of his Lime-kills, (kilns), Gathering, Filling, Carting, and Spreading their Master's Muck, and all other sort of Fuilzie (manure), fit for Gooding and Improving the Land. They are in like manner to work all manner of Work, at Barnes and Byres, to bear and carry the stacks from Barnyards to the Barnes for threshing, carry meat to the Goods (stock) from the Barnes to the Byres, Muck, Cleange and Dight the Byres and Stables, and to help to winnow and dight the Cornes."* We can quite understand and sympathise with his final comment when he says that *' No cottar wife of the present day would face such a range of duties with equanimity.'*

Women's Work

The onerous work undertaken by women, noted in the previous document of 1656, had been the common lot of women for centuries. For instance, a hundred years earlier in 1523, Sir Anthony Fitzherbert lists the work undertaken by a farmer's wife. He makes the list in his Book of Husbandry in the following manner: *'It is a wife's occupation to winnow all manner of corns, to make malt, wash and wring, to make hay, to shear corn, and in time of need to help her husband to fill muckwain or dungcart, drive the plough, to load hay, corn and such other. Also to go or ride to market to sell butter, cheese, milk, eggs, chickens, capons, hens, pigs, geese and all manner of corn. And also to buy all manner of necessary things belonging to a household and make true reckoning and account to her husband what she hath received and what she hath paid. And if the husband go to the market to buy or sell (as they often do), he then to show his wife in like manner. For if one of them should use to deceive the other, he deceiveth himself, and he is not like to thrive, and therefore they must be true either to other.'* [Pritchard 2003]. He is emphasising the need for close, honest collaboration to bring about success.

Even Sir Anthony, a man of that time, acknowledges that *'it may fortune sometime that thou shalt have so many things to do that thou shalt not well know where is best to begin. Then take heed which thing should be the greatest loss if it were not done and in what space it would be done; and then think what is the greatest loss, and there begin.'* [Pritchard 2003]. With the vast list of tasks it is no wonder he felt it necessary to write on the dilemma of knowing where to begin!

Early visual evidence of women at work in the fields can be seen in the Luttrell Psalter c1340. Here *'Reaping'* shows women cutting corn with hooks or sickles.

Concerns about the name Bondager

The name bondager and the role of bondagers in agriculture, together with what became known as the bondage system, had obviously developed and evolved from ancient words, needs, practices and customs. Many people are disturbed by the word bondager and immediately assume that slavery must have been involved. In early times some of the people who were on the very lowest rung of society were indeed slaves. These "serfs" were the property of the landowner and could be sold with the land. If they tried to escape they could be captured and severely punished.

Bondagers in early times and in later more recent times were not slaves. They entered into a bond or agreement with the landowner or farmer or hind and this was for a set period of time. This agreement or bond was usually for a year or sometimes for the bondager six months.

Michael Robson [Robson 1984] writes about the bondage system in the following way: *'Though there were people who thought that the term "bondager" for this provided female labour denoted something approaching a form of slavery, the "bond" and "bondager" seem to have applied rather to the condition laid upon the hind'* and he then quotes a minister from Westruther in the 1830s (New Statistical Account) as stating *'The class of servants here called bondagers are no less free and independent than other labourers.'*

Sir F. H. Doyle [Doyle 1844] also wrote about this confusion in 1844, and says that *'Cobbett towards the close of his life, attacked it,'* as a form of slavery but Doyle after collecting information for his report on employment in agriculture considered that *'this bondage is simply an engagement for a year, upon specified terms, it indicates, I think, some confusion of thought to speak of it as slavery.'*

Almost a hundred years later, in 1922, W. G. Davidson (he is related through his mother to William Fairbairn – see page 59 et seq.) writes to The Border Magazine [Davidson 1922] in response to an article entitled *'The Border Keep'*. He says *'Where the so-called "local" antiquary got his facts one would like to know. The "bondager" was not bound by law to the soil, nor yet "went with the farm". The custom mentioned is the now dead and gone "bondage system", bad enough in all faith, under which each ploughman or "hind" on a farm bound himself to supply a female worker, hence "bondagers", who might be his daughter or other relative. Failing such a stranger was hired. This system, as you readily guess, was the source of frequent scandal, remembering the type of cottages of the period.'* Obviously working life for many people in Britain was very hard, and life must have been a bitter struggle with many difficulties and disappointments but this was still not slavery.

This employment system, apparently old-fashioned and rooted in the past, prompts the question of whether farming practice was also lagging behind the times.

Developments in Agriculture

For many centuries agriculture had, in fact, remained much the same and it was not until the mid 18th century that change became more rapid. D. J. Rowe expressed the opinion [Bailey 1972] that the Open-field System and use of commons for grazing must have curtailed or hindered innovation, and that enclosure, whilst causing terrible hardship to some, did enable the innovative farmer to act on his own initiative and introduce new crops such as turnips, clover and grass. M. Flinn [Flinn 1966] notes that enclosure in Britain had been slowly taking place from the early middle ages and had begun to *'accelerate in the eighteenth century, until, by the mid nineteenth century, there was very little open-field land left.'*

D. J. Rowe also mentions population growth. In the last half of the 18th century population in England and Wales increased by approximately 50%. *'This was'* he says *'a rapid increase, after several centuries in which the rate of population growth had been slow, and it presented the problem of increasing the production of food stuffs'*. He does pose the question, however, whether *'population growth encouraged agricultural development or whether improved agricultural techniques and output enabled populations to grow?'* He leaves this question unanswered.

The government set up Royal Commissions to look at the state of agriculture throughout the land. William Marshall, *'an efficient farmer'* and *'agricultural publicist'* who had *'proposed the setting up of a national board of agriculture in 1787'*, praised the report *'General View of the Agriculture of Northumberland, Cumberland and Westmorland' (1794)* made by John Bailey and George Culley. These two men were noted agriculturists. John Bailey was land agent to the Earl of Tankerville at Chillingham Castle. He did much to encourage innovation and undertook the embankment of the River Till which ran through the Tankerville estate. George Culley was one of the renowned Culley brothers who, together with his brother Matthew, did much to further agriculture in Northumberland. The Culley brothers were born at Denton near Darlington into a small landed family. They spent time at Dishley as Robert Bakewell's earliest pupils, and moved to Fenton in Glendale in 1767. *'Their most lasting influence was on the breeding of live stock.'* [Northumberland 1922].

On a personal and human note William Marshall, mentioned previously, had suggested the setting up of a national board of agriculture and also agricultural colleges but he was given no credit for this. He was later very critical of some of the reports because he thought they were very rushed. Some of the reports were made over five or six weeks in winter, which he felt did not allow the reporters to become familiar with the areas covered. *'Of the three West Riding reporters, very capable farmers who had large estates in East Lothian, he said that much of the report "might have been written with nearly equal propriety, before the Surveyors left east Lothian?"'* To J. Bailey and G. Culley he offered *'considerable praise'* for their report on Northumberland. He was not the only writer on agriculture who is little remembered. D. J. Rowe mentions that in the late eighteenth century writers on agriculture, *'many not well remembered'* recommended *'long leases and draining etc.'* and also *'the creation of farmers' clubs, agricultural societies and shows, and the establishment of ploughing matches.'*

The report by John Bailey and George Culley *'concentrated on the farming of the advanced northern part of the county'* whereas they noted the southern area around Newcastle was generally unimproved. In 1847, T. L. Colbeck [Colbeck 1847] said that *'we now can, with much less grassland than formerly, actually feed more cattle as well as grow more corn'*. This was due mainly to the *'improved turnip husbandry'*. The Bailey and Culley report comments on the rapid improvements saying *'There are probably few parts of the kingdom where estates have made such rapid improvements as in this county; there being several instances of the value being more than trebled within the last 40 years. Many causes have certainly been aiding to produce this great effect; but the principal one is attributed to letting large farms, and leases for 21 years; by which means the tenants of capital were encouraged to make those great exertions, from which such advantages have resulted, not only to themselves and proprietors of the land, but to the community at large, from the very increased produce, and superiority of its quality.'*

In 1797, Bailey and Culley record the memories of Mr. Edward Nisbet, then near 90 years of age, who said that it was *'upwards of 70 years'* since Mr. Proctor, the proprietor of Rock, brought Andrew Willey, a gardener, to cultivate turnips at Rock for the purpose of feeding cattle. Andrew Willey later became a gardener at Lesbury.

Over the border they note that *'Mr. Pringle, formerly a surgeon in the army'* with an estate near Coldstream and William Dawson, of Frogden near Kelso, were interested in the best way to grow turnips. These best methods were based on Mr. Tull's book Horse-Hoeing Husbandry. Bailey and Culley comment dryly that Mr. Pringle using the best way, in 1756 or 57, was not followed by his neighbours but *'Mr Dawson (an actual farmer)'* working on the same principles in 1762 was immediately copied! The best methods were used in Berwickshire and Roxburghshire and were eventually taken up by various districts in Scotland. William Dawson, who died in Edinburgh in 1815, became known as *'the Father of Scottish Agriculture'*. The Hay family, landowners at Kirk Yetholm and in East Lothian, were also *'noted agricultural improvers'*. Draining, deep ploughing and the invention of useful machinery were all part of their experiments in the 18th and 19th centuries. [Yetholm 2006].

The foregoing demonstrates that there were many forward-looking men working to improve the agriculture on both sides of the border. They were aiming to develop not only the best crops but also the best methods and tools to carry out the work.

Turnips were first sown broadcast so the seeds were not confined to neat rows and this made hoeing them complicated and very expensive. This work was usually undertaken by gardeners and other men. Bailey and Culley record how *'Mr. Ilderton, about thirty years since, had the merit of first reducing the price of hoeing, by teaching boys, girls, and women, to perform the work equally as well, if not better, than men.'* Mr. Ilderton was obviously concerned about the quality of the work but cost seems to be the major factor. He organised the work by using '*a light plough, without a mould-board,* and with this *'he divided the field into small squares of equal magnitude, and directed the boys and girls to leave a certain number of plants in each square. In a short time they became accurate, regular and expert hoers; and, in a few years, all the turnips in the country were hoed by women and boys, at half the expence, and better than by men.'*

A serrated-edged sickle or heuk was used traditionally for cutting corn and this work was mostly done by women. From the mid Eighteenth century, in Scotland, the heuk was being replaced by a smooth-edged sickle. *'Robert Somerville noted that it had gained ground in East Lothian by 1805'.* At this time, the scythe was also coming into use as a tool for cutting corn. This led to theories being tested and there were for example *' extensive experiments to determine the comparative merit of scythe and sickle carried out on farms on the Dunglass estate in East Lothian in 1793,* and the *'detailed costings showed the substantial savings in time and labour achieved by using the scythe.'* This clearly demonstrates that there was a willingness to use systematic study in order to arrive at the best methods allied with the best tools.

An interesting article appeared in the Berwick Advertiser for 4 May 1833. It was given the heading "East Lothian" and it announces the intention to look again at the toothed hook in preference to the scythe hook. *'It appears from a communication in the Berwick Advertiser, understood to be from a respectable farmer, that many of the tennantry of the counties of Berwick and Roxburgh are of the opinion that the re-introduction of the old fashioned or toothed hook would be attended by many advantages in cutting down their crops. The author of said communication proposes that a meeting of those interested should be held at Dunse on high market day in May, and that if he finds this proposition is approved of, he engages to have ready for inspection a toothed hook of such a make and temper as he thinks will be best suited for the purpose of reaping. Here it may be mentioned that as the scythe hook is easier to work with, and from that circumstance popular with reapers, it will be necessary for farmers to show some determination, for unless that is done they will never be introduced. To the credit of an extensive farmer to this district it is said that no scythe hook is ever permitted with him'.* This demonstrates how arguments over the merits of one tool as against another can rumble on for many years. The article reveals that the workers would not readily go back to using the hook. This would be of great concern to the bondagers as, traditionally, one of their most important roles was to shear the corn.

Rev. Hastings Neville, the Rector of Ford in Northumberland, records that *'Mrs Burns, fifty years ago (about 1859), sheared with teethed hewk for Wm. Jobson, farmer of Turvelaws, near Wooler, who would not allow the sickle to be used, and his rule was that there should be three good handfuls to a sheaf. Even after the sickle came into use for wheat and oats, barley was still cut by hand shearing, whether with teethed hook or sickle; the left hand being used to hold the corn while being cut. Barley straw being weaker than that of wheat, would not so well stand against the stroke of the sickle'.* [Neville 1909].

Despite this lauding of older tools, ideas and technology were moving on. William Howatson remarks on how George Hope of Fenton Barns in East Lothian was *'one of the earliest and most enthusiastic proponents of the mechanical reaping machines'* and *'by 1860, East Lothian could boast 160 reaping machines.'* These machines could obviously save labour and the labour force needed for harvest was huge. *'In 1867 George Hope of Fenton*

Barns' 'needed to recruit only fifteen extra harvesters'. This was a much-reduced number as in the same year in Perthshire on a *'large unit' 'extra harvest labour'* was *'a hundred females'*. [Howatson 1984].

Figure 4. Hinds and Bondagers in Lowick. The working unit is clearly shown in this photograph – The hind with his pair of horses and his bondager. The bondager at the front was called Appelina Lyall and was known as Appie. Bart Stanton (aged 94) of Wooler remembers a family of four or five sisters who worked as bondagers. One was called Torie, which was short for Pretoria. (Mrs Hetha Bruce, Lowick).

In February 1866 (Berwick Warder) at the West Teviotdale Farmers' Club, Mr. Jobson of Humelknowes *'read an able paper on "The cheapest and best way of cutting corn crops".* He looked at the old toothed hook, sickle and scythe and finally the reaper. He said *'Taking all things into account, I feel no difficulty in awarding the palm to the reaper as by far the cheapest and best mode of cutting grain crops'.*

T. M. Devine noted that *'W. Hasbach dismissed regions where farm service and payment in kind survived as "conservative" and lagging the more advanced areas of the south'* but he takes issue with this assumption, and points out that *'Scottish farmers were among the most progressive in Europe and they were unlikely to be any less skilled in the deployment of labour than in other aspects of farm management'.* [Devine 1984 chap 1]. The contrast between the forward looking and experimental attitude of the farmers, in their agricultural practices, and the way the engagement of staff was rooted in the past, is very marked.

3. Contemporary Comments on the Bondage System

Landowners, farmers, vicars, schoolmasters and farm apprentices all commented on the bondage system. The pros and cons were analysed and discussed. Much was set down in print, but sadly, many more opinions and concerns were lost forever through not having been committed to paper or through the discarding of valuable documents whose significance was not appreciated.

William Marshall reported to the Board of Agriculture in 1808. [Marshall 1808]. He too looks back to a more feudal time when he writes under the title 'Work People'. *'The following particulars relating to the Northumbrian Peasantry, will afford matter of amusement, if not astonishment, to English farmers. The practice of Northumberland is doubtlessly, a relick of the vassal system, which still prevails in the more northern parts of Europe, where farm labourers belong to the land:- make part of the live stock of the farm. The practice of paying laborers, in kind, originated in the same necessity as that of paying landlords and clergy, in kind: practices that once prevailed, no doubt, throughout the island, and all Europe. How far it may still be right, in very recluse situations, where farm work people are a sort of fixtures to the soil, though they do not belong to it, I will not attempt to decide; but merely transcribe the Reporters account of the Northumbrian practice, at the close of the eighteenth century.'*

He goes on to provide more specific information later in the report. *'Through the greatest part of this county, and especially upon large farms, there are very few servants kept in the house (farmhouse); seldom more than two men and two maids; but the ploughman, carters, barnmen, shepherds etc. have each a house and garden, or yard, to themselves, and are generally married. The conditions of servitude for one year are:-*

		£	s	d
2	*cows kept, or money in lieu, at £3 each*	6	0	0
3	*bushels of wheat, at 5s. per bushel*		15	0
33	*Ditto of oats at 1s.8d. ditto*	2	15	0
12	*Ditto of barley at 2s.6d. ditto*	1	10	0
12	*Ditto of rye at 3s.4d. ditto*	2	0	0
10	*Ditto of pease at 3s.6d. ditto*	1	15	0
24	*lb of cast wool at 6d. per lb*		12	0
1	*Bushel of potatoes planted, a pig tethered, keeping hens etc*	2	4	0
	Carriage of coals, six cart-loads	1	0	0
	In all	18	11	0

They are bound to find a woman laborer to work for the following wages: for harvesting 6d. per day; for hoeing turnips, hay-making, scaling, weeding corn, etc. used to be 4d. per day, but was last year raised to 6d. per day.'

He also mentions the conditions for shepherds and stewards who are included in the system and often, as will be seen later, had to provide a bondager as part of their bond or agreement. *'In addition to the above conditions, the shepherd generally has as many sheep kept as are worth four or five pounds a year; but if he has any under-shepherd to keep to assist him, the number is increased accordingly. In the hilly districts, their sheep sometimes amount to hundreds, beside six or eight neat cattle……….An overseer, or head servant, has, in addition to the above as much money as to make his place worth £20 to £30 a year.'*

The above information comes from the work undertaken by J. Bailey and G. Culley which they produced in 1794. They also included the following information with regard to hoeing turnips: *'In this branch of labour, the women in the northern parts of the country excel; the writer of this note has at different times visited Norfolk, Suffolk, and all the principal turnip districts in the island; but never saw turnips so well hoed and completely cleaned, or kept in such garden-like culture, as on these borders.'* This shows that the women workers were noticed and their skill was highly praised and appreciated.

John Grey and Josephine Butler, his daughter, also commented on the system. Josephine wrote in the Memoir of John Grey of Dilston [Butler 1874] that *'the good state of the agriculturists of Northumberland, which good state is not directly traceable to the existence or non existence of certain customs prevalent elsewhere, and which undoubtedly exists in spite of certain indefensible parts of agricultural arrangements of that county, such as the "bondage system".'* She continues a little later, rather mysteriously, *'It was liable to great abuse, and that on some estates it was not abused, was owing, as I have hinted, to causes, some of which lie deeper and are more remote in their beginnings.'* Could she be hinting at chivalry?

John Grey wrote, in 1829, to J. C. Blackden at Ford Castle about the bondage system, where he says *'I regret that it has acquired this odious designation. I may engage a 'hind' at regular conditions. I may engage his eldest son, living in his house, at 9/- or 10/- a week; his second son, perhaps at 6/-; and his youngest at 8d a day, to work on occasions when I have work to do that he can perform; and this is respectably enough called a 'hiring'. But because I bargain with the 'hind' for the work of a woman in exactly the same way, namely at such times as I require it, it is called 'bondage'. The 'bondager', however, is not always a woman, but sometimes a boy, if it suits the hind better to employ one.'*

He later gave evidence to a Committee of the House of Lords in 1830 and stated that:
'It cannot be said that the occupation of the females is unwholesome, or beyond their strength. The healthful and cheerful appearance of the girls in the turnip or hay fields of the north, and their substantial dress, would bear a favourable comparison with those of any other class of female operatives in the kingdom; and their neat and respectable attire on attending their place of worship on Sundays would fill with astonishment, and perhaps envy, the female peasantry of Kent or Surrey.'

Farm pupils or apprentices were common and J. Bailey and G. Culley noted that farmers *'are seldom without pupils from various and distant parts of the kingdom, with whom they have very handsome premiums.'* At present there is *'the son of an Earl, and the son of a Baronet.'* An example of this is the farm apprentice who came to Lilburn Grange, Northumberland in 1842 (the 'Lilburn farm apprentice') and wrote a detailed diary of his time there. He was pleased with his welcome to the farm and wrote *'I came to Mr. Howey's on the 23rd of May from Newcastle and met Mr. Howey on the Road expecting me. I looked over the farm and found it was a very good one'.* Later in his diary he mentions the hinds being *'obliged to find a woman to work for them in the fields for women work in the fields the whole year they hoe the turnips shear the wheat/ that is they reap it/ and in fact do as much work as a good many men the men are alowed by their masters 8d in the winter 10d in the spring and 1/- in the summer for each woman and each man* must *find a woman to work without the woman here to work in the fields the work of the farms could not be carried on for the population is so thin that there are not sufficient number of men without the women to work the land and it appears to me most strange that this is the case for the country in this part is I should say one of the finest in the country and a very large inputting place the corn being sent all over England in large quantities.'* So this young man is impressed by the farming in Northumberland and surprised that so much work is carried out by women. He comes to the conclusion that the population density is low and this is the reason for the number of women workers. [NRO 851].

Hastings Neville writes at the end of the 19th century about the bondage system – *'This was an agreement made by the hind who was to inhabit one of the farm cottages, that in case he could not guarantee to the farmer as a worker another hand from his own family, he would provide one. This was generally a woman. She had board and lodgings in the hind's house, and the hind paid her wages. This was the "bondager". Her lot was harder than that of the other women on the farm. She had to work for the hind in milking and house work, and still do her full share of farm work. She was always more or less a stranger in the home, and nowhere is family life more exclusive than among our Border people. The sympathy of the people was always given to the hind in this case, because he had to pay a stated, or upstanding wage to the woman.'* His book was published in 1909 but Rev. Neville became rector of Ford in 1871 which gave him personal memories of many years on which to base his writing. He also states, in his preface, that the information about former times was *'carefully gathered from agricultural labourers themselves'.* [Neville 1909].

Rutherfurd's Directory of 1866 gives a very positive view of the bondager's life. *'The field has its charms for these women; their general strength enables them to do all that is expected of them; the high wages furnished a dress agreeable to their taste; and there is a lightsomeness in the half-yearly tenure and the coming market, which, inducing a change of place and company, fills up an existence of agreeable excitement.'* [Rutherfurd 1866]. Speaking in 1981, T. C. Smout concluded that *'the hind of South-East Scotland was the best paid and best fed of Scottish farm workers of the 1840s.* [Howarth 1998].

4.   Hiring Workers

This chapter includes information about fairs and hiring fairs, which were regular features of country life. These events would be extremely important in the lives of the farm workers, male and female, and their families. This was the chance to get away from the farm and the daily routine, to mix with a wider circle, to catch up with friends, to see shops and stalls of goods rarely seen, and be frivolous and carefree for a few hours. It is not difficult to imagine the contrast these events would give to lives led in relative isolation on the farm. With hiring fairs the prospect of a better situation, with slightly better conditions, and new companions, as workmates, were all to be enjoyed and savoured.

Early in the New Year workers were 'spoken to'. This meant that the farmer let the workers know whether they were needed for the next year, which would begin in May. New bargains for their labour could be made if they were staying on. An anxious question in January or February was – '*Has he spoken yet?*'

Sir Mark and Lady Barbara Goodson moved to Kilham in 1973 and were surprised to find that, for about the next five years, the steward came each year on 11 May to ask if everyone was to be employed for the next year - a continuation of the idea of being '*spoken to*'.

Richard Dunmore wrote that '*In the agricultural world, this was the time for hiring skilled workmen for the coming year. A hiring fair often known locally as the Statute Fair, or simply the Statutes, was held during Wakes Week* (Wakes Week was a North of England term for an annual holiday – usually associated with the industrial areas of Yorkshire and Lancashire). *The fairs origin was in the Statute of Labourers of 1351 – an (unsuccessful) attempt to freeze wages after the Black Death when, with labour in short supply, workmen began to demand their price for employment. By the 19th century workmen were still going to hiring fairs in search of new jobs and farmers were on the look-out for good workmen.*' [Dunmore].

The poster for the Cornhill Fair dated 1714 (Figure 5) demonstrates the structure behind the long established fairs, with Sir Carnaby Haggerston collecting the revenue from the fair and imposing law and order on those attending. A stiff penalty of forty shillings to one hundred shillings was imposed for breaches of the peace. This fair was to be held on 6 December 1714.

Over a hundred years later the Cornhill Hiring Market is described, in the Berwick Advertiser, for the 6 March 1852, in the following way. '*On Monday last, the 1st inst. being the hiring market, a numerous attendance of both sexes presented themselves, and in the course of the forenoon hiring went on very brisk, and few left without obtaining masters. The wages given for the summer half year were upon an average what had been obtained in former years, and all that we had an opportunity of conversing with upon the subject spoke very favourable of the result. In the afternoon of the day the village was all gaiety, in consequence of this annual reunion (as it may be called) bringing many of the country people in contact, and who testified their pleasure by treating each other to their fairing. It was a really happy and exhilarating sight to see so many joyous and smiling faces, and to listen to their loud and boisterous laughter. A football match was played in the afternoon in the Craw Green, near Coldstream, which was kept up with great spirit and amidst much hilarity till after 6 o'clock.*' This account gives a picture of a crowded market with bondagers and farm men quickly being hired but with no precise detail of wages. The pleasure of the occasion is clearly indicated and anyone selling gingerbread or sweets as fairings would do a brisk trade.

Figure 5. A poster for the Cornhill Fair dated 1714

St Boswells Fair, held at the village of St Boswells near Melrose, was also a very important and ancient fair. This fair was held on 18 July. Jean Lang notes that *'Before Lammas Fair, once held on the slope of the western Eildon, close to Melrose, eclipsed it, St Boswells Fair was the most important in the south of Scotland.'* She uses an account given in 1794 by the Rev. John Scade, the minister of the parish, to describe this fair. *'Great flocks of sheep of all denominations,'* *'black cattle are also numerous; and the show of horses has usually been so fine, that buyers come from many places, both of England and Scotland.'* *'Linen cloth was another article'* which, depending on the quality, sold for *'10d to 1s to 3s 6d, 4s and 4s 6d per yard.'* *'Booths (or as they are called, craims) containing hardware and haberdashery goods, are erected in great numbers at the Fair,'* and *'the money turned in the course of the day at this fair is guessed to be from £8,000 to £10,000 stirling. The Duke of Buccleugh receives a certain rate, or toll, upon sheep, cattle, and all other commodities brought into the fair for sale.'* The minister praises the sober and frugal inhabitants but complains that the fair being on a Saturday or Monday causes *'inattention to the religious observance of the sabbath'* and that *'The evil has been complained of, but no remedy has yet been applied.'* [Lang 1913].

By 1832 the fair had *'greatly declined'* and *' a gazetteer'* is rather disparaging in his remarks about the village, but concedes that the fair is still *'the resort of many salesmen of goods, and in particular of tinkers.'* He also remarks on the customary ceremonies which were still observed – *'the Fair was still officially proclaimed open by officials representing the Fair's overlord, his Grace the Duke of Buccleuch. At the door of a barn, adjoining the present blacksmith's house a representative of the firm of Messrs Curle and Erskine, Melrose, the Duke's lawyers, each carrying a halberd, and between them came a drummer gorgeous in knee-breeches, buckled shoes, green coat with brass buttons and a lofty "lum hat".'* David Stoddart, an ex-soldier, from Nisbet near Ancrum, was the last drummer. He was known as

'Black Davie' and he opened the Fair by beating *'a loud tattoo, and in a voice to be heard above all the din of buyers and sellers, he made the official proclamation.'* This he did *'for five shillings and his "denner".'* Another interesting point was that *"at one time rowdies at the Fair were tried and sent on to Jedburgh by cart, for a few days."*

Jean Lang compares the wares on sale at the time (in 1911) with those of the past. She says the *'Gimcrack watches, "swagger sticks," toys and ornaments, and sweets of rich aniline colours are the chief commodities on the stalls. The "kisses" of one's youth – dumpy, three-cornered things like pincushions, striped in pink and white, or in more sober cream and brown – have given place to modern confections. No longer can they aid the bashful ploughman to make his declaration, and he has to trust to "reading sweeties" (whose amatory conversationalism possesses none of the subtleties or symbolism of the triangular confection of olden days) to do his love-making for him. Gingerbread horses and horsemen, speckled with coloured caraway seeds, or richly gilded, no longer abound.'* She mentions shooting galleries, Aunt Sallies and merry-go-rounds, *'pawing horses all a-snort, driven by steam'* and *'urged on'* by *'racous strains of a gramophone'. 'Swinging-boats like their rivals the channel steamers take on board rosy-cheeked "bondagers" and their swains, and eject them after a brief but stormy passage, during which the pea-hen quality of the fair passengers' screams have made even the gramaphone appear pianissimo. They are pallid past recognition, but their courage is dauntless. Half an hour for recovery, and back they come.'* [Lang 1913]. Obviously they had come to enjoy themselves, and enjoy themselves they would, come what may!

The Penny Music Hall gets a mention where she describes *'the evergreen lady with very red cheeks and very golden hair, with whom all the callowest amongst the young hinds and shepherds are in love, as their fathers were before them.'* After an encore *'she picks kisses from her mouth and throws them at the audience with such force and with such a appearance of something hard and tangible, that her admirers intuitively duck their heads.'* Jean Lang brings the chapter to a close by speculating on the reminiscences back on the farm which she imagines might begin with *"D'ye mind yon yin at Codlin's last Bosil's Fair?"* [Lang 1913].

Michael Robson mentions that 'the variety of entertainment at Whittingham Fair near Wooler, held on St. Bartholomew's Day, 24 August, made it at least as noteworthy as St Boswells, *'with its rows of refreshment tents and gingerbread stalls, troops of mountebanks, strolling players and boxing booths; gangs of huksters and muggers displaying their varied assortment of merchandise'* and most importantly *'its crowds of fresh-coloured country lads and lasses, enjoying their annual holiday.'* He also mentions St. James' Fair, at St. James' Green, Kelso on 5 August and a fair at Broughton, Peebleshire on the 30 October. [Robson 1984]. Robson's Directory for Northumberland 1841 mentions *'A Fair is also held on Whitsun Bank, (Wooler) about a mile from the town, on the third Tuesday in May, at which great numbers of horses, cattle and sheep are disposed of.'*

Michael Robson says that these older fairs were *'originally intended to offer marketing opportunities for specific produce,'* but hiring did take place. The hiring was usually for the *'temporary labour needed for harvest'* and the general mood was that the fair was *'the recreational highlight of the year,'* an escape from the *'ordinary labouring round on the farm.'* [Robson 1984]. Mr Henley wrote in the 1867 Royal Commission, *'the fair is the holiday of the working man'* and he saw *'nothing objectionable'.* He noticed the *'usual enjoyments'* and *'happy faces'.* [Henly 1867].

Hastings Neville [Neville 1909] mentions St. Ninian's Fair at Fenton near Wooler. He mentions that country fairs were more important sixty years ago echoing the previous point made by Jean Lang. This fair was held on 27 September and very similar to St Boswells. Arranged as a street with *'refreshment tents kept by the publicans of the surrounding towns and villages, having the names of their signs on flags or streamers.'* He also mentions *'gingerbread made in moulds to represent the Royal Arms, men, horses and dogs; these being, par excellence, the "fairing" that was always expected by the young and old people who, for any reason, could not be present at the fair.'*

'There were also several games of chance going on that would not now be allowed. Thimblerigging was carried on by sharpers in the lanes and foot-paths leading to the fields,

and another game called prick-the-garter. Good marble players were much attracted to a pile of about a dozen pennies to be shot at for a penny a shot, all the coins knocked down being the reward. The thoroughfare was filled from end to end with an animated moving crowd; cheap-jacks driving a brisk trade, travelling musicians, and ballad singers, who sold for a half penny many an old song that doubt-less had its origin in the folklore of the North'.

'Everyone went to the fair that could ride, drive or walk. It was an annual event to which young and old looked forward; and although no doubt there were evils connected with it, and its extinction by the rise of the cattle mart at the railway station is not to be regretted, the pity is that there is nothing that can take its place, and reproduce its good features as a social festival suited to the country.'

Despite some hiring taking place at the *'long established traditional fairs'* the main hiring fairs *'were held at fixed times of the year'* and were *'related to the Whitsunday and Martinmas terms and thus fell in during Spring and Autumn'*. Many of these fairs *'originated no earlier than the eighteenth century. They were essentially markets at which the level of wages was fixed by demand,'* meaning that when workers were few wages could rise and where there were many workers wages could fall. [Robson 1984]. Mr Hindmarsh, of Ilderton, said to the 1893 Royal Commission that *'One advantage of the hirings of the hinds is that they can command the market price of wages. This meeting of hinds creates the rate of wage and they really fix it.'* [Fox 1893].

A much altered notice for hiring fairs at Hexham for 1779, 1784, 1789 and 1802 is an interesting document which demonstrates great effort to get the message straight and into the public domain.

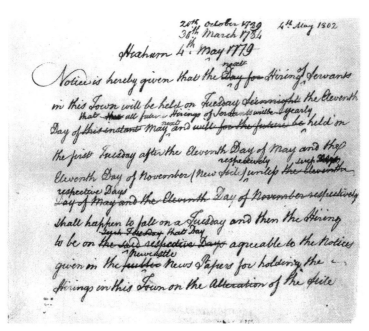

Figure 6. Hexham hiring fairs. A re-use of the same notice, with adjustments, for a number of years.

Transcription of Figure 6:

For the years – 1779, 1784, 1789 and 1802 – Hexham
Notice is hereby given that the next Hiring of Servants in this town will be held on Tuesday the Eleventh day of May next and that all future Hirings of Servants will be yearly held on the first Tuesday after the eleventh Day of May and the Eleventh day of November respectively unless such respective Days shall happen to fall on a Tuesday and then the Hiring to be on that Day agreeable to the notices given in the Newcastle News Papers for holding the Hirings in this Town on the alteration of the stile.

THE SOUTHERN COUNTIES' REGISTER, DIRECTORY, &c.

FAIRS.

The figures within parenthesis—thus (78)—occurring after the fairs, markets, and anniversaries, denote the page where the event is fully described; the letter *n* denotes that the fair preceding it has become nominal or defunct; where no figure or letter occurs, the event is not in the district, and the entry is made from other almanacs for convenience of reference; but for its existence or the accuracy of its date we do not vouch.

MARCH.

Alnwick, hiring, 1 Saturday
Berwick-on-Tweed, hiring, 1 Sat.
Cornhill, hinds' hiring, 1 Monday (484)
Dunse, hinds' hiring, 1 Tues. (549)
Ettrick, hiring shepherds, & sale of ewes, last Wed. (n, 417)
Galashiels, seed-corn, &c., 3 Wednesday (n, 430)
Gifford Tryst, last Tuesday
Hexham, stock, 25
Jedburgh, hinds' hiring, 1 Tuesday (248)
Kelso, hinds' and herds' hiring, 1 Friday (73)
Kelso Horse Fair, 2 Friday (73)
Lauder, hinds and herds, 1 Tuesday (519)
Melrose, hinds' hiring, 1 Mon.; ewes and other stock, Saturday before last Tuesday (129)
Morpeth, horses and cattle, 28
Peebles, hiring, 1 Tuesday
Selkirk, shepherds' and hinds' hiring, 1 Wed. (375)
Stow, ewes, seeds, corn, hiring, 2 Tuesday

APRIL.

Belford, last Wednesday
Carlisle, cat., Saturday nearest 20
Castleton, hiring, 2 Friday (236)
Ladykirk, linen cloth, plants, &c., 5 (n, 504)
Lauder, servants, 6 Tuesdays after 1 Tuesday of March (519)
Selkirk, hiring servants, 5 (375)

MAY.

Alnwick, 12
Berwick-on-Tweed, hiring, and horses, 1 Sat.
Castleton, hir., Frid. bef. 17 (236)
Dunse, hir. young men & women, 2 Tues. before 26 (549)
Falkirk, cattle and horse show, 3d Thursday
Greenlaw, cows, &c., 22 (n, 541)
Heriot House, sheep, cattle, and turnip-seed, Friday after 26
Hawick, hir. servants, 17 (305)
Jedburgh, cat and horses, 1 Tues. aft. 26; hir. serv., 1 Tues. (248)
Kelso, hinds' hiring, 1 Friday (73)
Langholm, cat., last Tuesday, o.s
Melrose, hiring young men and women, 1 Monday (129)
Norham, 3 Thursday
Peebles, 2 Wednesday

JUNE.

Dumfries, hor., Wed. after 17, o.s.
Dunse, cat., shp. & hor., 1 Thurs. (549)

Earlston, cat. and horses, 29 (507)
Gifford Fair, 3 Tuesday
Linton (Peeblesshire), sheep, 28
Melrose, cattle, 1 Wednes. (129)
Norham, 3 Thursday
Swinton, 3 Thursday (n, 608)
Yetholm (Kirk), sheep, 27 (157)

JULY.

Alnwick, last Mon.; wool, Saturday after 5
Coldingham, 2 Tuesday, o. s. (n)
Cornhill, lambs and wool, 3 (484)
Dunse, cat., sheep & wool, 2 Tues. (549)
Ettrick, lambs and wool 30, (n 417)
Galashiels, wool, 8 (430)
Hawick, wool, 1 Thursday after St. Boswell's; shearers, 1 Thursday after 26 (305)
Hexham, wool, 2
Jedburgh (Rink), 20, or two days after St. Boswell's (249)
Kelso, wool, 2 Friday (74)
Langholm, lambs and wool, 26
Linton (Peeblesshire), wool, Wed. after 18
Morpeth, Wednesday before 22
Peebles, wool, Tuesday after 18
Pennymuir, lambs and wool, 31 (229)
St. Boswell's, 18 (121)
Selkirk, shearers, 15
Stagshawbank, 5
Thirlestane, lambs, 30
Yetholm (Town), lambs, wool, &c. 2 Wednesday (n, 158)

AUGUST.

Berwick, hiring, 1 Saturday
Carlisle, cattle, 26
Dunse, cattle, sheep, and horse, 26 or Tuesday after (549)
Hexham, stock, 6
James', St. (Kelso), 5 (74)
Jedburgh, cattle, horses, shearers, 20, if Tuesday; if not, Tuesday before
Kelso, shearers' port every Monday morning during harvest
Lauder, lambs, Friday bef. 12 (n, 519)
Melrose, shearers, 1 Mon.; Lammas, 12; but if Saturday, Sunday, or Monday, Tuesday after (129, 130)
Newcastle, horses, cattle, and general business, 2 Wednesday
Peebles, Tuesday before 24
Stagshawbank, lambs, 5

SEPTEMBER.

Belford, ewes, 26

Carlisle, cattle, 20
Castleton, ewes and lambs, Friday before 2 Wednesday (237)
Cornhill, draft ewes (26)
Dunse, ewe tryst, 3 Tuesday (550)
Ettrick, tups and fat sheep 24 (n)
Hawick, tups, 20 and 21 (305)
Jedburgh (Rood Day), cattle and horses, 25 (249)
Kelso Union Agricultural Society's Exhibition of sheep, and sale and hire of Leicester and Cheviot Tups, 2 Thursday and Friday (47 and 89)—see note (613); Leicester and half-bred draft ewes and cattle market, 24 (74)
Langholm, sheep, 18
Moffat, 2 Friday aft. Falkirk Tryst
Peebles, Tuesday before 12
St Ninian's, 27

OCTOBER.

Alnwick, 1 Tuesday
Belford, hiring, 1 Wednesday
Castleton, draft ewes and lambs, Thursday bef. 2 Tuesday (237)
Earlston, cat. and horses, 3 Thursday (507)
Galashiels, general business, 11 (n)
Greenlaw, cows, last Thurs. (541)
Hawick (Tryst), horses and cattle. 3 Tuesday (305)
Jedburgh (Rink), 14 (obs., 249)
Lauder, servants, 4 Friday (519)
Melrose, ewes and other stock, Saturday after 1 Tuesday (130)
Morpeth, horses and cattle, 25
Norham, 2 Thursday
Peebles, 2 Tuesday
Penicuick, 1 Friday
Pennymuir, sheep and cat, 15 (229)
Rothbury, stock, 3
Selkirk, servants' hiring, 31 (375)
Swinton, 4 Tuesday (n, 608)
Stagshawbank, lambs, 24
Wooler, cattle, sheep, 17
Yetholm (Kirk), sheep, 24 (158)

NOVEMBER.

Alnwick, hiring, 1 Saturday
Berwick, hiring, 1 Saturday
Castleton, hiring, Friday before 8 (236); cattle and small lambs, 3 Friday (237)
Chirnside, last Thursday (n)
Dumfries, horse, Wed. before 22
Dunse, servants' hiring, 1 Tues.; cattle and sheep, 17, or Tuesday after (550)
Edinburgh (Hallow Fair), 2d Mon.
Ettrick (Little Fair), 3 Friday (n)
Hawick, cat., & hiring servants, (305)
Hexham, stock, 9; hiring, 11
Haltwhistle, cattle, 22.
Jedburgh, hiring, 1 Tuesday (248); cat. and horses, 1 Tues. (249)
Kelso, servants' hir., 1 Friday (73)
Langholm, cattle, 5
Melrose, servants, 1 Monday; cat. 22 (130)
Newcastle, cattle, last Wednesday; hiring, 1 Tuesday
Rothbury, stock, 1

Figure 7. The fair venues throughout the year. (from Rutherfurd's Directory: Fairs). [Rutherfurd 1866].

In Hexham the borough jury undertook to fix the date of hiring servants and that *'This ancient custom of hirings is still continued at Hexham. There are two in the year, one at Martinmas and the other in May, and this seemed to have been the case, through out the present century.'* [Northumberland 1896].

W. M. Swan the secretary of Long-Benton Agricultural Society writes about a fairly new 'Hinds' Hiring and says *'The Hiring for Hinds, established three years ago, having proved of such Importance to the neighbourhood, by the great increase of Engagements made each Year, will take place as usual.'* (Newcastle Courant, 3 February 1837).

A notice about the establishment of a hinds' hiring at Felton also appeared in the Newcastle Courant for 17 February 1837:

Hinds' Hiring.
At a meeting of the Gentlemen Farmers and Inhabitants of Felton and the Neighbourhood, it was unanimously agreed that Public Notice should be given for a Hinds' Hiring, to be holden at Felton on the last Friday in February; and that a HIRING will take place accordingly, and continue to be holden in the last Friday in February annually, by Permission of the Lord of the Manor. Felton, February 1st, 1837.

Each year reports of the various hiring fairs appear in the newspapers: some are very much to the point while others give interesting details and also venture opinions.

Berwick Advertiser, 9 May 1835:

Wooler Hiring.
In the hiring market the number of people was very considerable, though it continued rainy during the greater part of the day. There was a great demand for female servants, and many hinds had difficulty in getting one to hire, on account of the objections which girls generally have to working out. The wages of the female servants were rather higher – Some getting as much as £5.15s for the half year: but for men servants there was no material change, their wages were about the same as last year.

This report emphasises the demand for bondagers and that girls, as the reporter states, did not like working out and how this caused problems for the hinds. The higher wage rate for women reflects the shortage of women workers.

Berwick Advertiser, 18 May 1835:

Dunse Hiring.
The hiring market on Wednesday was well attended. There was great demand for female servants: but numbers of young men could not get places. Wages were from £3.10s to £4.10s some go to £5 –for women from £4.10s to £5.10s and a few we believe got as high as £6.

Female workers were again in demand and could ask for higher wages. Young men were not so in demand despite the lower wages. Cost was obviously not the only criterion when a farmer chose his work force. Available accommodation could have had some bearing on this situation.

Berwick Advertiser, 12 March 1836:

Alnwick Hiring.
There was a considerable briskness in the hiring for hinds at Alnwick on Saturday last at an advance of wages.

This brief report gives little detail but wages had risen.

Figure 8. A Hiring and Statute Fair in the North of England – notice the workers for hire standing round the market cross on the left.   (Illustrated London News, 12 November 1881)

The purely hiring fairs also attracted additional traders to the various centres. Michael Robson notes that *'Stall owners took up regular positions in the customary streets or market place where farmers and labourers gathered'.* He also notes how *'Hinds and shearers' 'were regularly hired at the fairs,'* but states that *'it was possible for the farmer to reach a private agreement on conditions for a further year with those already working for him whom he wished to keep on.'* [Robson 1984].

At the same time as new hiring fairs were being set up the Newcastle Courant carried an advertisement from an enterprising young man who was obviously wishing to take more control of his situation or at least try a different route to employment and promotion:

WANTS a Situation, as FARM STEWARD,   *March 17ᵗʰ 1837*
A young man who has been nine years in that Employment, and can have an unexceptionable character from any of the Gentlemen he has formerly served.
Application (if by letter, Post Paid) to Mr. Coxon, Star Inn, Alnwick, will meet with immediate attention.

The many aspects of these hiring fairs are covered in the article from The Illustrated London News, 12 November 1881. This short article gives a flavour of these fairs and includes an engraving of a Statute Fair (see Figure 8).

The *'yearly Statute Fair, with its appointment of hiring farm-servants, both male and female, who stand all day in the market place for personal inspection, is quite in character with the fashions and notions of the olden times.'* It names some north country ballads from *'Songs and Ballads of Cumberland and the Lake Country'* edited by Sydney Gilpin and published in Carlise in 1874. Three of the songs are *'Rosley Fair'*, *'Gigglesdown Fair'* and *'Croglin Watty'*. Those to be hired *'stand in the market-place with a sprig or a straw in their mouths'*. *'The honest poor fellow (Croglin Watty) who tells his own experiences in the prose interlude of this song'* (written by Robert Anderson).

> *"The wives," he says, "Com roun' me in clusters:"*
> *"What weage dus te ax, canny lad" says yen*
> *"Wey, three pun' and a crown; wunnet beate a hair*
> *o' my beard". "What can t'e dui?" says anudder.*
> *"Dui! Wey, I can plough, sow, mow, shear, thresh,*
> *dyke, milk, kurn, muck a byre, sing a psalm,*
> *mend car' gear, dance a whornpipe, nick a naig's*
> *tail, hunt a brock, or feight wer a yen o' my weight*
> *in aw Croglin parish. So, Watty is hired by a*
> *cross and miserly old dame, "wi' a kill-dried*
> *frosty feace".*

The article goes on to comment on the figures standing by the market cross on the left of the picture:

'It must be weary waiting in that position, when so little notice is taken of them by the comfortable farmers and farmers' wives strolling about in the foreground, and exchanging neighbourly and household talk with each other or bargaining over poultry, suckling pigs, and more important dealings in cattle.'

The article also mentions that the fairs are in decline and that *'the registry offices have had a considerable effect upon the public hiring of servants'.*

Another ballad is quoted with its chorus:

> *'Dairymaids and ploughboys gay,*
> *Don't be hired without good pay*

For you've to plough and make the hay,
And milk the cows at break of day.'

The article then makes a comment on social position:

The distinction between rich and poor is feelingly touched on: the farmer and his wife in bed drinking their wine, and the ploughboys and dairymaids *'compelled to rise when the wind does blow, and face the weather through wind and snow.'* But unpleasant though some aspects of the life maybe, the poet remarks that *'there are smiling faces up and down,'* *'Susan, Martha, and Sarah smart, and Matilda Jane in a carrier's cart.'* Of the same Sarah he finds occasion to add that she is the girl for a dairymaid.

'She can make the butter, cheese, and whey,
And dance with John on hiring day.'

5.   The Terms and Conditions and Personal Recollections

The hiring agreements that have survived from the 18th and 19th centuries are similar to the conditions of farm service   quoted in the section - The Bondage System – Its Origins - which was dated 1656. There is an agreement dated December 1745, almost a hundred years later, for a shepherd (Andrew Davidson) at Middleton Hall, Northumberland.   Although for a shepherd, not a hind, it is of interest because as well as including the usual permission to keep sheep he is asked to provide a number of workers for harvest work i.e. '*to doe Bondage when we have Occasion he must find us one Mower one Raker one Shearer*'.   The whole contract is beautifully written but has little punctuation, which makes it a little ambiguous in parts.

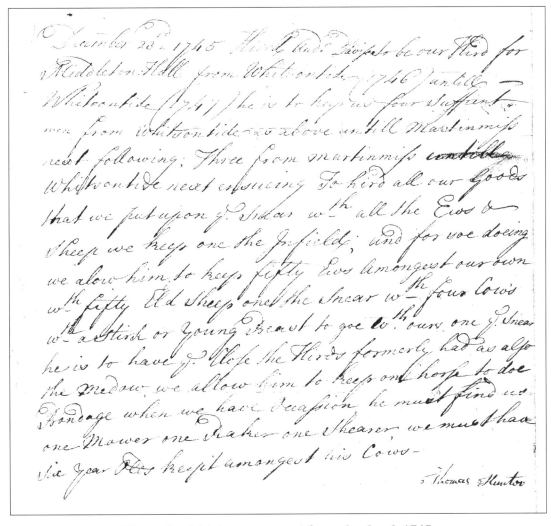

Figure 9. A hiring agreement for a shepherd. 1745.

Transcription of Figure 9:

December 23rd 1745 Hired Andr. Davidson to be our Hird for Middleton Hall from Whitsontide 1746 untill Whitsontide 1747 he is to keep us four sufficient men from Whitsuntide as above until Martinmiss next following; Three from Martinmiss until Whitsontide next ensueing To hird all our Goods that we put upon ye Snear with all the ews and sheep we keep one the Infield; and for soe doing we alow him to keep fifty Ews Amongest our own with fifty Old Sheep one the Snear with four Cow's with a stirk or young Beast to goe with ours one ye Snear he is to have ye Close the Hirds formerly had as also the medow, we allow him to keep one horse to doe Bondage when we have Occasion he must find us one Mower one Raker one Shearer we must have six year olds kept amongst his Cows.

Thomas Huntor

Another interesting early record is from the History of Northumberland [Northumberland 1899]:

'West Chevington, February 28th 1794. The bearer, John Mather, is at liberty to hire with who he pleases, to enter the 12th May.

Jos. Fenwick

This is a *'discharge note granted by Mr. Fenwick to one of his hinds'* which demonstrates that there were more written records than might have been supposed at this time. One agreement included the bondager to spin a spindle of linen yarn. Mr. Armstrong of North Charlton remembers amongst old papers for Middleton Hall that bondagers would get an allowance of wool. Also they were sent to the doctor's to be leeched once a year.

Below are a few records of hiring arrangements, some of which were hand written, and some were recorded on ready prepared printed forms which were usually headed up 'Memorandum of Agreement'.

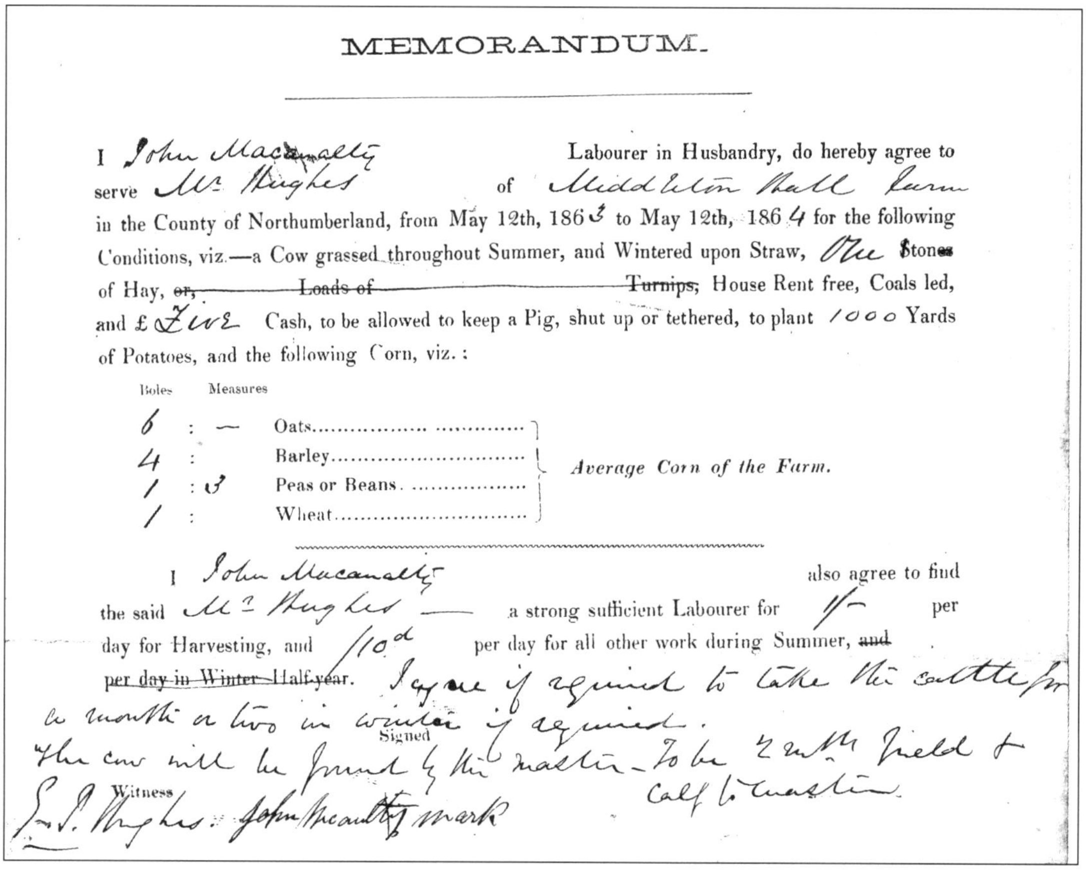

MEMORANDUM.

I John Macanalty Labourer in Husbandry, do hereby agree to serve Mr Hughes of Middleton Hall Farm in the County of Northumberland, from May 12th, 1863 to May 12th, 1864 for the following Conditions, viz.—a Cow grassed throughout Summer, and Wintered upon Straw, One Stones of Hay, ~~or, Loads of Turnips;~~ House Rent free, Coals led, and £ Five Cash, to be allowed to keep a Pig, shut up or tethered, to plant 1000 Yards of Potatoes, and the following Corn, viz.:

Bolls	Measures		
6	: —	Oats	Average Corn of the Farm.
4	:	Barley	
1	: 3	Peas or Beans	
1	:	Wheat	

I John Macanalty also agree to find the said Mr Hughes a strong sufficient Labourer for 1/- per day for Harvesting, and 10d per day for all other work during Summer, ~~and per day in Winter Half-year.~~ I agree if required to take the cattle for a month or two in winter if required. The cow will be found by the master – To be 2nd milk yield & calf to master.

Signed

Witness

E. P. Hughes : John Macanalty mark

Figure 10. John Macanalty's agreement with hand written additions. 1863.

Here John Macanalty is hired for the year from May 1863 to May 1864. The agreement is the usual complex list of payment in kind, some cash and to provide a strong sufficient labourer (the bondager). He also agrees to extra duties with the cattle if necessary. The cow is to be provided by the farmer and the calf and half the milk yield to go to the farmer. Very significantly on the reverse of this agreement is a default clause should John Macanalty be unable to provide a satisfactory bondager. John is unable to sign his name and uses a cross.

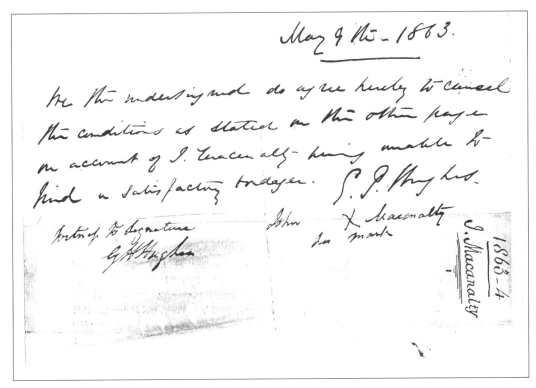

Figure 11. John Macanalty's default clause. 1863.

Memorandum of Agreement.

                                                                           John Angus agrees to hire and *Robert Rankin* agrees to serve the said *John Angus* as Hind, at *Whitefield* Northumberland, for One Year from the *13* day *Mays* 189*8*, during which time the said *Robert Rankin* shall, when working, be paid wages at the rate of *Seventeen* shillings and _____ pence per week, paid monthly. He shall also have *£2.8.0 instead of* _____ Potatoes.

The said *Robert Rankin* is to provide, when required, during the said term *Two* Women, who are to be paid *1/3* per day when working in summer; _____ per day when working in winter, and *2/6* per day when working at harvest work.

                                                             (Master) *John Angus*

                                                               (Servant) *Robert Rankin*

[COPYRIGHT.]

PRINTED AND SOLD BY J. J. JAMES, BOOKSELLER, MORPETH.

Figure 12. Robert Rankin's agreement to work as as a hind at Whitefield. 1893-94.

Robert Rankin's agreement is made on the 8 March 1893 (Hiring day) but runs for the year from 13 May 1893. Robert is paid totally in cash, with a cash allowance instead of potatoes. He is to provide two bondagers when required. Robert signs his name.

MEMORANDUM OF AGREEMENT.

Morpeth March 2 1898

Robert Rankin (if able to work) agrees to serve Mr. John Frater as Hind for One Year, from May 1898 to May 12 1899 for which he shall receive 18 per week, paid monthly 1000 yds potatoes

SECOND MAN.

Andrew 16 per week. 1000 yds potatoes

Steven 8 Potatoes.

To have 3 Women working at 1/6 per day in Summer, 1/3 per day in Winter, and per day in Harvest, or 20 days Harvest at 30 per day.

Robert Rankin. Andrew Rankin

John Frater

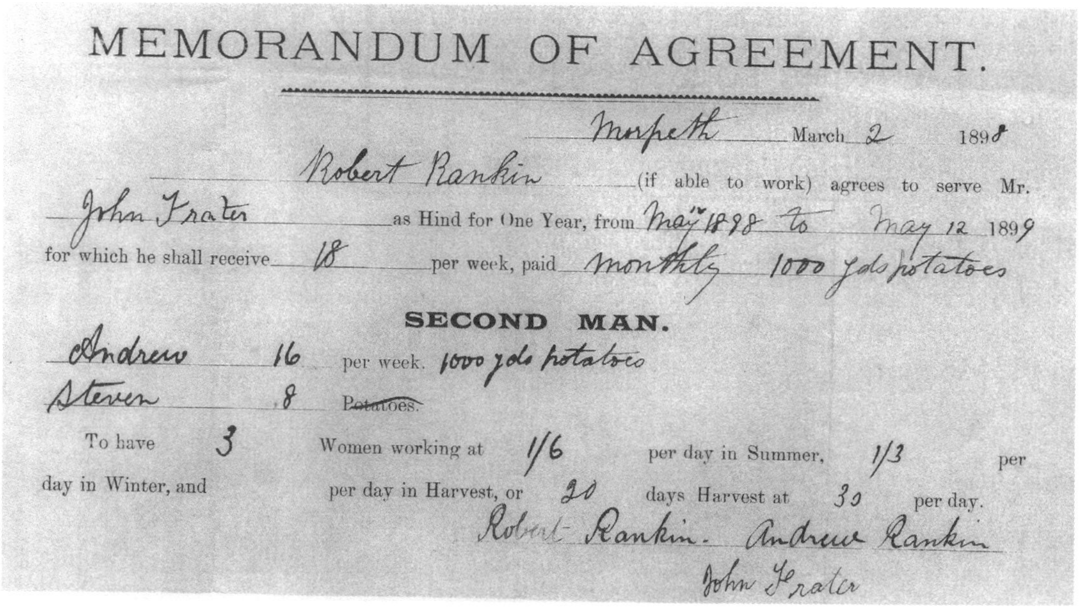

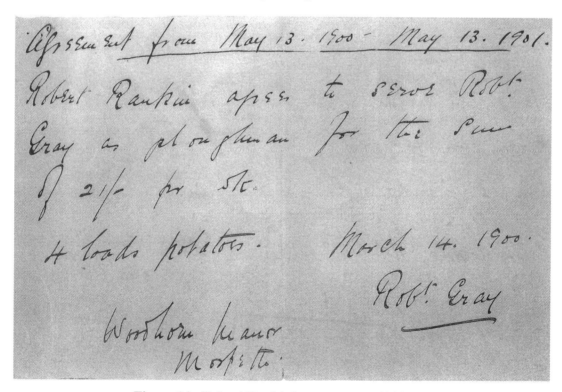

Figure 13. Robert Rankin's agreement. 1898-99.

This Memorandum of Agreement shows a family agreement with Robert Rankin making arrangements for two sons to be employed with him. Steven is probably employed as the odd laddie or turnip dick with wages to correspond. The three women workers are likely also to be family members. Robert and Andrew sign the agreement.

Agreement from May 13. 1900 - May 13. 1901.

Robert Rankin agrees to serve Robt. Gray as ploughman for the sum of 21/- per wk.

4 loads potatoes. March 14. 1900.

Robt. Gray

Woodhorn Manor
Morpeth.

Figure 14. Robert Rankin's agreement. 1900-01.

A year later Robert is working on his own with an increase in cash wages and potatoes by the load rather than a set number of yards. (A thousand yards of potatoes could represent approximately one sixth of an acre if the row was about 28" wide. The yield could be somewhere between ½ to a ton of potatoes. Thanks to my brother Lance for working this out for me).

We can only hazard a guess about what has happened to Robert and his family by the year 1900 to 1901. Perhaps there has been a family disagreement, tragic death or deaths, family members wishing to strike out on their own, or the working situation with John Frater was so difficult it was impossible to stay on and no family situation could be found for the next year. The other possibility is that John Frater himself had run into difficulties and the farm had changed hands.

We do know that in March 1901 Robert was seeking a reference from John Angus, for whom he worked in 1893. Robert obtains a good reference from John Angus and we learn that he had worked for John for six years.

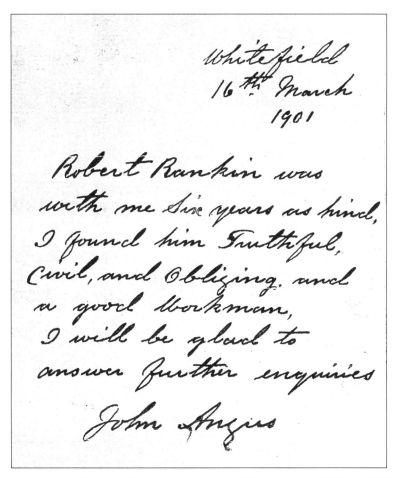

Figure 15. Robert Rankin's reference from John Angus of Whitefield. 1901.

When hiring his workers in the 1860s, Mr. Brown, a farmer at Yearle, noted the arrangements he made with his workers in his pocketbook. He demanded *'a sufficient woman worker'* from some of his workers, both hinds and shepherds. For instance John Dunn, a hind, provides a bondager. James Whittle, a shepherd, also provides a bondager. Robert Thompson, a hind, was to pay the Master 2d. a day, all the year, in lieu of a woman worker. Essentially this was a fine for being unable or unwilling to provide a woman worker. William Whittle, a hind, does not provide a bondager and does not pay a fine. Perhaps this is part of a 'family contract' and James the shepherd has provided the bondager.

These agreements demonstrate the importance of the women workers and their position as part of the male farm workers agreement or bond.

Finally we should also notice Jane Dougharty who has the Cote House and works as an outworker receiving the same wages as the bondagers but with some payment in kind of small wheat and potato land. We can only speculate as to whether she classed herself as a bondager, or was referred to as a bondager by the farmer or her fellow workers.

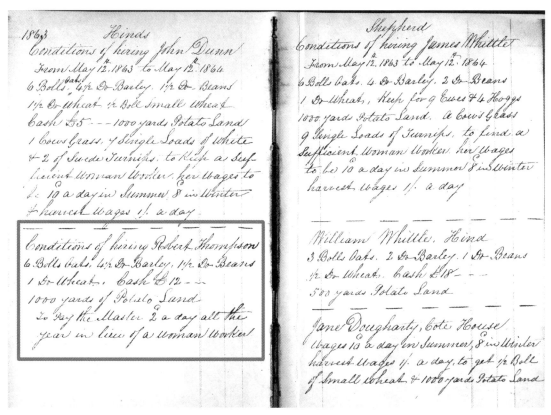

Figure 16. Mr. Brown's pocketbook – Robert Thompson.
(Anne & Derek Fairnington, Wooler)

Appendix to Chapter 5. Hinds' Wages over Time & Ten Years of Wheat Prices

Table showing Hinds' Wages in Cash and in Kind at different Periods								
	1821	1831	1841	1851	1861	1871	1881	1891
Money (stint)	£3 10s	£4 0s	£4 0s	£4 0s	£5 0s	15s a week	15s to 16s a week	16s and upwards
Corn Payments:								
Oats	30 bushels			36 bushels	30 bushels			
Oatmeal		60 stones	60 stones					
Barley	29 bushels	24 bushels	24 bushels	24 bushels	24 bushels			
Beans and Peas	9 bushels	12 bushels	12 bushels	12 bushels	12 bushels			
Wheat	6 bushels	4 bushels	4 bushels	4 bushels and 2 bushels of small wheat	12 bushels			
Potatoes	1 new boll planted.	1,000 yards planted.	1,000 yards	1,000 yards	1,000 yards	18 bags	1,000 yards	1,000 yards
Cow	Grazed in summer: 2 loads hay or turnips in winter.	Grazed in summer: 2 loads hay in winter.	Grazed in summer: 2 loads hay or straw in winter.	Grass in summer: 1 ton hay in winter.	Grass in summer: 1 ton hay with straw in winter.			
House	Free	Free	Free	Free	Free	Free	Free	Free
Coals	Led	Led	Led	Led	Led	Led	Led	Led
Flitting	Free	Free	Free	Free	Free	Free	Free	Free
Female worker	8d a day: 1s a day in harvest	8d a day: 1s in harvest, 24 days	8d and 10d a day:1s in harvest, 24 days	8d and 10d a day: 1s in harvest, 24 days	10d a day: 1s in harvest, 24 days	1s a day: 3s in harvest, 24 days	1s. 3d to 1s.6d a day: 3s in harvest, 24 days	1s.6d a day: 3s in harvest, 24 days

1893 Royal Commission. [Fox 1893].

Wheat Prices, average for the month of April in the years 1839 – 1849, taken from the London Gazette.

1839	70s.	1d.
1840	69s.	0d.
1841	63s.	11d.
1842	61s.	0d.
1843	46s.	5d.
1844	55s.	6d.
1845	45s.	11d.
1846	55s.	6d.
1847	75s.	10d.
1848	49s.	6d.
1849	46s.	0d.

Extracted from The Farmer's Magazine – Prompt Payment by Cuthbert W. Johnson, Esq., F.R.S. [Johnson 1850].

6. The Crucial Years

The Year 1837

1837 was a significant year in the Border area. It was in this year that agricultural workers made a concerted effort to get rid of the bondage system.

It would have been difficult for the hinds to take action much earlier because the Combination Laws made meeting together illegal. These laws emanated from the French Revolution and its repercussions. The British Government feared revolution from the disadvantaged masses, as it was aware of revolutionary enthusiasm and social dissatisfaction. Trade Unionism in particular was feared and the Combination Acts were passed in 1799 and 1800 to prevent men meeting together and forming combinations or unions. G. M. Trevelyan said that *'The laws were supposed to apply against combinations both of masters and men, but in fact the masters were allowed to combine as freely as they wished, while their employees were prosecuted for strike action.'* [Trevelyan 1944].

After much lobbying these Combination Acts were repealed in 1824-1825, so making Trade Unions legal.

The newspapers in February 1837 report a number of meetings and carry detailed items about pay and conditions. They also include lively letters, which dispute the situation.

A report appears in the Berwick Advertiser (4 February 1837) where three separate meetings are mentioned; at Swinton, Gavinton and Mitford and others are alluded to in the statement that the workers are *'forming themselves into a union to act along with the other unions now forming through the country'*. The account of the meeting at Swinton, marked by a cross by someone to highlight the passage, presents a detailed argument against the bondage system and is signed by *'upwards of 80'*. It clearly sets out, in separate points, the difficulties the hinds and their families encounter. If the arrangement with the bondager fails, due to the bondager falling sick or walking away from the situation, or indeed never having arrived to take up the position, or if found unsuitable, the hind still has to provide the extra labour. Thus the burden falls on the hind's wife who then has to *'turn out'* leaving the children unattended. The men state that their children are left *'to the mercy of bystanders, exposed to the fury of the flames and many dangers besides'*.

Providing a bondager must have been a tremendous responsibility and worry at the beginning of a year's work, until the bondager had shown her ability to work well and to fit in with the family. In the previous chapter we saw how a contract could be cancelled if the bondager was unsatisfactory. Secondly, the men give their calculations of the payment in kind and they add to this the money earned by the bondager. From this are deducted the expenses which arise from this arrangement, the bondager's wage and cost of boarding her, which also includes washing. These calculations leave the hind with less than half the gross amount to maintain his family. The men also resolve not to engage unless free of bondage, stacking and harvesting, which suggests they wish to be rid of the obligations which were usually set against the provision of a house. Finally they set up a society, with a fund to overcome the difficulties they foresee when some men are unable to obtain work on these conditions. The fund, it seems, was to be built up from a 5s. penalty incurred by any hind not adhering to the new terms the meeting had agreed.

BONDAGE.—A meeting of hinds residing in Swinton parish was held on Friday the 27th ult., in Swinton, to take into consideration the hardships they lie under with regard to bondage work; and resolutions to the following effect were adopted: " First, with regard to our being bound to produce a woman at pleasure, whatever circumstances we are under, whether sickness, or a breach of bargain with those we have engaged, or their not being suitable (hinders them from giving their services), our wives are obliged to turn out and leave our children to the mercy of the byestanders, exposed to the fury of the flames, and many dangers besides. Second, with regard to our income, we have first,

	£ s. d.
10 bolls of Oats, which for four or five years back will average at 17s 6d per boll,	8 15 0
3 bolls of barley, at £1	3 0 0
1 boll of pease, at £1 5s	1 5 0
1 Cow's keep,	5 0 0
Sheep Money	3 10 0
Potatoe ground, valued	1 10 0
5 Cart load coals, driven at 3s 6d per load	0 17 6
	23 17 6
Bondager's income through the year	6 10 0
Income in full	30 7 6
	16 12 0
	13 15 6

Reduction of yearly income

Bondager's wages	7 10 0
Board and washing, at 3s 6d per week	9 2 0
	16 12 0

By the above statement it appears that £13 15s 6d is the whole that we have to maintain ourselves and families, and we therefore agree conjunctly not to engage for the future unless being free of bondage free of stacking, free of harvesting, under the penalty of 5s, which will be laid into a fund to support those of the society who may not succeed in obtaining services." Signed by upwards of 80.

Figure 17. Swinton. Berwick Advertiser, 4 February 1837

The report of the meeting of hinds in the parish of Langton reveals that Gavinton, near Duns, has a school or at least a schoolroom and that this has been made available for the meeting. The term union is used in the report and the intent is to work together with *'other unions now forming through the country'*. Besides deciding *'unanimously'* to act against the bondage system they were looking for guidance and support from a *'general meeting of the hinds'* in the near future.

A meeting of the hinds in the parish of Langton took place on Wednesday the 1st inst., in the School room, Gavinton, for the purpose of forming themselves into a union to act along with the other unions now forming through the country which have for their object to abolish the present system of bondage—when it was unanimously resolved that the bondage to which they are at present compelled to submit is a great grievance, which they ought to get quit of as soon as possible and all present signed their names to act together, and to be guided by a general meeting of the hinds of the country, which is expected shortly to take place.

Figure 18. Gavinton. Berwick Advertiser, 4 February 1837

The report of the meeting at Mitford, which is close to Morpeth in the south of Northumberland, shows there was county-wide dissatisfaction amongst the hinds about their working conditions. The meeting was held in a public house and many hinds attended but we are given no indication of what, if any, decisions were made.

> A numerous meeting of the hinds in the parish of Mitford and its neighbourhood was held at Mr. Robert Thompson's, Plough Inn, Mitford on Saturday the 28th January last, for the purpose of considering the bondage system."

Figure 19. Mitford. Berwick Advertiser, 4 February 1837

William Brewis (1778-1850) of Throphill, a hamlet four miles west of Morpeth, wrote in his diary for 6 to 13 March 1837 that *'The Hinds hiring commenced on the first day of March at Morpeth. They through the course of the winter have been meeting and forming a kind of Union amongst themselves not to bind their wives or maids to what is commonly called bondage. It has made a great stir throughout the county, in many places, say Alnwick, Wooler, Rothbury, but,'* he concludes, *'at Morpeth they were more quiet'*. (The Northumbrian October/November 2004)

The Berwick and Kelso Warder (18 February 1837) reports on a similar meeting in Haddington in East Lothian where the term combination is used, rather than union. Whilst mostly about the hind this meeting does suggest wages for labourers and farm servants. Labourers should have 12s a week, which would be 2s a day. This seems high but is, perhaps, an attempt to secure and keep a casual labourer who is able to pay for his or her keep. The farm servant refers perhaps to the byre man or orra man or even a bondager when employed for the full year. This article also raises the question of exploitation and hours of work but makes no attempt to stipulate the hours.

> COMBINATION OF THE FARM SERVANTS IN EAST LOTHIAN.—At a meeting of the hinds, farm-servants, and labourers, lately held in the Town Hall, Haddington, the following resolutions were agreed to, viz. :—" L.10 sterling in money; a cow's keep, or L.6 allowed instead; 1½ quarters of Barley; 4-8ths do. of pease; 6¼ bolls of oatmeal, Dutch weight; 6 bolls of potatoes, 4 cwt. per boll; permission to keep a pig, five weeks' meat in harvest; free house and garden; coals driven; no bondager; labourers' wages, 12s. per week; farm servants, L.14 per year; also, that no undue advantage should be taken of the hours of labour expected from the servants." What may be the result of these resolutions, we know not; but it is undoubtedly a new position which that class of the community have assumed.

Figure 20. Haddington. Berwick and Kelso Warder, 18 February 1837

The reporter wonders about the outcome of the meeting and says *'What may be the result of these resolutions, we know not'* and he then indicates that this is the beginning of workers trying to influence their situation through joint action saying, *'but it is undoubtedly a new position which that class of the community have assumed'*.

At about the same time, in the Berwick Advertiser, a number of detailed articles appeared. One is a report of a second meeting at Ayton and two anonymous presentations, by *'A Farmer'*. The Ayton article reported on the *'loud' 'complaints'* against *'the hardships'* of *'this relic of feudalism'* which is, of course, the bondage system. Again the report helps to show how the hinds find the system difficult. *'The three-fold cord of bondage'* is detailed.

The first cord is the bondager herself but the second cord illuminates the complex situation and real difficulties the hind and family had in fulfilling his bond. Not only must the hind supply a bondager but if she is working in the fields and a stack needs to be carried then somehow another worker has to be found. This is usually the hind's wife and then the problem of childcare has to be solved. This seems an incredible burden to place on a hind when this kind of planning and organisation ought to be the responsibility of the farmer or foreman or steward. The third cord mentioned is, of course, harvest work.

The fear of not getting a place held many back from signing up to the *'Society'* and the meeting ended with *'everyone to engage on the best terms he could'*.

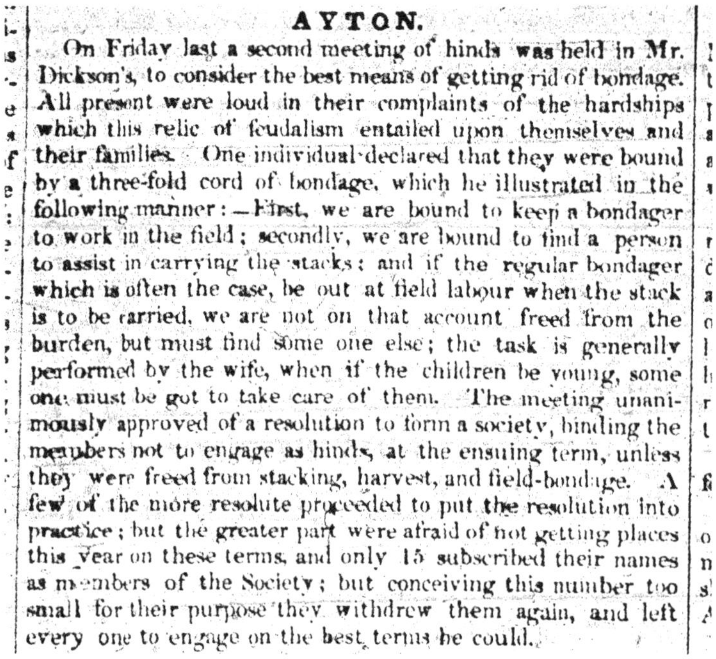

AYTON.

On Friday last a second meeting of hinds was held in Mr. Dickson's, to consider the best means of getting rid of bondage. All present were loud in their complaints of the hardships which this relic of feudalism entailed upon themselves and their families. One individual declared that they were bound by a three-fold cord of bondage, which he illustrated in the following manner: — First, we are bound to keep a bondager to work in the field; secondly, we are bound to find a person to assist in carrying the stacks; and if the regular bondager which is often the case, be out at field labour when the stack is to be carried, we are not on that account freed from the burden, but must find some one else; the task is generally performed by the wife, when if the children be young, some one must be got to take care of them. The meeting unanimously approved of a resolution to form a society, binding the members not to engage as hinds, at the ensuing term, unless they were freed from stacking, harvest, and field-bondage. A few of the more resolute proceeded to put the resolution into practice; but the greater part were afraid of not getting places this year on these terms, and only 15 subscribed their names as members of the Society; but conceiving this number too small for their purpose they withdrew them again, and left every one to engage on the best terms he could.

Figure 21. Ayton. Berwick Advertiser, 18 February 1837

The *'A Farmer'* articles are quite different. The first article is a simple table of the hind's income with the heading HINDS' CONDITIONS IN NORTHUMBERLAND. The bondage system is totally ignored with no mention of the provision of an extra worker or what duties this worker must fulfil. The writer challenges *'anyone to disprove its accuracy!'*

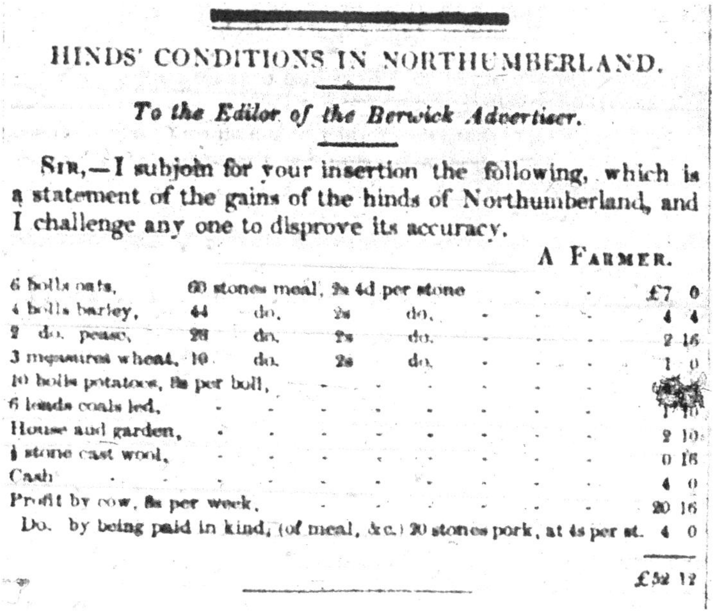

HINDS' CONDITIONS IN NORTHUMBERLAND.

To the Editor of the Berwick Advertiser.

SIR,—I subjoin for your insertion the following, which is a statement of the gains of the hinds of Northumberland, and I challenge any one to disprove its accuracy.

A FARMER.

6 bolls oats,	60 stones meal, 2s 4d per stone		£7	0
4 bolls barley,	44 do.	2s do.	4	4
2 do. pease,	28 do.	2s do.	2	16
3 measures wheat,	10 do.	2s do.	1	0
10 bolls potatoes, 8s per boll,			[illegible]	[illegible]
6 loads coals led,			1	10
House and garden,			2	10
½ stone cast wool,			0	16
Cash			4	0
Profit by cow, 8s per week,			20	16
Do. by being paid in kind, (of meal, &c.) 20 stones pork, at 4s per st.			4	0
			£52	12

Figure 22. Hind's Conditions in Northumberland. Berwick Advertiser, 18 February 1837

The second article is very long and from the Scottish side of the border. It is signed *'I am, sir, yours, &c. A Farmer – Banks of the Blackadder, February 1st 1837'* (Berwick Advertiser dated 18 February 1837) This article also enumerates the payment in kind and takes the bondager into the account. In this case the income of the hind stands at £40.9s.7d., which contrasts with the previous article which gives the hind an income of £52.12s. This is a very large discrepancy. Comparing the two sets of figures is very difficult as the writers choose to work in different ways. One gives prices per stone and the other by the boll. Potatoes are expressed in the number of yards planted or in bolls of seed potatoes. In one list the house and garden is valued £2.10s. and the other gives no cash value. This emphasises the intricacies of the system and also must provoke in us admiration for these men and their ability to make these complex business agreements.

The writer from the Banks of the Blackadder goes on to point out that the bondager will work in *'the house at bye hours'* so being useful in a way unaccounted for when just looking at the transactions in money. This usefulness might or might not be the case and there is some suggestion that not all bondagers were so helpful. Walter White writes *'and when, as sometimes happens, there is no work in the fields, he must still keep her, and she hangs about the home, sewing a little for herself if she can. As regards housework the testimony concerning her is she is not fond of it, or offering to assist the wife'.* [White 2006].

The writer from the Banks of the Blackadder continues by pointing out that not every hind needs to look outside his family for the bondager. Only '*one in every three or four'* has to hire a worker through the hiring fair. He also lists the days of work lost, such as *'hiring days, flitting days, preaching days, sick days, very wet days when little work is done, and at least three months in the middle of winter when one-fourth of each day is lost for want of light',* when valuing the hind's wage on a weekly basis. By thinking of various additional sources of income, the cow, its calf and potatoes the weekly 'cash' amount grows from 12s. to 15s. a week. He achieves this, partly, by reducing the year from 52 weeks to 48 weeks to take account of the lost days already listed and, not forgetting, the shorter winter days. He thinks that payment in kind is a great advantage with the hind receiving the same gains regardless of the crops' yields that year and wonders if the hinds value this as they should. He then launches into the objection to the bondage system and the letter becomes more abusive in tone as he asks, *'Do they imagine the farmers will give them the same gains without bondagers as they do with them? Not likely!'* Housing workers in the farmhouse, he says, is not an option. This had been the system when farms were smaller and the workforce was also small. In consequence of this, the only alternative to the bondage system is the "north country" system of erecting bothies - here he uses "north country" to mean northern Scotland. He then suggests this will result in *'filthy, drunken and immoral* habits' which contrasts strongly with the *'cleanliness, sobriety, and good moral conduct'* which he maintains is a direct result of the bondage system. This is due to the good, steadying parental influence on the young workers.

Barbara Robertson also writes about the bothy system and considers that *'Deprivation there undoubtedly was (in the bondage system) but compared with conditions that prevailed in the bothy system counties north of the Forth or in the lives of many urban workers, the Border farm servant, whether male or female, was certainly better off.'* [Robertson 1990].

TO THE

EDITOR OF THE BERWICK ADVERTISER.

Mr. Editor,—As I understand your valuable paper is pretty extensively read by the hinds, permit me through its medium to address a few lines to them. I have learned that numbers of the hinds have had meetings, and my own amongst the rest, for the purpose of combining to get their wages raised, but more particularly to resist keeping a worker (commonly called a bondager). The first thing that I shall state is the amount of income a hind has at present, and I will just take my own estimates which I suppose are about the average in this part of the country. Their gains then are as follow, viz.:—

10 bolls of best oats, at 22s per boll	£11 0 0
3 ditto of barley, at 24s	3 12 0
1 ditto of pease, at 30s	1 10 0
1500 yards of a drill of potatoes planted, at 3s 6d per hundred	2 12 6
Cow's grass	4 10 0
Fodder for ditto	1 15 0
500 yards of potatoes planted for ditto, at 3s 6d per hundred	0 17 6
4 double cart loads of coals driven, and more if they need them, at 8s	1 12 0
Sheep money,	4 0 0
Drink money,	0 10 8
Meat in the time of harvest, at least 30 days, at 6d per day	0 15 0
Supper barley, ¼ of a boll,	0 6 0
Worker's summer's wage, average about 96 days, at 10d per day	3 19 2
Ditto harvest wage, 22½ at 2s 2d per day.	2 8 9
Do. meat in the time of harvest, and working amongst corn after, 30 days, at 6d	0 15 0
Do. supper barley, ¼ of a boll	0 6 0
	£40 9 7
I have added the worker's summer and harvest wage to the hinds, but for that I deduct £4 for the wage he pays her, and 3s 6d per week for her meat, which I think quite enough considering that she does always something in the house at bye hours, £3 17s	8 17 0
	£31 12 7

The above statement is only applicable to such hinds as are under the necessity of hiring maidens: those who can furnish a worker from their own family, are much better off, and I consider that there is not more than one out of every three or four who is obliged to go to the market to hire a worker. To the above statement I might have added several little advantages a hind has over a labourer who resides in a town, but shall pass these over. Taking the above sum of £31 12s 7d and dividing it by 52 weeks, it will be found that a hind has upwards of 12s per week upstanding wages through the year; but were I to take from these 52 weeks, all the time that a farmer loses through the twelvemonth, such as hiring days, flitting days, preaching days, sick days, very wet days when little work is done, and at least three months in the middle of winter when one-fourth of each day is lost for want of light, there would not be more than 48 weeks in the year that could be counted. According to this calculation they get upwards of 13s per week. But the above is not the real income of a hind; to the above sum of £31 12s 7d should be added at least £3 more as profit on his cow, £1 5s for her calf, and £3 more on the produce of his potato ground. If these sums are added together, they will amount to £38 17s 7d as real income, which gives him within a few fractions of 15s per week. From the above statement (which I consider moderate for this year), it appears a hind has decidedly the advantage over every other labourer in this country, with the exception of shepherds and stewards. As hinds are paid chiefly from the produce of the farm are they really so blind as not to see that when the prices of grain, &c., are low, they only suffer along with their masters; but when prices are high, like this year, they are often greater gainers than their masters?—the number of bolls they have to dispose of being always the same, while their masters may have little to sell from the badness of the crops. But it appears that their low wages are not the only thing they complain of. The great outcry is the hardship of keeping a *Bondager.* If they are determined to get rid of this burden, what do they think will be the consequence? Do they imagine farmers will give them the same gains without the bondagers as they do with them? Not likely! But what is to become of the workers (who are their own sons and daughters)? Do they suppose that farmers will take into their houses the additional number of 12 or 15 young men and women? That is what they will never submit to do. What then is to become of them? For my part I can see no other way of accommodating them, and at the same time getting our out-work carried on, but by adopting the north country system, and that is by erecting bothies for them: and what turn will this serve them?—will it not engender filthy, drunken, and immoral habits, as it does in the north country? What, I would ask, is the cause of our hinds and their families being so respectable in their station in life, of their superiority over the farm servants in the north country for cleanliness, sobriety, and good moral conduct? Nothing but the *Bondage* system; or, in other words, their being brought up under their parents' roof, and under their immediate superintendance. There is no doubt servants have just as good a right as their masters to meet and discuss their grievances; but I would warn them to consider well what they are about. How long is it since they could not get places when they were thrown out of employment, and when labourers of almost every description were trying to get hindings? Will these days never return again, do they think? And besides, do they not suppose that such of their masters as pay them well, and otherwise use them well, will not be disgusted at their conduct? I could say a great deal more on this subject to shew its absurdity, but will conclude by advising the hinds to take care what they are about, and to look at the dilemma into which they are landing themselves. I have not heard of stewards joining the hinds in this absurd business, but am not a little surprised at shepherds making the same outcry about the hardship of keeping a worker, and will be very short with what I have to say to them. According to the present price of stock a shepherd has at least £5 more than a steward, and £10 more than a hind, therefore they are fitter to keep two than a hind is to keep one.

I am, sir, yours, &c.

A Farmer.

Banks of the Blackadder, Feb. 1st, 1837.

Figure 23. Banks of the Blackadder. Berwick Advertiser, 18 February 1837

The writer from the Banks of the Blackadder continues his letter with more warnings, and despite acknowledging the rights of servants to meet and discuss their grievances, he raises the spectre of unemployment. *'How long is it since they could not get places?'* and suggests this situation might return. Farmers who *'pay them well'* and *'use them well'* will be *'disgusted at their conduct'.* He also attacks shepherds who have joined the hinds in the protest. As we know, shepherds were sometimes asked to keep another worker.

This letter does not go unchallenged for in the Berwick Advertiser (4 March 1837) there is a lengthy reply from *'An Advocate for the Abolition of Bondage'*, Swinton Parish, 27 February 1837. The writer suggests that the letter was meant to *'intimidate'*, and he sets out to *'correct some errors and absurd ideas'*. He takes issue with the figures given and considers many of them to be exaggerated. The work allotted to pay for the hind's house far outweighs the value of the *'almost ruinous cottage'* - £3.13s.9d being the value of work as against £1.10s. his valuation of the cottage. These exaggerated amounts would, he suggests, add up to £12, which could be deducted from the 'extravagant statement' of £31.12s.7d. or £38.17s. The profit from the cow is dismissed because, as he points out, the profit *'in many instances a hind has of a cow's skin'*. He also derides the attitude towards the shorter winter days that can hardly be laid at the door of the hind but instead *'the ruler of the seasons'*. (Might he be a minister?) He urges the *'hinds and farm servants'* to *'stand firm and steadfast'*.

Figure 24. An Advocate for the Abolition of Bondage. Berwick Advertiser, 4 March 1837

In March the newspapers report on the fairs as usual. The Berwick and Kelso Warder (4 March 1837) comments on the number of farm servants which are more than usual and that they were *'generally engaged on the same terms as formerly; a few only receiving a little additional wages'*. The reporter speculates that this calm successful hiring market *'will prove fatal to the combination to which we adverted a few weeks ago'*.

Hiring Markets.

DUNSE HIRING MARKET.—At this market, on Wednesday last, the number of farm servants in attendance was greater than on any similar occasion for many years past, and they were very generally engaged on the same terms as formerly; a few only receiving a little additional wages. The business of the market went on very quietly, and, in all probability, the result will prove fatal to the combination to which we adverted a few weeks ago.

Figure 25. Dunse. The Berwick and Kelso Warder, 4 March 1837

The Berwick Advertiser also reports on the Dunse (today's Duns) Hiring, (Wednesday, 1 March 1837) mentioning how quietly everything had proceeded. *'Some irritation' had been expected because of the 'unions which had been formed throughout the county for the purpose of abolishing bondage'.* This report also detailed the *'additional wages'* as 10s. to £1 sheep money *'and 2d. per day on bondagers' wages'.*

DUNSE.

The hiring market at Dunse for engaging married farm servants took place on Wednesday the 1st instant. Some irritation was expected to have taken place betwixt the hinds and their masters on account of the unions which have been formed throughout the county for the purpose of abolishing bondage. The whole however went off very quietly, no stand having been made on that subject. Hiring was brisk, and an advance of from 10s to £1 has been obtained on what is called sheep money; and also 2d per day on bondagers' wages.

Figure 26. Dunse. Berwick Advertiser, 4 March 1837

The same edition of the Berwick Advertiser reported on Wooler hiring market which was held on Friday 3 March 1837. On this occasion because *'a strike'* to *'repeal'* the *'bondage system'* was expected *'few masters were present'.* The writer then goes on to report a very significant event. *'We have heard of two gentlemen who engaged their servants without the bondager.'* A caveat to that is *'the servants agreed to shear during the harvest'* so covering one of the aspects of a bondager's work.

Wooler hiring Market, which took place yesterday, was numerously attended by servants; but as it was generally supposed that a strike would be made for the repeal of the "bondage system" few masters were present, and consequently little hiring was affected. We have heard of two gentlemen who engaged their servants without the bondager, but the servants agreed to shear during the harvest.

Figure 27. Wooler. Berwick Advertiser, 4 March 1837

The Newcastle Courant (10 March 1837) also reported the hirings. *'Kelso Hiring Market - On Friday last the attendance of married servants at the Kelso hiring market was greater than for many years past; a considerable number from Northumberland being present'.* The date of this hiring seems to have been the same as the Wooler hiring, and two days after the Dunse hiring. The attitude of the farm servants at the beginning of proceedings was described as showing *'a disposition to demand higher rates',* but few obtained the increases mentioned before of 2d. per day for bondagers and £1 per annum additional stint or sheep money. It concludes by remarking that many left *'without having obtained situations'* even upon the old terms. These workers, no doubt, felt discouraged by the outcome and would be fearful for the future of themselves and their families.

KELSO HIRING MARKET.—On Friday in last week, the attendance of married farm servants at the Kelso Hiring Market was greater than for many years past, a considerable number from Northumberland being present. At the commencement of the market, the servants shewed a disposition to demand higher rates than has lately been current in the district, and in a very few instances obtained, we believe, a rise of 2d per day on the wages of bondagers, and L.1 per annum additional stint money. The greater part of the engagements entered into, however, were on the old conditions, and many servants left the market without having obtained situations even upon these terms.

Figure 28. Kelso. The Newcastle Courant, 10 March 1837

The story continues to unfold in the papers published on 11 March 1837. The Melrose report is brief and no mention is made of any attempt to demand more money or to abolish the bondage system.

MELROSE, MARCH 4.—At our hiring market for married servants held here to-day, there was a good turn out. Wages, so far as we heard, were the same as former years, and a good deal of business was done.

Figure 29. Melrose. Berwick and Kelso Warder, 11 March 1837

The reports on the Berwick hiring market are lengthy and full of drama in both the Berwick and Kelso Warder and the Berwick Advertiser. The description in the Warder (11 March 1837) indicates a very large gathering, which was on the whole pretty well behaved. The men who had their coat tails cut off would be very upset as a mutilated best coat would be a financially serious occurrence as well as a humiliating one. This seems to be a strange way of showing objection but was repeated elsewhere so perhaps was an accepted way of taking *'revenge'*. Some *'hooting'*, *'one or two pugilistic recoutres'* and scaring the masters' horses were the other demonstrations made at this fair. The reporter says that *'nothing of a serious nature took place'* although the police *'were on the alert'*. The outcome was that farmers near to Berwick hired hinds without bondagers, relying on casual labour being available from the town. Other farmers made private arrangements or paid the increases mentioned previously – 2d. a day for the bondager and a *'slight increase in wages'* (perhaps the £1 stint money mentioned before). The reporter concludes *'by the redress of every grievance on the part of the masters, the good sense of the servants will soon convince them of the injudiciousness of sudden and ill-formed combination;'* and he looks to things very quickly returning to normal.

BERWICK HIGH MARKET.– Saturday last, the High Market for the hiring of servants was held in Berwick, and the concourse of people from all the surrounding districts was immense, so great an assemblage not having taken place in the town for upwards of nine years. In Hyde Hill, the principal place of rendezvous, the people were literally wedged in, and it was with the utmost difficulty that carriages could make their way through the dense mass. The cause of this great influx of people was attributed to the few engagements that had been made at Wooler, Dunse, and the other hiring markets in the neighbourhood. The hinds appeared generally determined to resist the system of bondaging, and throughout the day evinced their resolution by hooting at such individuals as they supposed were inclined to take employment on the usual terms. On one or two persons whom they suspected, they took a species of revenge by cutting off their coat tails, but, with the exception of this, and one or two pugilistic rencontres—common to almost all fairs—nothing of a serious nature took place, not even a riot requiring the interference of the police, who were on the alert. There were some indications of hostility to the masters, discovered occasionally in the scaring of their horses as they passed through the crowd. With regard to the hiring, little was done upon the whole. Some farmers, in the vicinity of the town, hired a few hinds without bondagers, calculating on a ready supply of workers from Berwick, when needed. Those at a greater distance engaged their hinds either privately on the old terms, or openly with an advance of 2d a day for bondage labour, and a slight increase of wages.—We have no doubt, that by the redress of every grievance on the part of the masters, the natural good sense of the servants will soon convince them of the injudiciousness of sudden and ill-framed combination; and that, in a week or two, when the present excitement subsides, they will return cordially to their employment.

Figure 30. Berwick. Berwick and Kelso Warder, 11 March 1837

The reporter for the Berwick Advertiser (11 March 1837) mentioned the *'unprecedented number of servants'* at this market, due, he says, to a *'greater portion of the hinds having left their situations on account of "the bondage", and their refusal to engage on these terms at Kelso and Wooler Fairs'*. He includes the interesting information that a *'Mr. G. Rea Jnr., of Wooler,'* visited this hiring fair in the morning. He *'addressed'* the *'multitude'* from *'the window of the Peacock Inn'*. Mr. Rea spoke about the injustice of the bondage system and urged the hinds to stand firm. (The Peacock Inn stood at the junction between Hide Hill, Silver Street and Sandgate where The Bank of Scotland now stands.)

BERWICK UPON TWEED.

BERWICK HIRING MARKET.—In consequence of the greater portion of the hinds having left their situations on account of "the bondage," and their refusal to engage on these terms at Kelso and Wooler Fairs, an unprecedented number of servants were in attendance at our market on Saturday. The weather during the day was remarkably fine. In the forenoon the multitude were addressed from the window of the Peacock Inn by Mr. G. Rea jun., of Wooler, who enlarged upon the injustice of the bondage system, and recommended the hinds to stand firm and unflinching and the farmers would be obliged to yield. Nearly all of them acted up to this advice, and consequently there was very little hiring. When any of the farmers who were in favour of bondage appeared, they were received with hooting and cheering, but no violence was offered. One hind who had engaged himself on the former terms, was denuded of the tails of his coat; but no bodily harm, we believe, was sustained by him. A very few agreed to provide a bondager as formerly, and some compromised the matter; but the far greater portion returned home unhired. Those who were engaged without bondagers were generally such as had large families—the farmers supposing that in these cases they would be secure for labourers. An advance of 2d per day on the worker's wages was generally acceded.

Figure 31. Berwick. Berwick Advertiser, 11 March 1837

Hastings Neville wrote in his book, first published in 1909 [Neville 1909], about the breaking of the bondage system. His story closely resembles the newspaper accounts but with the passage of time, sixty years or more, perhaps some details had become mixed up. Wooler was the place where farmers first hired their hinds without the bondage condition but the *'commotion'* and speech from the window of an inn seems to have happened in Berwick.

CORNHILL.

COALITION BETWEEN THE FARMERS AND HINDS.—On Monday last the quarterly market was held at Cornhill, at which an unusually large number of hinds were present. They were on two or three different occasions harangued on the grievance of bondage in the course of the day. The [illegible] farmer we believe who acceded to their terms was Mr. Tulip of Westfield, who had no sooner done so than he was elevated in a chair and carried by them in triumph up and down the market. A strong excitement was evinced when it was learned that any one had hired subject to the old rules of bondage, or where any one offered himself for hire even though an advance of wages was stipulated. Immediately all were at work, and with the assistance of such means as were at hand his coat was made a spencer. Nothing could exceed the ridiculous appearance of the parties thus cropped, of whom there were not a few. We understand Mr. Thomson of Pawston, while endeavouring to save a person to whom even more than this was threatened, was relieved of his watch, some one having taken the advantage of the pressure to appropriate it to himself.

Figure 32. Cornhill. Berwick Advertiser, 11 March 1837

Another notable event took place at Cornhill and was again reported in the Berwick Advertiser (11 March 1837). The report was entitled *'Coalition between the Farmers and Hinds'*. At this *'quarterly market'* there was again a large gathering and they were, as the reporter put it, *'harangued on the grievances of bondage'*. He then describes how a farmer, believed to be Mr. Tulip of Westfield, who went along with the demands *'was elevated in a chair and carried by them in triumph up and down the market'*. The reporter also notices that if a hind was willing to be hired on the old system, although with *'an advance of wages'*, he was given the same treatment as those in Berwick; his coat was *'made a spencer'*. The haranguing, the chairing of Mr. Tulip and cutting of coat-tails would stir up very strong feelings which could easily spill over into violence. Mr. Thomson of Pawston, for instance, was *'relieved of his watch'* whilst endeavouring to save someone under threat of having more than his coat-tails cut! This must have been a very memorable meeting which would be talked about for a very long time.

The whole hiring season must have been the talk of the area for many weeks. There was the worrying time leading up to the hirings, and then the dissection and discussion of what had actually happened. No doubt there would be some bad feeling and recrimination amongst the workers, and farmers would, very likely, resent the uncertainty and disturbance, which had resulted in a rise in wages. In the Berwick and Kelso Warder (25 March 1837) under the heading "Local Intelligence" (the heading for local news) there is, surprisingly, no direct reference to the recent troubles which has obviously died down. The reporter says *'upon the whole, engagements have been made satisfactory to both parties'*. The *'advance of wages'* he suggests *'upon proper application, was cheerfully yielded by the farmers'*. An unusual statement, considering the previous news items and letters. Perhaps he is trying to diminish the hinds' meetings, the letters and the demonstrations at the hiring fairs and suggest that all the fuss, had actually been unnecessary.

Berwick and Kelso Warder, 25 March 1837:

Local Intelligence
The season for hiring farm servants is now nearly over, and upon the whole, engagements have been made satisfactory to both parties. Throughout the northern parts of the county of Northumberland, the hinds have obtained an advance of wages, which upon proper application was cheerfully yielded by the farmers.

This seems to mark the end of this determined attempt by the agricultural workers to combine together in a form of union, and force some change in their hiring conditions.

Sir F. H. Doyle writes in his report [Doyle 1844] *'Mr. Jobson, of Chillingham Newton, whose local situation rendered him independent of it, yielded to the wishes of his men, and hired them at certain wages, with regular employment for the year; and singular enough, before the year was out, they desired one and all to be replaced on the original footing; in fact there can be no doubt that, owing to the thinness of the population, the great farmers who have suddenly sprung up on the borders find some such system necessary in order to carry on their agricultural operations, and the labourers receive an equivalent for submitting to it.'* Due to the isolation in which these farm workers lived it was difficult for them to achieve and maintain a united front. Also, perhaps the advantage of this system was only fully appreciated when a new system was introduced.

Again the bondagers themselves get little mention and we must just imagine how keenly they would follow events. They would have been interested in the final outcome and how this would affect their own circumstances.

Life after 1837

No doubt, life for many soon got back to normal but for some their lives were to change forever when they emigrated to Canada. In June 1837 150 people *'mainly farming families from the Glendale area of Northumberland and from the Borders, boarded the Sunderland-built 450 ton ship Cornelius, which left Berwick for New Brunswick in Canada. The ship had been chartered by the Stanley Land Company, which promised both land and work. But by the time they arrived in Canada in July 1837 after a month-long voyage, this was no longer available.*

However, the provincial government stepped in to help the arrivals and they were offered 100 acres of land each in an area known as Harvey settlement.

Friends and relatives were persuaded to join them. In 1850, a number of other families arrived and took up a 1,000-acre block of land which they called Tweedside.

Harvey and Tweedside became one continuous settlement and was peopled by emigrants from the Borders and Glendale areas and, to this day, the name Tweedside lives on in New Brunswick.' (The Journal, 18 August 2007).

These people had already been through a traumatic hiring season and then made the courageous decision to emigrate. It is easy for us to imagine how desperate they must have felt on learning that the Stanley Land Company had got into financial difficulties, but luckily help was given.

The number of emigrants had been growing over the previous five years and these emigrants were now not only made up of mechanics, farm servants and small farmers but also *'enterprising agriculturists'* with substantial capital. (Berwick Advertiser 3 June 1837)

The report two years later, in the Berwick Advertiser (9 March 1839), shows that the old routine continued and this hiring market at Berwick was a particularly happy occasion:

Hiring Market – On Saturday last our market was attended by an immense number of agricultural servants. The weather throughout the day was exceedingly pleasant, and a great number of country people visited the town for amusement in addition to those in quest for situations; in short the latter number seemed to be the minority. We do not remember the occasion when the market was more numerously attended. The appearance and deportment of the whole could not be equalled but in Great Britain; and was matter for great gratulation (congratulation). *The demand for servants was equal to the number present, and we believe all met with engagements on terms similar to those of late years.*

Other items from the newspapers continue to give some idea of life at this time.

On 16 March 1839, a week after the last newspaper report, the Wooler hiring market is featured and the reporter notes the lack of people at the hiring market. Despite the obvious reasons that this market was the last of the season, and the weather was poor, the writer also mentions other reasons which include emigration and the lure of the big town.

Berwick Advertiser, 16 March 1839:

Wooler High Market.
This market was held on Thursday the 7th instant. We never saw such a thin market here before: perhaps it may be accounted for by the stormy weather, and it being the last of the hiring markets. We understand the hinds were all quickly hired, and that a number of farmers are still in want of hands. This class of men are not so numerous as they were a few years since; emigration has thinned them considerably, besides many of them have removed to Newcastle and other manufacturing districts, where they obtain better wages than they receive in agricultural employment. We have however some reason to suppose that their morals are far from improved by the change: Their simple and natural mode of life so highly conducive to the improvement of the health and the heart, renders them easily led away by bad example, too much of which abounds in more populous districts.

This report is rather patronising in tone, but enables us to have an insight into the attitude of the times, as well as the information about how employment patterns were changing. The farm workers, we find, were looking to improve their circumstances and widen their horizons. The year of 1837 may still have been having some influence on the situation in 1839.

These two hiring market reports are very general, with no specific detail of the wages agreed, although in Wooler hinds were scarce.

In 1840 the weather seems to have been the major factor in the poor turn out for the Kelso Hiring Market and it is notable that the word bondager is replaced by the term 'women'.

Berwick Advertiser, 21 November 1840:

Kelso
At our market of Friday last, owing to the very unfavourable state of the weather, the attendance of both masters and servants was considerably less than usual. The rate of wages were higher than last year, and were as follows:- Women for the half-year, from 40s. to 50s. and some were as high as 60s. Men from £4.10s. to £6. Lads from 30s. to 50s. according to age.

The agricultural report in the Berwick Advertiser (28 November 1840) confirms the exceptional state of the weather:

East Lothian.
The weather has been unfavourable for out-door labour since our last; repeated and heavy showers of rain having rendered the ground too wet to allow of it being readily worked, which has been extremely embarrassing for the farmers, and may be of a serious consequence. In so much as on the clay soils, it is impossible to get the wheat into the ground, which will now have to stand till spring, as the more than ordinary state of the soil, joined to the advanced period of the year, is against the probability of anything further being done in this part of the season.

Hiring continued to be noted in the Berwick Advertiser with an interesting comment in March 1848 that for two years the prospect of work on the railway had led to higher wages and gains, but in this year things were back to normal. At this time the railway was under construction with the Royal Border Bridge being built between 1847 and 1850. This bridge was designed by Robert Stephenson and was *'built by 2738 men, 180 horses, and two Nasmyth steamhammers to drive in elm piles'.* [Strang 1994].

On 13 October 1849 the Wooler correspondent reported the *'corn crops safely secured'* and the potato crop good and suffering from less disease than other local areas. Seven months later the weather was again so unusual that we get an even longer report in the Berwick Advertiser for 11 May 1850. Here it links the corncrake and cuckoo together demonstrating that they were equally common, at that time, in the border area.

Berwick Advertiser 11 May 1850:

The weather.
The night, which closed the first week of May, was more like a night of February than of the month of the cuckoo and the corncrake. The snow was in some places more than an inch in depth, and there were several very severe hail showers. Since then the weather has been gradually getting milder, but the temperature of the atmosphere in the morning and evening is still not at all calculated to awaken summer thoughts. We believe fruits and flowers have suffered considerably. Dunse, Kelso and Hawick have experienced weather equally rigorous, and in some situations the snow is still on the ground. The growth of young grass has received a considerable check, and the young lambs have felt it very severely.

Jack Lowrie (1910–2005), a farm worker at Doddington for 59 years, recalled that corncrakes were once common. Only cuckoos still visit Dod Law.

Most hiring fairs seem to run smoothly but occasionally there was trouble which had to be dealt with. In the following case the troublemakers were allowed to sober up overnight, in prison, and then were sent on their way. Notice again that the word bondager is not used and also that 'females' were in short supply.

Berwick Advertiser 15 November 1851:

Dunse Hiring Market.
The hiring for single servants took place at Dunse on Tuesday last. The attendance was considerably less than former years, no doubt caused, in a great measure by the Berwick market having so shortly preceded that of Dunse ; and as in Berwick, the demand for females was very brisk, and in many instances the parties in want of them had to leave the market without engaging. So far as we could learn, wages, for those capable of farm work, were from £2 to £2 10s. For men, according to age and capabilities, wages ranged from £3 to £4 10s; and in a few instances to £5. The country people enjoyed themselves in a very harmless manner throughout the day, and the only parties with which the police had to interfere were thimble riggers, garter prickers[1] and others of a similar sort; who from becoming intemperate, had to be immured in prison, but were all discharged the following morning, and ordered to leave the town.

These games of chance were mentioned, by Hastings Neville, in his account of St. Ninian's Fair at Fenton.

The Lilburn farm apprentice previously quoted in chapter 3 who came to study at Lilburn in 1842, made copious notes about the hiring system. He also offered some thoughts of his own having knowledge of farming practices in the south (a lace making area). *'The Hinds are engaged from May day to May day and the conditions are as follows:*

		£	s	d
6	Boles of Oats at 16s/=...................	4	16	0
4	Boles of Barley at 20s/=.................	4	0	0
2	Boles of Peas at 25s/=....................	2	10	0
½	a Bole of Wheat or (3 bushels) at 40/=	1	0	0
	Potatoes 1000 yards of =.................	2	0	0
	Coales leading............................	2	0	0
	Wool 10 or 12 lbs of......................		10	0
	Cow kept for them.........................	6	0	0
	Money in Cash.............................	5	0	0
		27	16	0
	House and Garden........................	2	10	0

Then he is obliged to find a woman to work in the fields. When the weather is bad they remain in the House and the Hind is not allowed anything by the master, the Hind engages a

---

[1] ***Thimblerig** (1825) – thimble trick*
A swindling game usually played with three thimbles and a pea which is ostensibly placed under one of them; the sharper then challenging the bystanders to guess under which thimble the pea has been placed, and bet on their choice. Hence Thimblerig – to practise the cheat of the thimble; To cheat in a juggling manner.

***Thimblerigger** (1831) A professional sharper who cheats by thimblerigging.*

Garter Prickers
Garter – the band used in 'prick the garter.' Whence the game itself 1827.
Pricking the garter (also prick-the-garter): a swindling game (see fast and loose).

***Fast and (or) Loose** (1557). An old cheating game played with a stick and a belt or string.*

Source: The Shorter Oxford English Dictionary on Historical Principles.

woman for a year to work for him and the wages that the woman receives is from £8.10.0 to £9.0.0. The Hind feeds them the same as the rest of his family and washes for them.

The Hind is allowed by the Master for the woman from 1ˢᵗ of April to 1ˢᵗ October.

	£	s	d
6 months at 5 shillings per week =	6	10	0
1ˢᵗ of October to the 1st of April 4s/ per week =	5	4	0
And for the Harvest 2d a day more than ordinary wages - The Harvest being about 20 days say		3	4
	11	17	4
Wages gain – by the Hind to find a woman	9	0	0
	2	17	4

This illustrates the best possible situation when the bondager is fully employed all the year. He then goes on to show how rarely this ideal situation arises, and how this theoretical £2.17s.4d. can, in reality, be much less.

'So that the Hind has to board and keep a woman and washing for her for £2.17.4 but perhaps the weather may be such that she cannot go to work for 5 weeks in the year so that only £1.17.4 is left to the Hind and in this part 5 weeks is the lowest that can be allowed for the bad Weather for there are almost always more than that of rain and snow that they remain Idle. So it appears that the Hinds have to keep a woman a year to feed her and wash for her for £1.17.4. Add the £27.16.0 the wage of the man the total £29.13.4 to keep a wife family and Bondmaid for a year but he has out of this to find His coals cloths and Pocket Money. How much better therefore would a man be if he had 10s/- per week and I have no doubt that the Farmers would give them it but by the bye a Farmer will <u>not</u> hire many a man that does not find a Bondwoman.' [NRO 851].

A common attitude to the system was 'Pity the poor hind who has to feed the bondager the whole year!' Another complaint, this time by the hinds, was *'The woman only earns her wages, we meat and wash her for nothing.'* [Henley 1867]. Hastings Neville notes that *'The sympathy of the people was always given to the hind'* the reason being *'he had to pay a stated, or upstanding wage to the woman.'*

The Lilburn farm apprentice sums up his thoughts about the position of the hinds in Northumberland when he writes, *' I now after due consideration think that the South County (country) labourouys are much better off than they are in the North if a (Hind has) Bondwoman to find and has an old wife he is much wise off but if he (the Bondman) Hind has a wife that can and is able to work in the fields they will do well enough. The South County men often get £29 & £30 a year and the wife makes lace which will be wath 3 or 4 pounds more.'* [NRO 851].

Earnings of up to £34 certainly seem a lot better than the £27.16s. – but generally agricultural labourers in the south of the country seemed to be living in more wretched conditions than those in the north and this is noticed by many commentators.

An article written by Cuthbert W. Johnson, Esq. F.R.S. in The Farmer's Magazine 1849-50 discusses the benefits of payment in cash or kind. *'Payment of cash once a fortnight, late on a Saturday night, and then perhaps in an alehouse'* is to be deplored as the family is likely to suffer under these circumstances.' (He is writing about the southern counties of England). He then goes on to endorse the *'ordinary practice in the north of England'*, which he says is *'still more advantageous to both parties if the labourers wages were paid partly in kind and partly in money.'*

He then goes on to quote Mr.John Grey of Dilston [Johnson 1850] who says the aim of the hind is to ensure that the payment in kind covers things such as *'meal, potatoes, cheese, bacon, milk, etc. and notwithstanding what the economists say about money being the only proper medium of exchange for labour, as well as other things, the custom of paying farm labourers in kind works for both master and servant.'*

The payment in kind is sometimes qualified with *'In corn Average of the farm.'* There is a Middleton Hall (Northumberland) document which states this in the farm steward's agreement. Dr. Shirra Gibb says *'It was understood he (the employee) was to be content with the quality of the produce given to him as his "Gains" (The common name given to this part of the wage.) so long as it was grown on the farm. In practice, however, he got the best, and on more than one occasion I bought in better meal and barley than we were able to grow on the farm for the "Hinds' Gains."*

John Grey also considers the *'social virtues',* of the system of family contracts, which mean the family stays together. The children do not have to leave home to go to work and are guided by their parents, and the elderly are not left to the care of the workhouse. This point is made more than once by John Grey when contrasting the situation in the south of England with that of the north of England.

Desperate poverty was described in two letters from The Morning Chronicle. The areas were Devon, Somerset, Cornwall, and Dorset, and the problems were overcrowding, poor diet, and shortage of work. Some of the problems were caused by too many labourers seeking work, due to the decline of lead mining. Many farmers were small farmers 30, 40, or 50 acres with too little capital to improve their farms. Some, the writer says, very critically, are *'not fit to be labourers'.* The wages also seem to be shrouded in mystery as farmers were reluctant, unless closely questioned, to state clearly what part of the wage was made up by a cider allowance. This, the writer says, is basically a *'truck system.'* The men cannot afford to spend 1s.6d. a week on cider, but they are obliged to do so. The cider was, of course, mainly drunk in the fields so there was no family benefit. Children were given cider also, and one boy of eleven had said *'I wouldn't work without my cider'.* So *'By the time they reach maturity they are accomplished drinkers'.* Not a sensible situation for the children and not a fair system for the labourer and his family.

A really major problem was that the work, for the south country labourers, was not constant. A labourer's wife said her husband earned 7s. a week *'when at work',* as did her son. Food was very meagre with sometimes water, a little fat and bread turned into *'broths'.* There were usually long walks to work because accommodation was not on the farm. Cottages had probably been removed to minimise the poor rate. The coming of mining to Linskard led to overcrowding but there was no will to build houses in case the mining did not last. Overcrowding led to a real threat of cholera.

In Northumberland and the Scottish Borders the yearly contract and 'upstanding wage' must have helped when compared with labourers working on more precarious day to day basis. However, the bondage system continued to cause discontent and, at times, there was agitation for change.

Attempts were made, at various times throughout the 19th century, to form a farm servants' union. Combinations and societies formed in 1837 were all part of this desire by the workers to be more organised. Many of these attempts were unsuccessful and short lived, for example, an unsuccessful union in Dunbar in 1860 and a more successful society in 1865 which *'started in Midlothian'* and *'spread to the Lothians, Peebles, Berwickshire and Perth'.* [Fenton 1987]. The Scottish Farm Servants Union was eventually formed by Joseph R. Duncan in 1912. In England Joseph Arch set up the National Agricultural Labourers Union in 1872.

Rutherfurd's Directory (1866) adds an interesting Addendum to its article on the *'peasantry'* which had been written in 1864:

'Last autumn (1865) the peasantry of the district began in earnest to agitate for its removal (the bondage system), and with a great amount of ability and prudence have not only carried their purpose, but have, as a rule, carried with them the sympathy of the public, and the goodwill of the farmers in the change.

The new system, which is variable and cannot be considered as yet definitely settled, beginning with the May term of this year (1866), is, that the hind having daughters engages them (the daughters) to do the ordinary field work, but at increased wages – thus, some farmers have engaged the whole family by paying the father 50s. or 60s. for each daughter he keeps at home, who are to be paid 10d. to 1s. a day as formerly; while others have hired with this difference – the daughters to be paid at the rate of fourteen or fifteen pence per day, but with no gratuity to the father, which brings their wages almost equivalent. In some instances strangers have been hired at the increased wage, but these cases are exceptional. Without doubt, the system now lies with the hinds themselves, to abolish or otherwise.' [Rutherfurd 1866].

The Year 1866

The year 1866 deserves a chapter to itself because the very concise passage in the Rutherfurd's Directory with the phrase, *'began in earnest to agitate'*, does not do justice to the amount of effort and determination shown, once more, by the agricultural workers.

The newspapers for 1866 carry many accounts of the situation in Northumberland, the Lothians, and the Scottish Borders, as the year moves forward towards the yearly hiring fairs. A very important problem for agriculture, at this time, which receives great prominence in the newspapers, was the continuing occurrence of cattle plague or rinderpest. Here too letters and articles appear in every newspaper emphasising the *'gravity'* of the *'ravages of the rinderpest'*. There had been a hope that the winter weather would bring some relief but this had been dashed. Government action had been weak – the wisdom of the Board of Trade and the *'vigour of the Home Office, has failed us like a broken reed.'* Slaughter of animals with the disease and those that had been in contact with diseased animals was part of the Government's Cattle Plague Bill. Buildings had to be disinfected and there were restrictions on the movement of cattle.

An attempt was made in 'Bambro'shire' (nowadays the area around Bamburgh) to curtail hunting but this was roundly decried by X.X.

FOXHUNTING AND RINDERPEST.

SIR,—About three weeks ago, a petition was circulated through Bambro'shire, which succeeded in obtaining some eight or ten signatures to it, requesting the Earl of Wemyss not to hunt in the neighbourhood, lest the infection of the cattle plague should be carried by his hounds.

If those who signed that petition were really afraid of such a thing happening, I do not blame them in the least for protesting against foxhunting, but would like to see them a little more consistent with regard to other courses by which rinderpest might be brought.

If it were possible for it to be proved, I durst venture a bet to a considerable amount, that for every foxhound belonging to the Earl of Wemyss that has, for the last three months, been within one mile of a diseased beast, there have been one thousand rooks, one thousand pigeons, and one thousand birds of other descriptions within fifty yards of one, and which have afterwards spread through the country over an area of at least ten square miles; and yet I do not believe, nay, I am quite sure, that not one of those who signed the anti-fox-hunting petition ever thought it worth the trouble of expense of giving a lad threepence a day to prevent those birds from alighting among their cattle. Besides this, I could enumerate half a score of ways much more likely to spread rinderpest than foxhunting, not of which is there a single effort made to prevent, even by the ten who were so anxious to stop their neighbours' amusement. Why this should be, I cannot tell. Several causes have suggested themselves to my mind, none of them, however, is flattering to human nature, the preversity of which is certainly great.—Yours, &c.,
X. X.

Figure 33. Foxhunting and Rinderpest. Berwick Warder, 16 February 1866

Court cases also arose from the restrictions placed on the movement of cattle.

Newcastle Courant, 9 February 1866:

Alnwick Petty Sessions.
On Saturday, Joseph Crisp was charged with having removed seven oxen from Hazon, in the Parish of Shilbottle, to Warkworth Station, on the 8ᵗʰ ult. without an order. Defendant is a farm servant to Mr. John Hogg, of Hazon. Mr. Hogg having sold the cattle, and not having been able to obtain an order at Alnwick for their removal on the Saturday proceeding, and it being of importance to have the cattle forwarded to the purchaser, he got a written certificate from Mr. Longstaffe, of Bank House, and Mr. Tate, of Guyzance East House, two neighbouring farmers, stating that the cattle were healthy, which certificate Crisp handed to Mr. Cranston, the station master, when he took the cattle to Warkworth. In defence, it was urged that neither Mr. Hogg nor the defendant had seen the order made by the magistrates at the Petty Sessions and published in the newspapers. The Bench, taking into consideration the difficulty there appeared to have been in this case in obtaining an order of removal, imposed only the mitigated penalty of £5 and costs.

Another Court case, reported in Berwick Warder 2 February 1866, was in Jedburgh and for a similar offence. Walter Amos, butcher, Hawick, had been seen driving cattle through the Parish of Lilliesleaf, without having a certificate saying the beasts were free from disease. Again there was difficulty in obtaining a certificate and the case was dismissed.

A week later the Newcastle Courant, 9 February 1866 includes a report of a meeting to be held in Wooler to organise local action against the cattle plague:

Wooler
A meeting was appointed to be held at the Board Room, Wooler, on Thursday, the 8ᵗʰ inst., to take into consideration the question of raising a fund to be applied to the stamping out of the cattle plague.

This problem of rinderpest would have been of great concern to everyone in the country but particularly for those living and working on farms. Landowners, farmers, farm men, women and children would all have had some concern and opinion about the plague. The work of closely observing the animals, the slaughtering when needed and the disinfecting of premises would have been the concern of the workers. Who would do the washing down and disinfecting of the buildings? It certainly seems to be a job that could well be allocated to the bondagers. Who, for instance, had noticed Mr. Amos in Lilliesleaf and reported him? The unease, gossip and finger pointing must have been rife, with everyone trying to cope with something they were horrified by and did not understand.

So we certainly have concern, perhaps panic, about hunting and rinderpest. X.X. is determined to continue hunting because fox hounds cannot be proved to be carriers of the disease. He suggests the petitioners would be better paying *'a lad 3d a day to prevent those birds* (rooks, pigeons and other birds) *from alighting amongst their cattle.'*

Despite these tremendous problems amongst the cattle of the area the hinds began once more to organise with a view to ridding themselves of the *'bondage'*.

The Haddington Feuing Market, 2 February 1866, was reported in the Newcastle Courant and also in the Berwick Warder 9 February 1866.

> FARM SERVANTS' WAGES IN EAST-LOTHIAN. — At the Haddington Hiring Fair on Friday, which in view of the agitation for an increase of wages at present going on among farm servants in adjoining counties may be regarded with some interest by farmers, we understand that a slight rise took place. In the lower districts of the county, where the wage is paid mostly in money, with an allowance of meal, there was an increase of from 30s to £2 a year, increasing the money wage from £16 to £18—in other districts, where the extras are greater, an increase of £1 was given; the custom is to give the hinds a cow's keep, the wages remain stationary—the money wage being from £12 to £13. The effect of the changes that have taken place has been nearly to equalise the rate of wages in the county, the hinds in the lower districts having hitherto been paid at a wage somewhat lower than has been given in the upper wards. The result of the fair formed the subject of discussion at the annual meeting of the East-Lothian Club in the afternoon, when a kindly feeling was generally expressed towards the farm servants.

Figure 34. Farm Servants' Wages. Berwick Warder, 9 February 1866

The East Lothian Club referred to was the Haddington Farmers' Club which held its meetings at the George Hotel, Haddington.

At this meeting, reported in the Berwick Warder of 9 February 1866, a *'kindly feeling'* was expressed by Mr. George Hope of Fenton Barns, who said *'The hinds had as good a right to endeavour to raise their wages as other people; and he would be very glad if they succeeded in doing so. At the same time it was for the farmers, as practical men, to get their work done as cheaply and as well as possible.' He thought that 'The recent agitation had been on the whole advantageous to the farm servant and he was glad to think it had been so.'*

Mr. Milne of Lugget said, on discussing the £2 rise in wages calculated by Mr. Gaukroger of Southfield , *'You were too low before'.* Mr Scot of Skirving said *'You are just coming up to what you should give'*

The concern then in East Lothian was more to do with money wages, and bondage was not mentioned.

The Newcastle Courant (23 February 1866) includes an article with the title *'The Border Hinds and Bondage Abolition'* which tells how meetings had been held throughout January and February and how the conclusion of this issue was imminent:

'The bondage question which has created so much interest among farmers and hinds for the last two months, is now approaching the time when a settlement must be made for one year at least.'

The Berwick Warder (9 February 1866) had a number of reports of meetings. The reports give the important points discussed but it is easy, for anyone who has attended a controversial meeting, to imagine the lengthy and perhaps heated arguments that lay behind the calm words used in the reports.

> ANCRUM—MEETING OF HINDS.—A large meeting of ploughmen and other farm-servants was held in the Cross Keys ballroom on Thursday evening—Mr. Anthony Dodds, Chesters, in the chair. The Chairman having briefly adverted to the present gains of the hinds, their prospect of speedily seeing the bondage system entirely abolished, and of obtaining more wages in future, called upon the meeting to express their sentiments—not upon the bondage system, for he knew they all wished it abolished —but upon the expediency of asking farmers to rid them of keeping a bondager, or in addition to this, to ask an advance of £5 annually on their present wage. After some discussion, it was resolved to ask only for the abolition of the bondage system. It was also agreed that hinds who had daughters able to work the bondage should receive 4s. a week from their masters for the keep of the bondager. After electing a secretary, treasurer, and other office-bearers, the meeting separated.

Figure 35. Ancrum . Berwick Warder, 9 February 1866

The Ancrum meeting was so large, it was held at the Cross Keys ballroom. The demand from this meeting was confined, in the end, to the abolition of the bondage system. A large amount (£5) of additional money was discussed, but the idea of asking for this was ultimately abandoned. The cost of keeping a bondager was also discussed and the value of this was considered to be 4s a week, the bondager in this case being a daughter and not a stranger. It is notable that the meeting consisted of ploughmen and other farm-servants. Can we infer from this that bondagers were included? Perhaps not, but it is an intriguing thought.

KALEMOUTH—MEETING OF HINDS.—On Thursday evening a meeting of agricultural labourers was held in a large granary at Kalemouth, kindly granted by Mr. Chartres, at which there would not be fewer than 300 present. Mr. A. Rutherford, Ormiston Mains, presided. The particular subject which received the chief share of the attention of the speakers was the bondage system. It was characterised as a disgrace to burden the poor hind with a bondager; but not only did the meeting demand its abolition, but they also agreed to ask a rise of £5 a year in their wages. A protection society was then formed, but we understand that very few joined—a general feeling prevailing that the meeting had asked too much. We have no doubt (adds our correspondent) the farmers will meet their labourers a short way, but the hinds are too extravagant in their demands.

Figure 36. Kalemouth. Berwick Warder, 9 February 1866

This again was a large meeting, with 300 agricultural labourers present, and was held in a large granary at Kalemouth. The demands here were greater than those decided at Ancrum because they included a rise of £5 a year. The reporter noted that few joined the newly formed protection society because, he thought, the *'general feeling'* was they were asking for *'too much'*. This shows that the workers, though anxious to improve their situation, were trying to be fair and reasonable. This would be a difficult balancing act between asking for what they thought was right but not jeopardising their employment.

MEETING OF FARM-SERVANTS.—A largely attended meeting of farm-servants was held in the Assembly Room, Tower Street, Selkirk, on Saturday night, to take into consideration the best means of obtaining a higher remuneration for their labour, and of getting rid of the bondage system. Mr. William Lewis was called to the chair, and briefly introduced the object of the meeting. Mr. William Hogarth, Fornielee, was then called upon to address the meeting. He spoke in condemnatory terms of the "bondage" with which he and so many of his brethren had so long been burdened. It was unnecessary for him to detail the many evils attendant on the system, as they were well known. A hind was compelled, in most cases, to go many a mile to hire a bondager, and when hired, it often happened that the master was not pleased with her; a few days' notice was then given, and the hind would have to look out for another bondager. Members of a hind's own family were generally excluded, so that the hired worker was in many instances an utter stranger, whose character might be good, bad, or indifferent. Was it fair, he would ask, that any man, whose house, consisted, as a rule, of only one habitable apartment, should be compelled to have a stranger sitting at his fireside, hearing and seeing everything that might be said or done in the family circle? No one, he thought, could be so bold as to stand up in defence of such a system. He would have the masters to hire the bondagers and otherwise to provide for them, and let the hind be free from all connection in the matter. As to the wages of hinds, he would not make any definite proposition, but considered that every man for himself should make an arrangement with his master. Several other speakers followed, all of whose remarks were more or less in favour of an increased remuneration, and the abolition of the bondage system. After considerable discussion as to the question of wages, it was resolved to leave the matter open, and it was declared that the meeting was of opinion that the "bondage system," in whatever form, was injurious to the interests of agricultural labourers; and that therefore all constitutional means should be used for its abolition. It was further resolved to hold another meeting on an early day for the purpose of forming a protection association.

Figure 37. Selkirk. Berwick Warder, 9 February 1866

Again this meeting attracted a large number of farm servants and it was held in the Assembly Room, Tower Street, Selkirk. This meeting raised some interesting points; particularly the difficulties that arose if the farmer was not satisfied with the bondager, which Mr. William Hogarth said *'often happened'*. This resulted in *'a few days notice being given'* to the bondager. The hind was then in the difficult situation of having to find another worker. Nothing is said about the bondager, and how she felt about her predicament and what she could do. Mr. Hogarth thought the farmer should hire the bondagers and provide for them. Several other speakers were called on and they too expressed similar opinions. The question of pay was more contentious; there was *'considerable discussion'* and the matter was left open. A protection society was to be established.

SWINTON.—The meeting of hinds here, as well as at Whitsome, was numerously attended, and at both meetings the chair was filled by a hind from New Horndean. We think the hinds in the Merse of Berwickshire could without difficulty get one more worthy of the honour amongst themselves, who could do them some credit in giving them sound advice in their consultations, they having as yet come to no resolution as to their actual wants. We would advise them to be moderate in their demands and to stick to one thing in the meantime, viz., get the " bondage system" completely abolished, then leave every one to make the best bargain he can with his employers. One thing appears to us to be absurd in the payment of the hinds of Berwickshire, good, bad, and indifferent being paid all alike ; to a good servant there is no encouragement, and to the bad there is no spur. It must be apparent to every one there is a great dissimilarity in their services, and we think it would be alike to the advantage of the master, as it would be to a good servant, to be paid according to their services. What will favour the farmer in the giving up of bondage, will be the larger supply of good servants, many young married men rather preferring to work at present at their own hands, at a much less average wage, than keep a strange woman in the house, breaking up all family privacy. These will all again turn attention to the plough, driving out older men to fill their places at draining.

Figure 38. Swinton and Whitsome. Berwick Warder, 9 February 1866

This report covered two meetings, but this time no definite resolution was reached, and the reporter suggests that the chairman was at fault for not giving *'sound advice'*. The reporter then offers his own advice and gives the opinion that hinds should not be paid the wage regardless of skill because for the *'good servant there is no encouragement and to the bad there is no spur'*. He also thinks that the abolishment of bondage will enable young married men to return to the job of ploughman. It is intriguing to think who this reporter might have been because he certainly has strong opinions and airs them freely.

The meetings were united in demanding the end to the bondage system and some were also determined to seek a £5 advance in the yearly wage. The farmers' were ready to accept the end of the bondage system, and it seems that this was partly due to *'good servants, many young married men'* choosing not to submit to the imposition and inconvenience of providing a bondager.

Letters were also appearing, at this time, in the newspapers. A letter in the Berwick Warder (2 February 1866) was from John Clay of Winfield, who also mentions the loss of *'our best men'* because of the bondage system. He acknowledges *'the hardship'* for the hind of hiring and housing a bondager but reminds the men that half the potato land always *'belonged to the bondager'* and this should be removed from the hinds *'gains'* and go with the bondager. Mr. Clay suggests the bothy system might help as a temporary solution for a year or two, when there would be a shortage of workers. He anticipates that the Irish lads would fill this gap, but he thinks the best solution and *'most helpful to society, would be to extend the family system'.* He takes issue with some of the language *'used towards the masters'* at the meetings and takes exception to Berwickshire being described as *'the most downtrodden county in Scotland'*. He disagrees with Mr. McLaren M.P. for Edinburgh who states that *'agricultural labourers had not advanced in prosperity these last twenty years'* and contrasts 10s. per week in 1840 against 15s. in 1866. He also points to improved cottages which he values at £7 per year, and the *'improved appearance of the dress of men, women and children, to be seen everyday, but more so on the Sabbath.'*

THE BONDAGE SYSTEM.

TO THE EDITOR OF THE WARDER.

SIR,—Regarding the "bondage system," the very name of it is quite sufficient to condemn it in this en, lightened age. It has, no doubt, been of long standings and has all along pressed heavy upon an industrious class of our rural population. In Berwick and Roxburghshires the bondage system is more deeply rooted than in any other county. Indeed, there are many counties where it is not known, so that it goes to prove that it is not impossible to farm without the system.

I would like to ask, What has the bondage system done for us? Less than nothing. We may be getting a few of not very first-class young married men to keep the bondager, with no little inconvenience and no small expense to himself. The effect and consequence of the system is, that it is driving many of our best men away from us as ploughmen, rather preferring to find employment in some other way than face the hardship of hiring a bondager into his house, who would take nearly all the gains that she would work for to meet her engagement, leaving little or nothing to pay for board and lodging. There is no doubt that the half of the potato land has always belonged to the bondager, and when the ploughman is relieved of the expense of her keep that half should be given up and transferred to the worker, either in her father's house, or wherever she may be kept.

In all changes there are difficulties to overcome, but if the bondage system was done away to-morrow (which I hope it will) there would be little or no decrease of workers. Nearly the same number would be in the country. But say there was to be a decrease. There is more than one way of meeting the difficulty. We may be obliged to commence the bothy system with Irish lads for a year or two. But the best mode, and the most healthful for society, would be to extend the family system, by getting our landlords to build more servants' cottages, which might be filled with widowed families that have been driven into towns such as Berwick and Kelso, who would be but too thankful to flee from the vice, temptation, and expense of a town life, and return to the quiet walk of a country life, again to get employment for their family in a more healthful and independent manner. They would soon find the advantage of this change, with the free house, garden, potatoes, &c., for all of which they pay a high rate in the town.

I have noticed at some of the meetings of the ploughmen language used toward their masters that will in no way help on their cause, such as was said at a meeting in Mid-Lothian the other day, that "Berwickshire is the most downtrodden county in Scotland," a statement that I cannot agree to. Take away the bondage system, and I have no doubt in saying that Berwickshire stands first in payment of gains, and that a very kindly feeling exists between master and servants.

I cannot agree to the statement made by Mr. M'Laren, M.P. for Edinburgh, that agricultural labourers have not advanced in prosperity these last twenty years. Was 10s. per week not a common wage in 1846? and is 15s. per week not as common a wage in 1866? To confute this statement you have only to look at the greatly improved dwellings, which have cost the landlord and tenant from £100 to £130 each, all now given to the servant free, which, at a common percentage on house property, would realise about £7 per year. Then you have the improved appearance of the dress of men, women, and children, to be seen every day, but more so on the Sabbath, when they are wending their way to the sanctuary to worship God.

Nor can I agree to the idea that there should be a combination to compel all the men to be paid alike—there is too much of the despot in it; in no other trade are men paid alike, and with our farm labourers why should it be different? A man with a family to carry on the work of the farm is a much more valuable servant, and therefore worth more than the man who has no family. The two men must come to their market value—if not, what is the use of having an active head and hands upon one?

As a farmer, I would advise the farm servants to get the grievance of the bondage system done away, and they would find that with their present wage—nearly amounting to £40, taking everything at prime cost—they are better off than a labouring man with £50 who has everything to buy at retail prices; and where they have families coming up their united wages will often exceed £100, as large an income as many a Dissenting minister.

With the above figures, I cannot see that there is any great room for the outcry that our farm-servants are underpaid. Let the servants come forward in a straightforward manner and state their demands, and it will be found that the sound principle laid down by Adam Smith, demand and supply, will regulate both parties.

JOHN CLAY.

Winfield, Jan. 23, 1866.

Figure 39. John Clay. Berwick Warder, 2 February 1866

John Clay's letter elicits a response from Adam Spence of Houndwood who could be a minister as he brings into the situation education and Christianity, when he writes about people being *'humanized by letters, and elevated by the light of Christianity'*. He is in favour of the workers cooperating together to help each other but thinks *'strikes or rigid combinations, will not be of permanent advantage to them'*.

Keeping a bondager results in a lack of privacy, which he recognises as a major problem for the hind and family, whether a young couple newly married or an older couple with a number of children. If this problem is too unbearable the remedy is often for the wife to take on the role of bondager and this results in other problems. Children are often inadequately cared for by another child, sometimes as young as eight and he also adds that *'household affairs'* deteriorate. He says *'there are various other evils which I need not here enumerate;*

and the bondager frequently has her share of those as well as the hind'. On first reading this I thought he was, unusually, offering some sympathy for the bondager but on reflection he is merely apportioning the blame for these unspecified evils.

THE BONDAGE SYSTEM.

SIR,—The manly and liberal letters of Messrs. Clay of Winfield, and Shaw of Skaithmuir, on the "bondage question," are well worthy of a cordial response from the hinds. It is a token for good when farmers are ready to consider favourably, any frank and honest statement by their servants, of grievances and wants that really exist. Esteeming it of great importance that good feeling be maintained between masters and servants, I shall, in order to promote this, state some things for the consideration of both parties.

While not going so far as some in denouncing the bondage system, I think it is a great burden, and a sore grievance to those who have not workers in their own families; but have to hire strangers, and maintain them in their own houses for this work.

In the cases of newly married couples, it is natural and proper that they should wish to have their own houses to themselves; and what a discomfort it must be to have a stranger constantly in their one apartment, during the time they are at rest, and when otherwise they could be alone. In other cases where there are several children, but none old enough to work, it is far worse to be compelled to lodge and maintain a full-grown person with their scanty accommodation, and limited means. It is then such a burden as has frequently compelled the hind's wife to go to the fields and do the work herself, and I have known cases where this has been done at the great risk of leaving their children under the care of another about 8 years old; and household affairs going to ruin.

There are various other evils which I need not here enumerate, and the bondager frequently has her share of these as well as the hind.

It is true that in carrying on farming operations workers must be had, but I quite agree with Mr. Clay that while this system has furnished one class of labourers, it has removed from being ploughmen many of the most thoughtful, steady, and skilful workmen; who, rather than keep a bondager, have betaken themselves to other occupations.

If, therefore, farmers could see their way to make as far as possible arrangements with those families who can furnish two or more workers; and thereby free those who have none, and who wish to be free; it would I believe be a great relief to many, and would go far to maintain between master and servant the good feeling that is so desirable. Under such arrangements, it would of course only be fair to give some compensation to those who provide the workers. There would no doubt be difficulties felt by both masters and servants; but remedies would gradually be provided, and the *present* bondage system would thereby be abolished.

It is difficult for a neutral party to speak of wages. Some of the computations of a hind's income are too high, and others too low. While fully aware of the large increase in wages that has taken place during the last thirty years, it may yet be submitted that this is scarcely in proportion to the increased quantity and value of the produce of the soil. True, the farmers having greatly increased rents are thereby the less able to give large increase in wages. But when the landlords are receiving so much more in rent, it is only fair that the hinds' wages should rise in full proportion. Many of our sober and industrious labourers have much struggling to "make ends meet," as the proverb goes; and while we think that some increase of wages is only their due, it would also in most cases be a great boon. It would, however, be a great mistake to abolish the "gains" and pay only in money. Corn, potatoes, and specially a cow, are of great value in a family.

It has been thought by some that when masters are wealthy it is a proof that there is something wrong, or that there is injustice to the servant. This, however, is fallacious reasoning. Unless there is clearly overworking, and underpaying, servants are far more likely to live comfortably under a master who has abundance, than if he had it not.

The working classes have it in their power to co-operate together, and thereby very much to assist each other, but strikes, or rigid combinations, will not be of permanent advantage to them. Everything has its marketable value. If therefore a people learn to do their work well, steadily, and faithfully, they will soon rise to their proper place; and above that place no artificial pressure or combination will long retain them. It is not only the amount of income but the way in which it is earned and spent that will give solid comfort. Dr. Chalmers once truly said :—" We believe it to be in reserve for society that of the three component ingredients in value, the wages of labour will at length rise to a permanently larger proportion than they now have either to the profit of stock, or the value of land, and that thus workmen will share more equally than they do at present with capitalists, and proprietors of the soil, in the comforts, and even the elegancies of life. But this will not be the achievement of desperadoes; it will be come at through a more peaceful medium; through the medium of a growing worth, and a growing intelligence among a people humanized by letters, and elevated by the light of Christianity."

This is the true way of rising, and we trust that the agricultural labourers—of whom as a class we would speak with the highest respect, for we are conscious of their worth—will clearly see that it is not only by a proper increase of wages but by good conduct and management along with these that they will be elevated, and kept in their elevation.

I am, sir, yours, &c.,
ADAM SPENCE.

House, Houndwood,
Feb. 1866.

Figure 40. Adam Spence of Houndwood. Berwick Warder, 16 February 1866

Financially, he says, wages have risen over the last thirty years but the value of crops have risen more. At the same time rents are higher making life difficult for the farmers but he still looks to a time when *'workmen will share more equally than they do at present with the capitalists.'* This writer is an idealist, but he does suggest a more flexible system which would allow good skilful, and steady workmen to work as ploughmen whilst declining to keep a bondager.

The next letter, from a hind, is very important because it marks a big change in the way this dispute, about the bondage system, is to be conducted. In 1837 the hinds did not make use of the newspapers to promote their point of view. This change may mark a gradual improvement in the standard of education for country people. Remember that in 1863 John Macanalty could not sign his name on his agreement and used a cross. The letter also indicates that newspapers were being more widely read. Through this the hinds, who could read and write, would naturally want to use this medium to state their case and defend their cause.

The hind disputes the value of the *'payment in kind'* in Glendale, an area with which he had been familiar. He also questions whether his house can be classed as free when obligations are set against it. For his house he must house the bondager, board her and wash for her, which costs 5/- per week, and also pay her £12 as a wage. By his reckoning he says, *'I am still paying for the free privileges at the rate of £13 per year.'* He also vigorously defends the position of the hinds who receiving an *'upstanding wage'* are paid when unable to work through illness. He feels they earn this privilege by working long hours. He details how the ploughmen work many extra hours in caring for their horses. They begin work at 4.30am in order to be ready and in the field for 6am. At night they are not totally finished until the horses are finally checked over and left for the night at about 8pm. There is also Sunday work with regards to the horses.

FARM LABOURERS.

SIR,—In looking over the pages of your paper my eye caught a glimpse of the words "Farm labourers," and I saw it was a letter from a correspondent, signed "Tenant," in which he holds forth a great deal of good advice to farm labourers, if he can only persuade them to take it as such. He says "the farm labourer in this district (Glendale) is, I consider, a well paid man." Now, in the district that "Tenant" writes from, the hind receives, in cash, corn, and potatoes, to the value of £23 11s; and, if he has not a cow, he receives other £8 instead, making in all (exclusive of house and coal cartage) 12s 1½d and 6-13th per week. And again, "Tenant" says, "some parts of his wages, he will always fail to appreciate till deprived of them, such as his cow, his free house, his potatoes, his free cartage of coals, &c., &c."

Something less than ten years ago, I was a hind in Glendale, and off a thousand yards of potato ground I had the immense quantity of five bags of potatoes. A man that would not appreciate a crop like that deserves a worse, seeing that it is only fifteen or sixteen bags short of what is considered a fair crop, and that the potatoes, in summing up a hind's wage, is valued at the least £4. These free privileges are things that I can never be deprived of. As for a cow, I have not got one. And, were I to say that I had a free house, and coals carted free, I would be guilty of a great falsehood. The word "free" means without expense. Then, how can this house, &c., be free when I am compelled to keep a hired woman, and give her board and washing, which is equal to 5s. per week, and £12 as a wage. Allowing her to win this wage from the farmer, I am still paying for these free privileges at the rate of £13 per year; were I to pay for this house, &c., in money, it would only cost me £6; and then I would be rid of keeping this woman about the house. I think I have made a plain statement of the rate at which a farm labourer enjoys these free privileges, upon which "Tenant" places so much value. If a hind does not appreciate these privileges he is very ungrateful, seeing that he pays so dear for them, considering them to be free.

Your correspondent says that "if the farm labourer is paid like other labourers, in cash, he must expect, like other labourers, to receive that cash only when working for it, &c." "Tenant" must know that other labourers never start work before six o'clock in the morning. A man that has horses to go with, must be up at half-past four to get his horses watered, fed, &c., be yoked in the field at six o'clock, must continue work till eleven or half-past eleven, he comes home with the horses, and, after getting them fed, he has fodder, such as straw, &c., to provide to serve till the morrow at the same time; he leaves the stables again at half-past one, goes on till six p.m., and before he gets home, &c., it is half-past six o'clock. He has them to attend again at eight o'clock, every day, Sunday included, and if a man was sick for a day or so in the year, your liberal correspondent would keep his pay off him, after all this extra labour.—I remain, your obedient servant,
    A BAMBURGHSHIRE HIND.

Figure 41. A Bamburghshire Hind. Berwick Warder, 16 February 1866

The situation must have been the major concern for all those on the farms with much mulling over, by the fireside or in the stable, of the possible outcome. The stress and worry would increase as the time of the hiring fairs approached. There would be, perhaps, high expectations and unrealistic hopes. Newspapers were also raising expectations with speculation about wages.

The Lauderdale Report includes a short summary of the labour situation. It states that:

'Hinds will be hired on various footings this season; but it is believed that all will be engaged at an advance of wages, whatever the arrangements in regard to "bondage" and "gains" may be.'

The letters published in the Berwick Warder (23 February 1866) are interesting, as there seems have been some contact between the two farmers. This is revealed by the *'Tenant'*, as he seems to be writing in response to *'A Bamburghshire Farmer'*, when in fact they are both published in the same paper. The other possibility is that the "farmer's" letter had appeared in another newspaper which had been published earlier.

Letters to the Editor.

FARM LABOURERS.

Sir,—Your impression of last week contains a letter signed " A Bamburgh... ...re Hind," which does not give a plain stat... ...ment of facts. To prove this, it is simply ne... ...cessary on my part to inform you the wages, &c., paid to hinds on our farm.

First, with regard to the potatoes. The hinds have their choice, just before the potatoes are taken up, of either twelve hundred yards as they stand, or two hundred and forty stones. Your correspondent writes as though five bags of potatoes was quite a common affair, whereas it will be seen that it is the hind's own fault if he takes them, as he has the choice of two hundred and forty stones.

The next point to which he objects is the bondage system. He says that he pays £12 a year for the bondager's wages, and calculates her lodgings, &c., at 5s. per week. This is a very high calculation for wages, and as to the lodgings, &c., it is of no account whatever in a family. But your correspondent writes as though he received no pay for the girl's labour, whereas, we pay the hinds, bondage wages at the rate of 1s. per day

in summer, 1s. 6d. per day in harvest, and 10d. per day in winter. That this is amply sufficient is easily proved when it is remembered that single women take what are called "bondage houses," which are free of rent, with, say a hundred and twenty stones of potatoes, and wages in many places at a 1s. in summer, 10d. in summer, and 8d. or 9d. in winter; and on this they live, providing themselves with clothing, food, &c. Surely then, a wage of 1s. 6d. in harvest, 1s. in summer, and 10d. in winter, ought to keep the hinds from grumbling.

His next assertion, that hinds "must be up at half-past four," &c., is full of subterfuge, from beginning to end. The fact is, it is only in the long summer days that they require to be early astir. In winter they are not up earlier than an hour before daylight, and are home about four o'clock p.m., and after bringing out the straw, &c., have no more to do until eight o'clock, when they have half-an-hour's work, foddering, &c. In summer a hind works from six till eleven o'clock, and from two till six o'clock. Your correspondent must remember that most town operatives have to work in winter as long as in summer by means of gaslight, whereas the hind, except the half-hour at eight o'clock, is done at dusk. And, again, in summer, he is relieved from his foddering duties as the horses are turned out to grass at six o'clock. Trusting that you will favour me by the insertion of these facts in your widely-circulated journal, I am, yours, &c.

A BAMBURGHSHIRE FARMER.

Feb. 13, 1866.

Figure 42. A Bamburghshire Farmer. Berwick Warder, 23 February 1866

This *'Bamburghshire Farmer'* may think that the way the potato *'gains'* are given on his farm is very fair, but there is an element of chance in the decision the hind must make. He reacts strongly to the meagre *'5 bags'* of potatoes, the hind mentions in his letter, and this seems to set the tone for the whole of his reply. In particularly the farmer's attitude to the bondager, and her intrusion into the life of the hind, shows a total lack of empathy and he dismissively writes *'as to the lodgings, etc., it is of no account whatever in a family.'*

He defends his arguments about the cost of keeping a bondager by citing the case of *'bondage houses'* where single women manage to support themselves on a much smaller daily wage than the bondager receives. They receive a cash wage, free house and potatoes.

He also objects to the hind's estimate of the hours worked and contrasts the hours worked by *'town operatives'* under gaslight. He mentions the shorter winter days but fails to mention the work at busy times, which could extend the day of work considerably. He states the lunch hours to be from 11am till 2pm whereas the hind says 11/11.30am till 1.30pm. To work on the land, with animals and through the different seasons obviously requires flexibility. The complex situation requires give and take from both employer and employee.

SIR,—I felt pretty certain that the statements of a "Bamburgh Hind," in your columns, would not go altogether unchallenged ; and I could have wished that some other pen than mine should, in addition to "A Bamburgh Farmer," have endeavoured to show the fallacy of his statements and arguments. I cannot acknowledge the rights of a Bamburghshire hind, even suppose he has been in service in Glendale within ten years, to claim to be a better judge of the value of wages in this ward than myself, who am, and have been for several years, a resident and considerable employer of labour here. Notwithstanding his apparent dread of being guilty of a falsehood, I fear that your Bamburghshire correspondent has been led by partiality into some mis-statements,—to use a mild term. In the first place, he sets down the value of the corn, cash, and potatoes received by our hind at £23 11s. Now, the allowance of corn very usual is one boll of wheat, four bolls of barley, two bolls of beans, and six bolls of oats. At the present time this amount of corn, of good quality, could not be bought at less than about £16, add to this £6 cash, and £4 for potatoes, the total will be £26. I consider £4 a low estimate of the value to a hind of his potatoes. According to your correspondent, the Bamburghshire farmer, he offers his hinds 240 stones of potatoes, and I do not think that this is an unfair estimate of the amount which they receive in this part of the country. I should like to know what a hind would have to pay for his 240 stones if buying them at a retail price? I fear it would be nearer £6 than £4. Your correspondent's paragraph about his five sacks of potatoes is as little worthy of notice as my letter would be if I valued his corn wages at the war price of corn. I entirely deny the truth of the statement that it costs a hind five shillings a week to board and otherwise keep a hired bondager. Were this the case, I am perfectly certain that the system would long ere this have exploded of necessity. If it costs five shillings a week to board every grown member of a hind's family—even taking the men at the same rate as the women - and a hind's earnings only amount to 12s. 1½d. per week, I fear there will be little left for clothing, schooling, &c. ; and yet I do not know a class of people better clad than our hinds. The Bamburghshire hind values the keep of a cow at £8. I fear that few who have one now, will be disposed to give it up in exchange for £8 a-year. Of course, the value of a house and garden varies much, but I consider that £4 per annum is not an excessive rent where the labourer has assured to him the advantage of residing close to his work. The cartage of coals also varies much in cost from the difference in distance from coal pits. I have no hesitation in saying, that most of the hinds I have had in my employ have cost me fully £2 5s. per annum for the coal cartage. The question of hours of labour is fully dealt with by the "Bamburghshire Farmer." I am only induced to write this letter by a wish to place the matter fairly before your readers, and would again express my opinion that, all things considered, a Glendale hind is not an ill paid man, when it is remembered that, after once entering on his place, he draws his wages every day whether he be working or not, whether he be sick or well his pay is safe, and he has no need to fear that his wife and little ones will be without their bit and their sup for one whole year at any rate, and there are few other labourers who are in such a position.—I remain, Sir, yours faithfully,

TENANT.

Glendale, Feb. 16, 1866.

Figure 43. Tenant. Berwick Warder, 23 February 1866

The letter from the 'Tenant' begins with a regret that no one other than himself and the 'Bamburghshire Farmer' had written to challenge the statements in the hind's letter. He suggests that some inaccuracies with regard to the value of gains 'had been led by partiality' which he likens to a farmer like himself calculating the value of 'corn wages at the war price of corn'. (Corn prices were high during the Napoleonic Wars due to scarcity when corn could not be imported because of blockades.) He calls the hind's valuations of gains 'mis-statements' and then underlines his meaning by qualifying 'to use a mild term'. He has no comment to make on the inconvenience to the hind of having to keep a bondager but writes in strong terms about the cost of the bondager's keep saying that if it was as high as the hind stated (5/- per week) the system would have 'exploded of necessity'. He considers the 'Glendale hind' to be 'not an ill paid man' which is an interesting comment as he seems to draw back from saying the stronger 'a well paid man'. Finally he reminds the reader that the hind gets an 'upstanding' wage, and that the hind's 'wife and little ones are secure for the year'.

THE BONDAGE SYSTEM — A HIND'S EFFIGY BURNED.—A hind, residing within a few miles of Jedburgh, who had lately joined a hind's protection association, thereby declaring himself opposed to the bondage system has nevertheless re-engaged with his present employer to keep again two bondagers. He has thus rendered himself unpopular amongst many of his neighbours—so much so, that on Monday night about 300 of them assembled near his cottage door and burned his effigy, amidst much hooting and derisive cheering.

Figure 44. Hind's Effigy Burned. Berwick Warder, 23 February 1866

From these letters detailing the pros and cons of the system we move on to a more surprising and dramatic report which appears under the local news for Roxburghshire. This item reports an alarming incident near Jedburgh where a hind's effigy is burnt.

The stress and strain of the whole situation for this man and his family must have been tremendous. He had obviously felt strongly enough to join the *'hind's protection association'* but was unable, in the end, to forego the chance to continue his present employment, even though it involved providing two bondagers. Was he persuaded or browbeaten by his employer? What part did the two bondagers have to play in this situation, if any, and what part did they play in the dramatic incident?

The appearance of *'about 300'* angry *'neighbours'*, noisily expressing their displeasure, must have been extremely frightening without the additional horror of the burnt effigy. As no injuries are reported, the aim of expressing their sense of betrayal, once achieved, seems to have been sufficient. The gathering together of so great a number of people, to carry out this protest, would be quite a task when communities were widely scattered.

The correspondence continues to appear in the newspapers as February comes to an end and the *'hiring month'* of March begins. The Berwick Advertiser for the 2 March 1866 had on its front page an advertisement for William Fairbairn's prize essay.

Figure 45. Prize Essay. Berwick Advertiser, 2 March 1866

Rutherfurd's Directory (1866) records that *'the agitation received considerable impetus by the Rev. John Thomson, of Rosalee, Hawick,'* offering *'a prize of £30 for the best essay by farm stewards, shepherds, ploughmen and their sons and daughters in the counties of*

Roxburgh, Selkirk, and Berwick, on the Evils of the System, and suggestions for their removal," which was still further advanced by the publication of two of the essays.'

William Fairbairn's essay won first prize, and was entitled *'Evils of the Bondage System and the Best Mode of Removing them'*. It carried the motto – *"Forced from home are all our pleasures, to increase another's treasures."*

Mrs Williamson's essay won second prize, and when published in 1869 as part of *'Voices from the Plough'* was entitled *'The Bondage System'*. Earlier in Rutherfurd's Directory (1866) it is noted under the title *'Bondage and Bondagers: Remarks on the evils of the system with suggestions for their mitigation and removal'*. Mrs Williamson chose the motto *"Is not this the fast that I have chosen?..... to undo the heavy burdens and to let the oppressed go free, and that ye break every yoke?" Isaiah lviii. 6.'*

The essay competition seems to have taken place in 1865 or earlier and the preface to William Fairbairn's essay, when published in 1865, named the three adjudicators as Rev. Tait, Kelso, Rev. MacGregor, Newton and Rev. Stewart, Peterhead. The adjudicators state that *'in several respects,'* the essay winning the second prize *'approaches very nearly in merit'* the first prize-winner. The names of the writers were unknown to the adjudicators until the judging was complete. The fact that one of the winners was a woman must have been quite unusual and perhaps caused a bit of a stir!

Both essays deal with the problems in separate sections, and the similarities between the two essays suggest that some guidance had been given as to the structure of the essay.

A number of ploughmen, farm stewards and shepherds are also quoted in "Voices from the Plough". These men had attended the Annual soiree of the West Teviotdale Ploughman's Association where John Thomson had acted as chairman. In all four hundred and thirty people attended the event, including Mrs Thomson and *'several gentlemen of note'*. The report of the event, made by the Hawick Advertiser, formed the basis for the pamphlet "Voices from the Plough".

The prize-winning essays and the speeches include many interesting details which will be included as the story of 1866 continues to unfold, and also in further sections of this book.

The Alnwick Mercury (3 March 1866) published a letter from W. C. of The Hoo, Welwyn, Herts. The writer is a Northumbrian and obviously takes a keen interest in his *'native and much loved county'*. He is familiar with many areas of England and believes that the standard of pay for the agricultural labourers in Northumberland compares favourably with those in other counties. The root of the problem he identifies as the *'bondage grievance'* and feels that in an age of improvement this bondage system is an anachronism. Northumberland's reputation is damaged by retaining this system of employment and if it is not abolished this time more trouble will ensue.

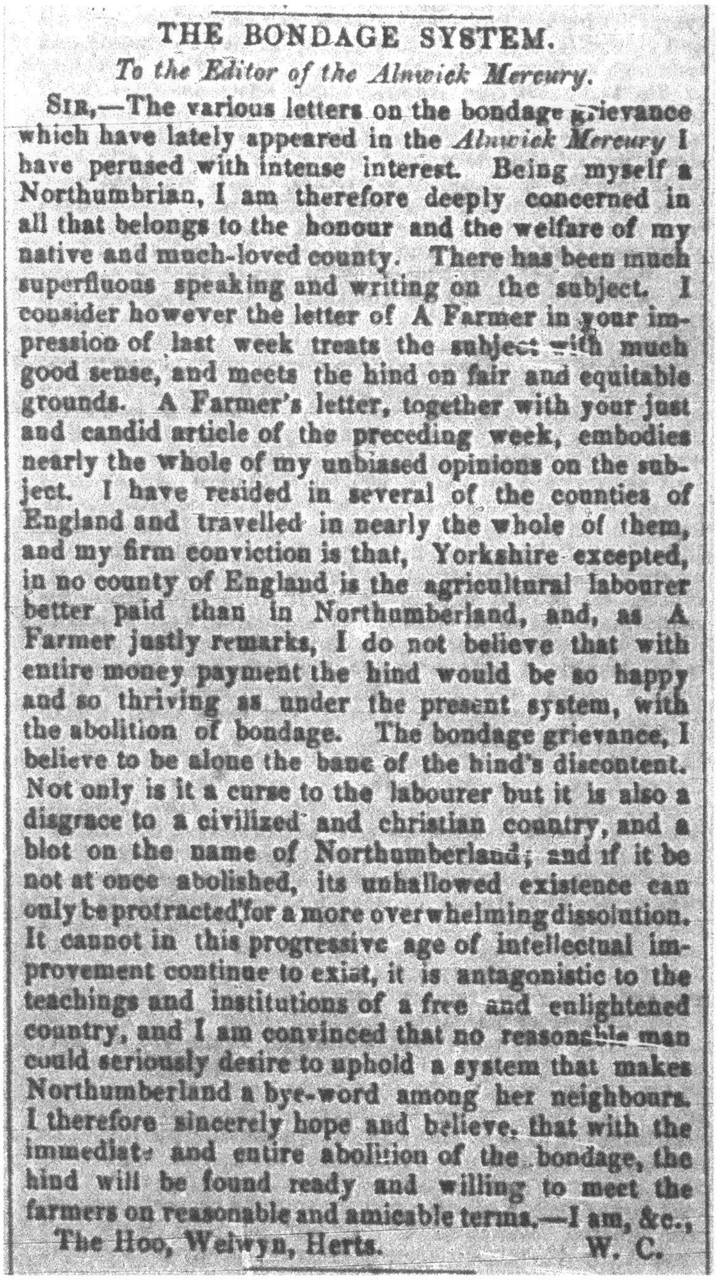

THE BONDAGE SYSTEM.

To the Editor of the Alnwick Mercury.

SIR,—The various letters on the bondage grievance which have lately appeared in the *Alnwick Mercury* I have perused with intense interest. Being myself a Northumbrian, I am therefore deeply concerned in all that belongs to the honour and the welfare of my native and much-loved county. There has been much superfluous speaking and writing on the subject. I consider however the letter of A Farmer in your impression of last week treats the subject with much good sense, and meets the hind on fair and equitable grounds. A Farmer's letter, together with your just and candid article of the preceding week, embodies nearly the whole of my unbiased opinions on the subject. I have resided in several of the counties of England and travelled in nearly the whole of them, and my firm conviction is that, Yorkshire excepted, in no county of England is the agricultural labourer better paid than in Northumberland, and, as A Farmer justly remarks, I do not believe that with entire money payment the hind would be so happy and so thriving as under the present system, with the abolition of bondage. The bondage grievance, I believe to be alone the bane of the hind's discontent. Not only is it a curse to the labourer but it is also a disgrace to a civilized and christian country, and a blot on the name of Northumberland; and if it be not at once abolished, its unhallowed existence can only be protracted for a more overwhelming dissolution. It cannot in this progressive age of intellectual improvement continue to exist, it is antagonistic to the teachings and institutions of a free and enlightened country, and I am convinced that no reasonable man could seriously desire to uphold a system that makes Northumberland a bye-word among her neighbours. I therefore sincerely hope and believe, that with the immediate and entire abolition of the bondage, the hind will be found ready and willing to meet the farmers on reasonable and amicable terms.—I am, &c.,

The Hoo, Welwyn, Herts. W. C.

Figure 46. W.C. Alnwick Mercury, 3 March 1866

A letter from '*A Northumberland Ploughman*' takes issue with a '*Mr. Farmer*' and his calculations with regard to the value of the hind's '*gains*'. He is at pains to be respectful but wishes to put the case before not only the farmers but the public. He seems to suggest that there is a feeling that the farmers are not willing to enter into a face-to-face discussion with the hinds. John Redpath, farm steward at Haymount, also felt the farmers were secretive. Speaking to the Teviotdale Ploughman's Association he said, '*Their plans are being matured, as surely as ours, with this difference – ours are public and not secret; they work upon the hole-and-corner principle*'. [Thomson 1866].

The '*Northumberland Ploughman*' adds some humour to his letter. He writes how his '*gudwife*' could use the 'mythical' £1 a week which the farmer had written about. He says '*she thinks she could buy a hind's income* (2s. 6d. a day according to the farmer), *and an extra new frock to some of the weans, and back 7d. or 8d. per week out of it.*'

Finally he becomes a bit more combative and asks the farmer to '*sharpen his memory*' and '*state the truth*'.

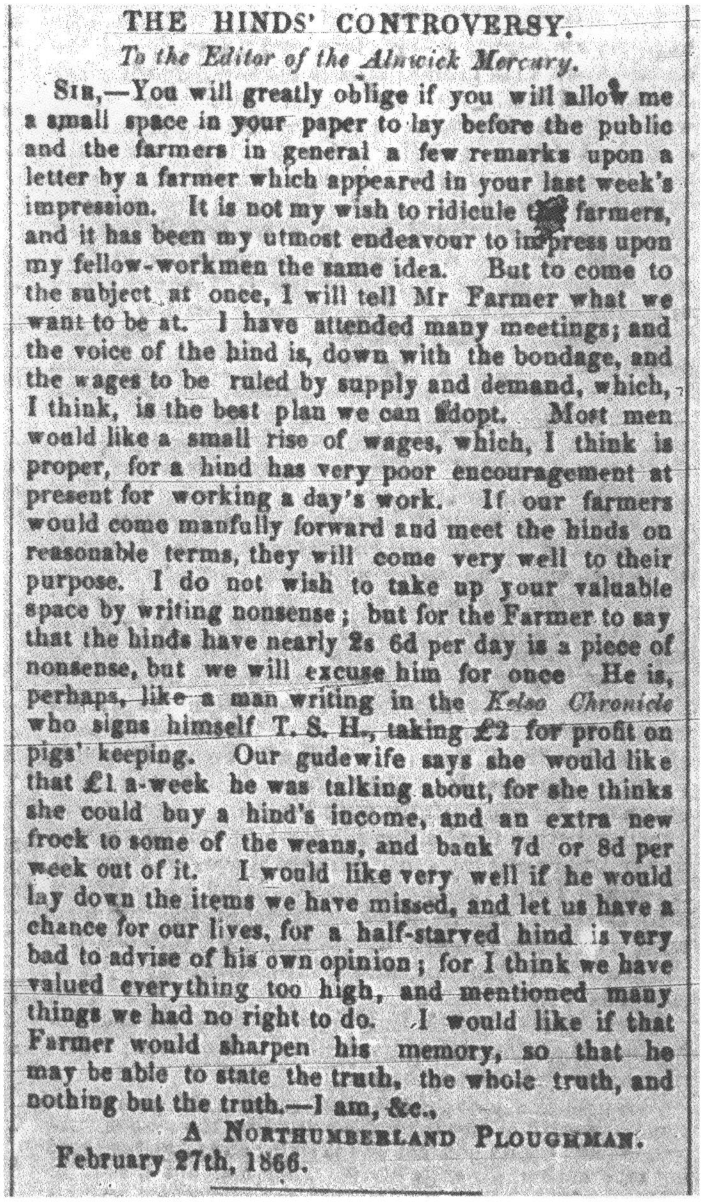

THE HINDS' CONTROVERSY.

To the Editor of the Alnwick Mercury.

SIR,—You will greatly oblige if you will allow me a small space in your paper to lay before the public and the farmers in general a few remarks upon a letter by a farmer which appeared in your last week's impression. It is not my wish to ridicule the farmers, and it has been my utmost endeavour to impress upon my fellow-workmen the same idea. But to come to the subject at once, I will tell Mr Farmer what we want to be at. I have attended many meetings; and the voice of the hind is, down with the bondage, and the wages to be ruled by supply and demand, which, I think, is the best plan we can adopt. Most men would like a small rise of wages, which, I think is proper, for a hind has very poor encouragement at present for working a day's work. If our farmers would come manfully forward and meet the hinds on reasonable terms, they will come very well to their purpose. I do not wish to take up your valuable space by writing nonsense; but for the Farmer to say that the hinds have nearly 2s 6d per day is a piece of nonsense, but we will excuse him for once He is, perhaps, like a man writing in the *Kelso Chronicle* who signs himself T. S. H., taking £2 for profit on pigs' keeping. Our gudewife says she would like that £1 a-week he was talking about, for she thinks she could buy a hind's income, and an extra new frock to some of the weans, and bank 7d or 8d per week out of it. I would like very well if he would lay down the items we have missed, and let us have a chance for our lives, for a half-starved hind is very bad to advise of his own opinion; for I think we have valued everything too high, and mentioned many things we had no right to do. I would like if that Farmer would sharpen his memory, so that he may be able to state the truth, the whole truth, and nothing but the truth.—I am, &c.,

A NORTHUMBERLAND PLOUGHMAN.

February 27th, 1866.

Figure 47. A Northumberland Ploughman. Alnwick Mercury, 3 March 1866

A letter in the Berwick Warder (2 March 1866) replies to the letter from the *'Bamburghshire Farmer'* (Figure 42). Here the*'Bamburghshire Hind'* is obviously *'stung'* by the farmer's reply and strongly defends his arguments. He feels his experiences with regard to the allowance of potatoes are as valid as the farmer's. The bondage system is, he says, *'hideous'* despite the *'whitewashing'* and this would be echoed by many men and their families. Mrs Williamson highlights one difficulty for the hind when she says he is *'well aware that the demand for bondagers is fully greater than the supply, and this induces him to be less strict about whom he admits into his family'.* She gives an instance *'but lately witnessed'* of *'a hind pleading with a girl, who was an entire stranger to him, to take the arles money, as if he had been pleading for dear life'.* This scarcity of bondagers obviously affects the wage the bondagers can demand. William Fairbairn confirms the figure, disputed by the farmer, of £12 a year whereas Mrs Williamson gives the greater figure of £7 for the half year.

Andrew Broadwood, shepherd of Drinkstone, would agree with the *'Bamburghshire Hind'* that to dismiss the boarding of a bondager as *'no account whatever in a family'* is just not true. Andrew writes about the pleasure of having *'all the hearth to call our own'.* He enjoys being able to speak freely of joys and sorrows and says *even the bairns seem to ken the odds, for they toddle about and seem to enjoy the pleasure of their own fireside. Likewise the very cat seems to ken.*

"*For she sits purrin' on the hud,*
No the least feared she need to scud,
For there's nae bondager noo to pu' her lug,
Or gar her mew."

The length of the working day is also given a thorough review, with the hind standing his ground with regard to the hours of work, when working with horses.

FARM LABOURERS.

SIR,—Your paper of February 23 contains a letter from a correspondent signed "A Bamburghshire Farmer," in which he charges me with the grave offence of not making a plain statement of facts. To prove this on his part, he considers it simply necessary to inform you of the wages, &c., paid to hinds on "our" farm. The first thing he finds fault with is the potatoes. Your correspondent says that I, a Bamburghshire hind, wrote as though five bags of potatoes were quite a common affair. "Bamburghshire Farmer" would condemn me for speaking of a bad crop of potatoes on the farm—that was a farm in Glendale, where I was living when I had this crop, and, to show that I am entirely in the wrong, he gives you the wages, &c., that hinds receive on what he calls our farm. In pointing out to me that I was in the ditch, he has come too near the edge and fallen in himself. I cannot for my part see why the farm should not be held up as an example just as much as our farm. He says that his hinds have their choice of twelve hundred yards or 240 stones of potatoes, &c. If five bags are uncommon, twelve hundred yards are as much so. I only know of two places where the hinds get any more than the ordinary lot of one thousand yards, and in the case I referred to I had no choice whatever. I got my thousand yards of ground, found my own seed, hoed them, and had them to take up, and was rewarded by five bags of potatoes for my trouble. I may here state that it was such crops as that which were the means of introducing this new system of getting the potatoes off the field by the bag or by weight, a system which I have never had the privilege of enjoying till the present year. An attack is made upon me concerning the bondage system. Your correspondent asserts that I have given a very high calculation for wages, viz., £12 a-year for a bondager. He must remember that it is not a housemaid that I am speaking of, but a bondager; and were he to go to any public market and try to hire one, they would be more sparing on him than on me if the calculation as to wages was not ready made to his hand; he would find £12 the lowest, instead of being so high as he asserts. Next, as to board, washing, &c., he says, "It is of no account whatever in a family." It is against both law and reason to say that a hind, with a wife and four or five children to feed, clothe, and his children to educate out of his small wage, that he can feed and maintain a healthy young woman, that he has no use for whatever, over and above his own family, and never take it into account. If your correspondent succeeds in establishing this as a fact, I for one will say that fact is stronger than fiction. Your correspondent next says that I wrote as though I received no pay for the girl's labour; this is a wrong representation. I said most distinctly that I allowed the girl to win this wage, £12, from the farmer, although I did not mention the wage per day, which is 10d. per day all the year, harvest excepted, when it is 1s. 6d., making proper allowances for broken time, &c. I cannot see that she can win any more than this £12, allowing the house and coals leading as part of her wage. I said I was paying at the rate of £13 per year for house, &c., valuing her board, &c., at 5s. per week; and were I to pay for house, &c., in money, it would only cost me £6 at the highest. In spite of all the labour and whitewashing which your correspondent has bestowed upon the bondage system, it will still show its hideous form. He considers my statements as to a hind's duties, hours. &c., full of subterfuge; he says it is only in the long summer days they require to be early astir. Now, from March till October, a hind must be up at half-past four; but these are facts too well known to be shaken by any assertion that he can make to the contrary. In winter, if we are longer in yoking sooner loosed, &c., it is taken off our dinner time; we are only allowed one hour in the stables. He speaks of town operatives working the same hours in winter as in summer; but most all tradesmen drop work at an early hour on Saturday afternoon and they have their liberty till Monday morning, whereas a hind has his duties to attend to both Sunday and Saturday. If the horses are at grass, there are plenty fields that have no water in them; thus on a Sunday the horses are to water twice at least. He says in summer a hind is relieved from foddering, &c., as the horses are turned out to grass at six o'clock. We do not take them out of the yoke till six, and then they are put into the stable and fed; we go back at eight o'clock, dress them down, and then take them to the field. If your correspondent has any more remarks to make, I hope he will make the truth more apparent, and then facts will not have such a striking resemblance to fiction.—I remain, Sir, your obedient servant,

A BAMBURGHSHIRE HIND.

Figure 48. A Bamburghshire Hind. Berwick Warder, 2 March 1866

The newspapers on the 9 and 10 March 1866 carried further letters and the usual reports of the hiring markets. The letter from '*A Bamburghshire Farmer*' sets out the situation, as he sees it, with a good deal of empathy for the hind and his wife and family. He does consider, however, that the '*gains*' should not be undervalued and the upstanding wage is very important. Operatives in town do not have this privilege. He also mentions the present hardships in farming – Rinderpest and low corn prices.

THE BONDAGE SYSTEM.

...,—The agitation among farm servants for an ad-
... of wages has assumed various phases, and in the
...-east of Scotland it has been resolved into a strug-
...r the abolition of the bondage. At some meetings
...ds it was agreed to ask a rise of £5 a year in addi-
...but the major and more reasonable part of the
...hmen ask only for their present gains, with the re-
...l of the bondage grievance. The bondage system,
...is called, is no doubt an anomalous arrangement;
...any respectable farmers have at once co-operated
...the ploughmen with a view to have it removed. Ac-
...ng to this method every married ploughman is bound
...vide his master with a sufficient worker, and if no
...r daughter or sister can "work the bondage," the
...man must hire a "fremed" woman to board in his
..., to whom he must pay a wage, and who gets
...the master one shilling for every day she works in
...er, tenpence in winter, and extra pay in harvest.
...age paid by the hind to the bondager is not less
...£12 a year, and the utmost she can earn in money
...ut £14, so that the hind has only £2 of money for
...oard, and often not so much. According to the
...al calculation, indeed the house and garden, with
... a thousand yards of potatoes planted, were in-
...d for the bondager's board; but this has been lost
...of by the hind, so that now he regards the gains
...his own, while the bondager's board comes all out
...is scanty exchequer. As the ploughman is paid
...y in kind, it is difficult to compute his exact in-
...; but a seemingly fair calculation makes the com-
...average income of hind and bondager amount to
...£48 to £50, of which about £22 must be allowed
...he bondager's wage and board, leaving the hind
...less than £30 to support himself and his family.
...calculations make the hind's wage only £27 a-
...after deducting the bondager's board and wages;
...s much depends on the cow and the potatoes,
...he price of grain, the exact sum can hardly be esti-
...d.

...e burden of bondage is chiefly felt by the plough-
...from his marriage till some one of his family grows
... work the bondage; and the grievance becomes
...y a tax upon marriage; while hired as a single ser-
...or working conjunctly with his father an able-
...d man will have probably £33 a-year, but imme-
...ly on his marriage, unless the young wife work the
...age, which is very undesirable, his wage is reduced
...out a fourth of its amount, while the young cou-

...ave the discomforts of a stranger constantly at
...fireside, and probably sleeping in the same room,
...nothing but a few boards between them. The
...s manifold worse if the bondager be disagreeable,
...he lives of the newly married pair are embittered
...not only a stranger, but one in whom they have
...nfidence, eating at their table, cumbering their
...stic hearth, dressing and undressing, and sleeping
...e same room, and then perhaps telling abroad what
...hear or see in the privacy of the domestic circle.
...case becomes worse when three or four children
...in succession; for one of the first questions asked
...ondager in the market is about the number of
...en; and many refuse to enter a house where
...are "half-a-dizzen bairns." The hardship les-
...when a family grows up, so that one of themselves
...undertake the bondage; and, where masters are
...erate, large incomes are made by the united earn-
...f a ploughman's family. In one instance a family
...rwickshire has been known to make £160 a-year.
...ving now commented at considerable length on the
...burgh Hind's" grievances, permit me to make a
...emarks on the advantages which he possesses over
...nics in towns. Your correspondent "Tenant"
...effectually disposed of the question of the free
...and coals lead that it is unnecessary to make any
...ations on these points. A "Bamburgshire
..., must, however, remember that he gets all his
...ces and corn at prime cost. If he was living in a
...he would find these commodities rather dearer
...he expects. Another very great privilege which a
...possesses is that he has full wages all the year
..., even if from sickness or other cause he does not
...a week. I have known instances in which a hind
...ot wrought a day for months, and yet he received
...ay all the time. At the present moment I could
...instances in which hinds have been ill many
...hs, and are receiving full pay. Can a "Bamburgh-
...Hind" give me an instance that will bear com-
...on with this among town operatives?
...conclusion, let a "Bamburghshire Hind" consider
...the present time, the farmers can give a larger
wage than they do give. Farms are letting very high
at present, owing to certain would-be-farmers coming
out of town to spend their money in the country. The
rinderpest is among cattle, and corn is absolutely given
away. How then can a farmer afford higher wages?
Apologising for occupying so much of your space, I remain, sir, yours most respectfully,
A BAMBURGHSHIRE FARMER.
March 3, 1866.

Figure 49. A Bamburghshire Farmer. Berwick Warder, 9 March 1866

The letter signed J. T. takes a more hectoring and unpleasant tone. He sneers at the hind and likens him to Rip Van Winkle, saying *'has your correspondent been asleep these last ten years?'* He dismisses the financial hardship of keeping a bondager based on figures arrived at from discussions with other hinds and also his own ideas of days worked in a year. He raises the question of the bondager doing housework for the hind and family. This is open to different interpretations, and he paints a rosy picture when he says the bondager *'is a positive boon to the hind when the amount of household work she performs is taken into consideration.'* He gives women in *'bondage houses'* as an example of women working outside all day and washing and baking, etc., until 11pm. William Fairbairn did not share this optimistic view of the relationship between the hind, his wife and the bondager. Strictly speaking the bondager, being hired by him, was the servant of the hind but any attempt to impose this hierarchy on her would, he says, *'excite a sneer of contempt'*. They *'care very little about household work'* and it is *'far from being rare to see them sitting with hands folded, or gossiping about their neighbour's houses, while, it may be, their mistress is over head-and-ears in work'*.

The question raised by J. T. of the need for more housing would meet with Mrs Williamson's approval, as she thought the solution to a shortage of workers when the bondage system was abolished would be more '*bondage houses*' although she does not use this term. She says '*We have seen the families of hinds, when deprived by death of their husband and father, obliged to remove to a town, and the elder children to work in a factory for the support of the mother and younger children, and thus their labour is lost to the farmer. Were houses easily obtained in the country, the town would not be so often resorted to.*'

FARM LABOURERS.

SIR,—Your correspondent, "A Bamburghshire Hind," whose letter appears in your last impression seems suddenly to have discovered that Northumberland hinds are, to use a common expression, "working for nothing and finding their own food." To prove that this is the case at the present day your correspondent gives the quantity of potatoes he once had, in Glendale ward, ten years ago. Why does not your correspondent go back at once to the time of the Saxons, and say "because hinds were slaves under Saxon rule, they are slaves at the present day?" The argument is the same as that which he employs, it is only carried a little further, that is all the difference. Your correspondent must assuredly be at a great loss for argument when he publishes the quantity of potatoes which he happened to have ten years ago in Glendale, and so lead neutral parties to infer that the quantity which he receives at the present day is similar. Perhaps, however, your correspondent has been asleep these last ten years, and has suddenly awoke, and written the letter which appears in your last issue; it so he is quite excusable. That the quantity of potatoes, which a hind receives has increased as much during the last ten years in Glendale, as in this neighbourhood, plainly appears from the sensible letter of your correspondent "Tenant," which also is contained in your issue of last week. It may be true that a "Bamburghshire Hind" knows of only two instances in which twelve hundred yards is the nominal quantity which a hind receives, but I know many places in which the nominal quantity is one thousand yards, and the real quantity twelve hundred. But if your correspondent has suddenly awoke from a ten years' slumber, it is quite possible that he may not be aware of this fact.

The "hideous features" of the bondage system is the next point of your correspondent's attack. I re-assert that £12 a-year is a high calculation for wage paid by the hind to the bondager. From inquiry among hinds I have come to the conclusion that £10 10s. a-year is a much fairer calculation. Let us see, then, how much the bondager earns for the hind by her farm work.

106 days at 1s. in Summer, reckoning her to work five days per week	£5 6	0
24 days in harvest at 1s. 6d.	1 16	0
26 weeks, five days per week at 10d., in Winter	5 8	4
	£12 10	4
Paid bondager for wage	10 10	0
Balance in hind's favour	£2 0	4

It thus appears that the bondager, working only five days a week, earns upwards of £2 more than the average paid to the bondager by the hind. On many large farms the bondager is employed six days in the week instead of five; as she is employed indoors, in the barn, &c., when it is too wet for her to work in the fields. In such cases she earns for the hind, a considerably larger overplus than the sum I have calculated. In large families the bondager is a positive boon to the hind when the amount of household work which she performs is taken into consideration. It may be thought that, after working all day, she will be unable to do much household work at night. This is a mistake: if it was true, how would women who have "bondage houses" do, who work out all day, and do all their household work at night? One of this class informs me that she is frequently up washing, baking, &c., till eleven o'clock, p.m. Again, there are many hind's wives who work bondage work, leaving no one to take care of the house, and they, too, must do all their household work at night; how do they manage to get it done, if an able young woman cannot work at night after a day's out-door work? The fallacy of the argument that bondagers cannot work in the house at night after working in the fields during the day, is thus rendered obvious. I hesitate not then to say that the bondager is well worth her board and lodging, when the household work which she performs is taken into account; and it therefore follows that the hind has all that she earns more than her wages for clear profit.

Your correspondent does not seem to be aware of the fact that most factory operatives in towns work from six till six, summer and winter, with perhaps an hour at dinner, and a quarter of an hour at breakfast time. As, however, your correspondent "Tenant" is of opinion that in my last communication I gave a very fair statement of facts on that head, it is unnecessary for me to say any more on the subject. I may, however, simply observe, that certain farmers in this neighbourhood are also herring-curers, and that their hinds have in the herring season extra long hours; but for this, I understand, they have extra pay.

It is gratifying that some of the most respectable farmers have willingly met the ploughmen in an honest effort to abolish the grievance. The hiring markets have not yet come on, but on many farms the ploughmen are already re-engaged. In some cases the bondage is retained with an advance of about £2 in money, but the fact that many enterprising farmers have done otherwise, is an earnest that the system is doomed to perish. As the hiring markets are approaching, and as some farmers may be in doubt how to proceed, it may be worth while to state the terms on which one Berwickshire farmer has engaged his ploughmen. The money promised is £20 a-year, a cow is kept, with an allowance of turnips in winter to the extent of four tons, a thousand yards of potato ground are allowed, and there is a free house and garden, with breakfast and dinner, but not supper in harvest. The bondage is abolished, but to any daughter able and willing to work, there is a promise of fifty shillings a-year, with one shilling per day for every day she works, and with three shillings a day besides breakfast and dinner during harvest. By this method the gains of the hind and the female worker are kept separate, and the worth of each will be regulated by demand and supply. Whether or not a sufficient supply of workers will be maintained remains to be seen; but with the scarcity of cottages all over the district this is very doubtful. As an ultimate remedy for the bondage, more houses are required; and considering the oppressive character of the system, farmers should aim at its utter abolition, and demand from the landlords additional house accommodation where any number of able and willing workers could be maintained. For more than twenty years there has been a great and growing diminution of population in the counties of Roxburgh and Berwick, till now the *minimum* has perhaps been reached, and the agitation among the hinds may possibly open up great social questions, prominent among which will be the erection of more houses.—I am, &c.,

J. T.

Figure 50. J.T. Berwick Warder, 9 March 1866

This next letter with its picturesque language paints an idyllic picture, which we know from previous letters, is not at all the case. His picture does, however, raises new insights into the complex situation - the fact that the hind can feel he is a farmer himself with his varied responsibilities to 'a cow and a pig, a garden and a few drills of potatoes. This is probably very important to the hind, giving him self-respect and enabling him to take pride in his work as a ploughman. Also, he mentions that the hind no longer has to drive *grain or coals during the night, and along bad roads'* which had been the case evidently, for former generations.

He acknowledges the problems of the bondage system, particularly for the young ploughman raising his family. The bondager is portrayed in the usual way as an imposition and also as someone who knows her value and will not work for a hind with *"half-a-dizzen bairns"*.

The proposed new system, the family hiring, is given in detail and he feels that separating the *'gains'* of the hind and bondager will be a big help towards ending disputes.

FARM SERVANTS IN THE BORDER COUNTIES.

Hardly any class of men is more sedate in a general way than the ploughmen, and especially the ploughmen of the south-eastern border counties. With their "coo," and their "soo," and their "tatties," and their comfortable load of meal set down at regular intervals, they have the necessaries of life at prime cost, and though they have little money, and seldom get a new black coat, there is no apparent reason why they may not "whistle and sing at the ploughin' o't." Without any great advance in the nominal value of their gains, their condition has greatly improved within the last thirty or forty years. The cow's produce is now worth twice as much as it was then; the sheep-money as it is called, has risen from 50s. to £5; the burden of wives having to shear for the house and to carry the stacks in winter has been remitted; and the hind has no such driving of grain or coals during the night, and along bad roads, as the hinds of a former generation had. The average gains of the hinds now are about 10 bolls of oats, 3½ bolls of barley, 1 boll of peas, 1600 yards of potatoes planted, a cow kept, 4 carts of coals, a free house and garden, with £5 in money, making altogether about £33 or £34 a-year at a moderate computation. With these gains, and with the pleasurable consciousness of being farmers to the extent of a cow and a pig, a garden and a few drills of potatoes, the hinds have reared families and kept the band in the nick, and had a tolerably easy if not a very splendid or elevated existence.

But "the trail of the serpent" is over even the most charming pictures of human felicity; and the one crook in the lot of the Border hind has been "the bondage system." The constitution is peculiar to the counties of Roxborough and Berwick, though it has partially spread into the counties adjoining. It is a mode of securing female labourers for the farm by having married ploughmen *bound* to furnish the master with a sufficient worker to be hired, boarded, and paid by the hind, but paid by the master, for the time she works, at the rate of 1s. a day in summer, 10d. in winter, with extra pay in harvest. This mode of securing workers has become a kind of necessity in the district, as there are no female bothies, and few extra houses whence female workers can be drawn, and also a strong aversion to have them boarded in the farmer's kitchen. For the farmer it has worked well, but to the hind it has always appeared a "bondage" to be endured only till there was some probability of having the whole fabric razed to its foundations.

The maledictions of hinds have not been without foundation, but in some cases the complaints have been exaggerated. The economical part of the grievance has been more apparent than real. In the primary arrangement provision was made in the hinds' gains for the woman's board, for the free house and half the potatoes were understood to be her perquisites, but this arrangement has been forgotten, and as the bondager would not earn more than £14 a-year, while her wage has been at least £12, the idea has become general that her board came almost entirely out of the hind's scanty gains. But the bondage system has other aspects even more oppressive. A young ploughman gets married, and unless the young wife can work the bondage, a woman must be hired to board in the house and work the bondage. Many of the houses are now commodious, but many are otherwise, and in these cases the hired woman must sit at the same hearth with the married pair, eat at the same table, dress and undress in the same room, and sleep at a distance of a foot or two without any other partition than the thin boards of the box bed. When the young people are blessed with five or six children, the case becomes worse, for few young women will hire into a house with "half-a-dizzen bairns," unless at a rate which the hind cannot give without injury to himself and family. The hardship is less when a son or daughter grows up to work the bondage, but for the first fourteen or fifteen years of a ploughman's married life he struggles amid difficulties that furrow his cheeks and turn his hair prematurely grey.

In the hirings now in progress the farmers have recognised the grievance, and a very general modification has been granted. On many farms the bondage in the case of hinds who have no workers of their own has been abolished. The gains of the hind have been fixed at something like £35 a-year, with no deduction for anything except that they pay for the coals they consume, which the master drives home without expense to the hind. In the case of hinds who have daughters able and willing to work, remuneration is promised equivalent, on the average, to about £19 10s. The arrangements vary slightly, some giving about three-half-pence an hour for all the work performed, with extra pay in harvest; others giving six shillings a-week, with from fifty shillings to four pounds at the end of the year, with extra pay and food in harvest; and some retaining the old system, with £2 additional to the hinds, but all coming to about the same point of allowing £34 to £35 for the hind, and £19 to £19 10s. for the female worker. Relief is thus granted to those who have no workers of their own; the vicious principle of mixing up the gains of hinds and bondagers is avoided; and, on the whole, peace and good feeling is more likely to prevail among the hinds of the border counties.—*Farmer*.

Figure 51. Farmer. Berwick Warder, 9 March 1866

So many anonymous letters! Although letters to newspapers today are sometimes signed in a similar way or the name and address is withheld, generally correspondents do not hide their identity. In 1866 many of the correspondents hid their identity and we can only assume that they felt the need to be secretive, and this was perhaps a means of escaping any reprisals. Even the more fervent letters can only give an inkling of the atmosphere at this time. John Thomson, in January 1866, when speaking in Lauder to the '*Great Meeting of Ploughmen*' reminded them that they '*the ploughmen*' had as much right to '*liberty of speech, liberty to search for the truth, know the truth, speak the truth, and defend the truth.*' The meeting concluded with '*loud cheers of "Down – away with the bondage!"*'

In '*Voices from the Plough*' John Thomson includes [Thomson 1869] some verses written by Andrew Wilson, '*An aged ploughman now living a Lilliesleaf*'. In one verse he calls the ploughmen to action when he writes:

'*Then come, all ye ploughmen these lines who may read,*
By the braes of the Ettrick and the banks of the Tweed,
Around by Mid-Lothian, where 'er ye may be,
Join the loud chorus, and sing it with me.
Chorus
Then away with Old Bondage – away with it now!
To this old feudal system we never can bow.
We'll march to the station, take Liberty's train,
For we ne'er will be burdened with Bondage again.'

Fairness was the concern of John Redpath's (farm steward, Haymount) when he complained about an unruly meeting where he said '*two gentlemen wanted to address the meeting, and both were cried down before we could gather what they had to say*'.

So - lots to discuss and dispute; sometimes with raised voices. With hiring approaching, nerves and tempers would be stretched to the limit.

After the months of discussion and agitation, particularly against the bondage system, there was naturally going to be keen interest in the outcome of the hiring fairs.

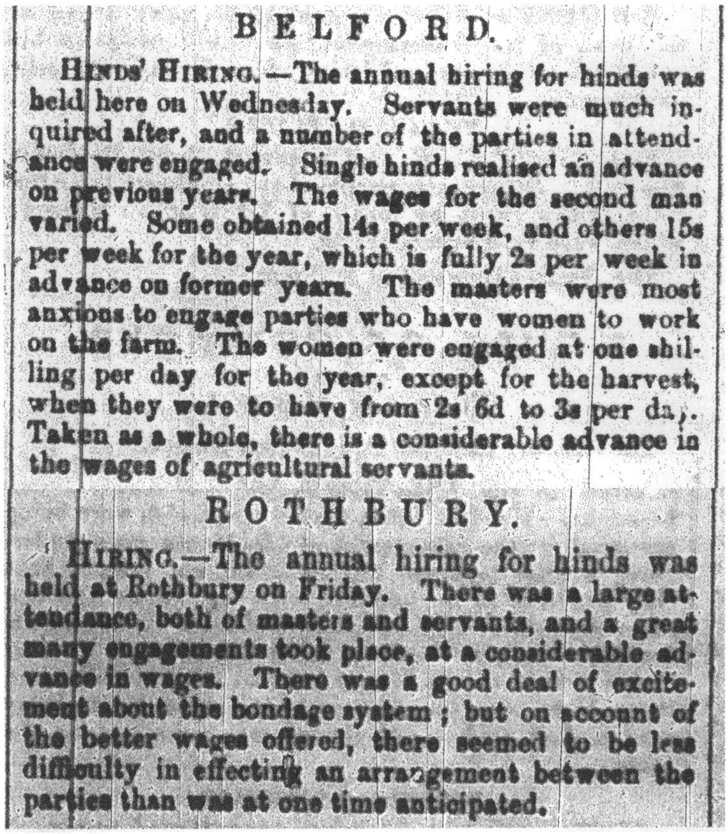

BELFORD.

HINDS' HIRING.—The annual hiring for hinds was held here on Wednesday. Servants were much inquired after, and a number of the parties in attendance were engaged. Single hinds realised an advance on previous years. The wages for the second man varied. Some obtained 14s per week, and others 15s per week for the year, which is fully 2s per week in advance on former years. The masters were most anxious to engage parties who have women to work on the farm. The women were engaged at one shilling per day for the year, except for the harvest, when they were to have from 2s 6d to 3s per day. Taken as a whole, there is a considerable advance in the wages of agricultural servants.

ROTHBURY.

HIRING.—The annual hiring for hinds was held at Rothbury on Friday. There was a large attendance, both of masters and servants, and a great many engagements took place, at a considerable advance in wages. There was a good deal of excitement about the bondage system; but on account of the better wages offered, there seemed to be less difficulty in effecting an arrangement between the parties than was at one time anticipated.

Figure 52. Belford & Rothbury. Berwick Advertiser , 9 March 1866

The Rothbury reporter notices the atmosphere at the hiring fair and says there was '*a good deal of excitement about the bondage system*', whereas, the Kelso reporter comments on the exceptional and '*very large attendance of masters and men.*'

Dunse hiring fair, being the focal point for the county of Berwickshire, had also generated a lot of interest. The reporter says the weather was unfavourable which is an understatement for there was heavy snow and cold wind, which lasted the whole day. Despite this the crowds were described as '*monster*' and '*immense*'. This reporter also describes how the end of the bondage was announced with '*tuck of drum*' and this had caused '*great excitement*'. He also noted that this had a '*considerable effect on the unfortunate hinds who had no families.*' These men, whilst apparently being relieved of the requirement to provide a bondager in the old way, were now at a disadvantage when farmers were looking for and showing preference for families who could provide the workers they needed. These men continued to hire women to work with them and the Dunse report makes this clear when it states that '*hinds without families, and who have to employ workers, were also engaged on the same terms, but with an advance of 30s. to £3 for the board of those they employ.*' This also shows the men had successfully made their point about the cost of keeping a bondager in their home.

KELSO.

KELSO HIRING MARKET, FRIDAY, MARCH 2.—At the hiring market for married farm-servants held to-day there was a very large attendance of masters and men, the expected change in conditions having induced almost every one having any interest in the matter to be present. There was considerable difficulty at first in effecting engagements, and to the last it was a dull market, a good many remaining without engagements. The understanding was apparently general that the bondage in its old familiar form was to be abolished, and the men, most in request were those with daughters who were able and willing to work. The general rate of engagements was as follows:— For men without workers the terms remain without alteration. For those who have workers the arrangements are various. In one or two cases we hear of women being engaged at the rate of fourteen pence per day all the year round; and for three-quarters of the year this was the general rate of remuneration for women, with the current rate of wage in harvest. In other cases the wage is one shilling per day, with from two to three pounds in addition. In some cases four pounds were given, but some deduction in another form leaves the actual wage very much the same as others. There were a very unusual number of men open to engagements, many of whom will ultimately remain in their present places, but they wished to see the market before making engagements. Still there will be a great deal of flitting. Though the crowd of people was so large, everything was conducted in a most orderly manner.

Figure 53. Kelso. Berwick Advertiser, 9 March 1866

The wages, of about £19.10s. for women workers, which had been speculation in the last letter, seems to have been correct but the way this was paid could vary. The reporter at Dunse says that 'bargains being numerous and diversified we cannot report the advance with precision.'

Due to these changing circumstances the Kelso reporter noted a high turn out 'of men open to engagement'. Many of these men would very likely 'remain in their present places' but were sensibly attending the market to obtain a thorough understanding of the situation before committing themselves to an agreement.

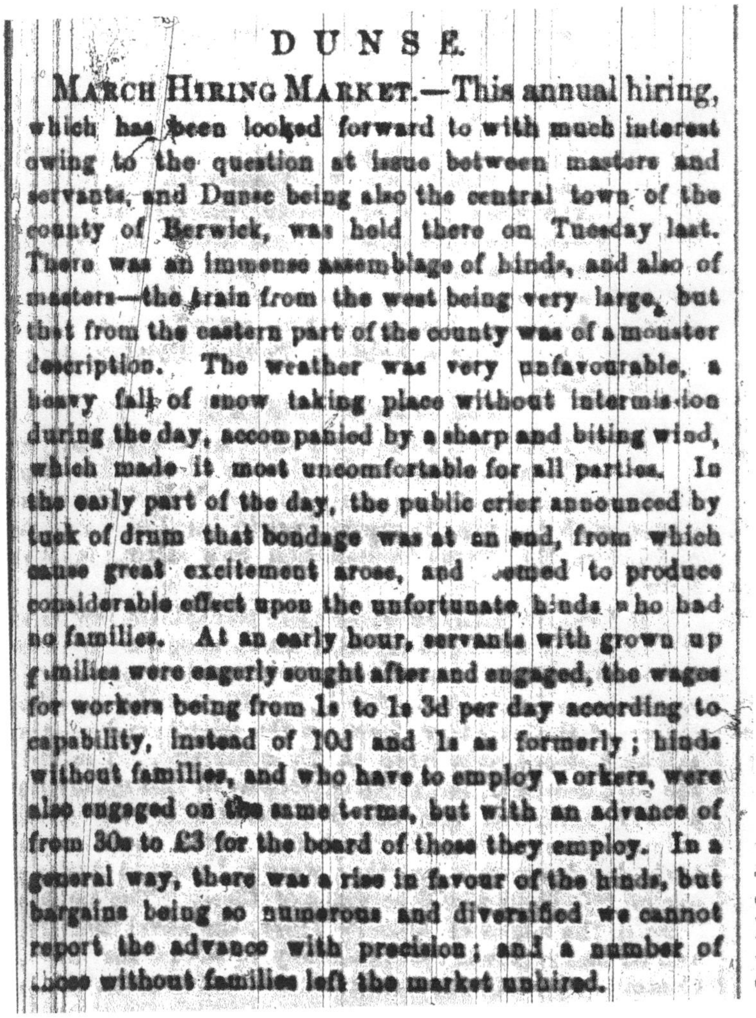

DUNSE.

MARCH HIRING MARKET.—This annual hiring, which has been looked forward to with much interest owing to the question at issue between masters and servants, and Dunse being also the central town of the county of Berwick, was held there on Tuesday last. There was an immense assemblage of hinds, and also of masters—the train from the west being very large, but that from the eastern part of the county was of a monster description. The weather was very unfavourable, a heavy fall of snow taking place without intermission during the day, accompanied by a sharp and biting wind, which made it most uncomfortable for all parties. In the early part of the day, the public crier announced by tuck of drum that bondage was at an end, from which cause great excitement arose, and seemed to produce considerable effect upon the unfortunate hinds who had no families. At an early hour, servants with grown up families were eagerly sought after and engaged, the wages for workers being from 1s to 1s 3d per day according to capability, instead of 10d and 1s as formerly; hinds without families, and who have to employ workers, were also engaged on the same terms, but with an advance of from 30s to £3 for the board of those they employ. In a general way, there was a rise in favour of the hinds, but bargains being so numerous and diversified we cannot report the advance with precision; and a number of those without families left the market unhired.

Figure 54. Dunse. Berwick Advertiser, 9 March 1866

It is noticeable that many of the 'hiring' reports moderate their language to fit the changing times. They were beginning to use *'changes in conditions'* and *'women workers'* instead of the *'bondage system'* and *'bondagers'*

Berwick hiring market led to a *'dense throng'* of people gathering in the market place on Hide Hill and again some were there purely to get an understanding of the changing situation. The reporter admits that abolition of the *'obnoxious'* bondage system has not happened but the *'modifications'* amount almost to abolition. The *'family system'* mentioned in Rutherfurd's Directory (1866) is being established and the hind, without family to work in the fields, is no longer obliged to employ and house a stranger. This being so we have already seen that hinds were still hiring women workers when they could, with a cash allowance for board. There were problems for some, probably due to a lack of women workers, and at Dunse a number of men without families left the market unhired.

After the stress of the changing situation, the holiday atmosphere must have brought welcome relief and kept the high street stalls busy until the evening. Unfortunately, there were some people intent on profiting from petty theft, and a number of pockets were picked. On two separate occasions pocket watches were stolen, and although no violence was reported, the young man found near Mr Hogg's public house may have been assaulted.

Berwick Advertiser March 9th 1866

Berwick Hiring Market- On Saturday, the annual market for hiring hinds in this district was held. In consequence of the agitation for the abolition of the bondage system there was an unusually large attendance of both masters and servants, the market place in Hide Hill being crowded by a dense throng for several hours. Although most, if not all of the farmers had come prepared to make concessions, considerable difficulty was experienced at first in effecting engagements; but as the day wore on, and matters having been fully discussed by the parties interested, engagements became brisker, and comparatively few left without being hired. Several also, who proposed remaining with their masters, attended the market to learn the terms of engagements, which also were to be binding in their cases. During the day the bellman was sent round the market giving intimation that women workers were not to hire under 1s 3d a-day and 3s a-day during the harvest time. From the terms agreed upon generally, it would appear that the obnoxious bondage system will henceforth undergo modification amounting almost to total abolition. In no case was it made a condition by the employers, who undertook to hire female outworkers for themselves, deducting their allowance from the lump sum given to the hinds for their joint wages. In the terms for men without workers there was no alteration. For those who have workers various arrangements were made, the servants most in request being such as daughters able and willing to work. In a few cases women were hired as from 1s 2d to 1s 3d per day all the year round, while in the majority this was the remuneration given them three quarters of the year, with 3s a-day during harvest time, and the usual gains. In some instances, the amount was 1s per day, with from £2 to £3 added. Generally speaking, the wages of the female workers may be said to have risen from £2 10s to £3. The new arrangements will chiefly benefit the females and hinds without children able to work the fields, the latter of whom found the allowance made to them for a bondager insufficient, while they were subjected to the additional annoyance of taking a stranger into their household. The weather in the forenoon was cold and rainy, but it cleared up as the day advanced, and many of the country people stayed in the town till the evening. There was the usual stalls in the High street for the sale of gingerbread, etc., and a number of "Cheap Johns, "and other attractive marts. Several people are reported to have been robbed of money and other articles, but no trace of thieves have been discovered. A young man was found by the police on Saturday night, lying in the yard adjoining Mr Hogg's public house in High Street; his albert chain had been cut and the silver watch (value £4) to which it was attached, was taken away. Another man, while in the said public-house, fell asleep, and when he awoke his watch, for which he had paid £5 a few weeks since, was gone. In the afternoon there was the usual horse market in Hide Hill, Mr Campbell, horse dealer, sold nine. Cart horses brought from £25 to £40; harness horses from £35 to £45; and ponies, from £12 to £15.

Figure 55. Berwick. Transcript - Berwick Advertiser, 9 March 1866

Payment in kind or the hind's '*gains*' was still the accepted method of payment but the Newcastle Courant in February had noted that farm servants at Peebles were agitating for fortnightly cash payments.   Payment totally in cash was certainly one of the issues under discussion.

WOOLER

Hiring Market -- At this hiring on Thursday, there was a large attendance of hinds, who made a strong stand to get free from bondage and a rise of wages. Hiring was somewhat dull; but in general men were hired without the bondage condition. Those with working daughters, however, were most readily hired. The terms for female workers was, as a rule, 1s per day all the year round, but 3s during harvest.

Figure 56. Wooler. Transcript - Berwick Advertiser, 9 March 1866

Wooler Hiring Market shows the men continuing to make a strong stand against the bondage condition but '*those with working daughters, however, were most readily hired'*.

Also in the newspaper, was an additional report, which dealt with the *'Nine Hours' Movement'*. This was obviously a third reason for agitation amongst the hinds, although it seems to have been given little prominence in the newspapers. The reporter is very sanguine about labourers on individual estates meeting with their employers and receiving some relief from their long hours of work.

As we have seen, some of the letters written by the hinds give a good indication of the particularly long hours worked by men who were in charge of horses. We have also seen the resistance by farmers to acknowledge that these hours were excessive. A farmer correspondent points out that those long hours did not apply to wintertime when daylight hours were short. He reminded the men that in factories work continued in lamplight to maintain the length of the working day. This idea might well be contradicted by the men. They certainly worked by lamplight to get their horses ready in the dark mornings and to settle them for the night. Also dinner hours in wintertime were confined to one hour to take account of the shorter working days - see the letter from 'A Bamburghshire Hind' in Figure 48.

Berwick Advertiser March 9th 1866

The Nine hours' Movement – We noticed in our last impression that a meeting of the labouring men of Dunse and district had taken place early in February for the above object, and that a memorial was drawn up, and a deputation had been appointed to wait upon the properties and tenant farmers, to lay their claims before them. The result of this appeal has been of a varied character, as although in almost every instance the deputation was received with courtesy and kindness, yet only one of the gentlemen waited upon unhesitatingly gave in his adherence to the wishes of the deputation, and it now seems to be generally agreed that the best plan that can be adopted to further the views of the memorialists will be for the labourers on the different estate, &c., to memorialise their employers individually, and we have no doubt that the men who adopt this plan will be received by their employers equally as cordially as were the deputation, and on stating their grievances, we feel confident their condition will be ameliorated as far as possible lies in the power of the gentlemen so appealed to. We believe that for the some time the nine hours' plan has been existence on the estate of Ayton Castle, Kelloe, Blackadder, and Swinton, and has found to work admirably.

Figure 57. The Nine Hours' Movement. Transcript - Berwick Advertiser, 9 March 1866

It is interesting to note that the *'nine hours'* plan was working on the *'estate of Ayton Castle, Kelloe, Blackadder and Swinton'*.

The Lauder report for the fair on the 6 March 1866 shows the expectations of *'all round rises in wages'* noted earlier did not materialise. Also note the miserable weather.

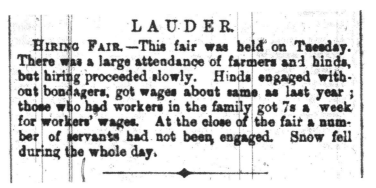

LAUDER.

Hiring Fair.—This fair was held on Tuesday. There was a large attendance of farmers and hinds, but hiring proceeded slowly. Hinds engaged without bondagers, got wages about same as last year; those who had workers in the family got 7s a week for workers' wages. At the close of the fair a number of servants had not been engaged. Snow fell during the whole day.

Figure 58. Lauder. Berwick Advertiser, 9 March 1866

The biggest demonstration made by the hinds seems to have been at Alnwick and this was extensively reported in the Alnwick Mercury and the Berwick Warder on the 10 and 9 of March respectively. These reports give a lively picture of the day and the excitement that pervaded the vast group of people. The Newcastle Courant of 9 March 1866 also reported the Alnwick Hiring saying that *'So large an assemblage of hinds was never seen in Alnwick before, about 2000 came by rail alone'*.

Everyone was keyed-up to take action and make a strong demonstration against the bondage system but the size of the crowd perhaps overawed many and the possibility of failure was already being mooted when Gilbert Turnbull stepped forward and the meeting got under way. The cash wage was first discussed with the wild figure of £15 shouted out from the crowd. He deals with this with humour and fairness. The bondage issue came next with the strong feeling in the meeting that if the farmers wanted women workers '*let them* (the farmers) *hire them'*. He creates some amusement over the food the bondager will eat and he says 1/- a day will only pay for her dinner and there is still breakfast and supper to provide.

Robert Rutherford, Farm Steward, Courthill, remarks on how little money is often left over after paying the woman worker. He has sometimes found it to be just 1s. 3d. a week and this is to feed '*a strong out-door worker.'* [Thomson 1869].

Gilbert Turnbull says, '*Mind, now, lads, none of you hire to-day to find a bondager. If you do, I hope when you come to hire your bondager at May-day, she may ask you £12 for the half-year.'* This is, of course, double the going rate and he is speaking tongue-in-cheek, a joke, but also a warning of displeasure.

William Campbell also spoke strongly urging the men to stand together. Both of them mention the lack of a wide coat or greatcoat and they say that keeping a bondager so drains their resources that they cannot afford a greatcoat. William says he only has a plaid which suggests that the plaid is second best in his opinion. Perhaps the plaid, though traditional dress, is considered old-fashioned. He is adamant in his opinion that the workers must not hire by the week for cash and therefore lose the benefit of the upstanding wage.

THE BONDAGE SYSTEM.
MEETING OF HINDS.

Seldom does our ancient little town present the crowded and lively appearance it did on Saturday last, occasioned by the large influx of farm servants to the hiring market. From an early hour the hinds kept streaming in from all quarters, and by eleven o'clock the centre of the town became densely packed, rendering the locomotion of passengers next to impossible. The reason of this great assembly, we need hardly tell our readers, was the anxiety of the Northumberland hinds to rid themselves of that system of working known by the name of bondage. It was generally understood that something would be done on Saturday to effect this desirable object, and accordingly large numbers of the hinds wended their way to Bailiffgate, the place of rendezvous, for the purpose of hearing the opinions of those who were to address them, and if possible coming to some resolution in the matter. For a while there seemed to be no one among the crowd possessed of the necessary zeal and earnestness to assume the self-consituted leadership of the movement; and rumour with her thousand tongues was quite busy in circulating the report that "it would all come to nothing." Some wiseacres were among those present, who had seen a similar agitation verify the above prediction. This, however, we are glad to say proved an exception.

After waiting anxiously for an hour or two, during which time several ineffectual attempts were made to draw out the minds of the bystanders and thus to constitute a meeting, a brawny son of the soil more confident of his oratorical powers than his brethren, and whose name was Gilbert Turnbull, mounted the paling at the entrance to Bailiffgate and addressed the multitude as follows:—Now, lads, what are we come here for? What about the money—what are we to have? ("15," — hear, hear, and cheers.) No, no, I like to look at both sides, and we must consider the farmers as well as ourselves. If I could get £15, it would be right enough; but that would be more than they can give. (Hear, hear.) We must look for something less than that. For my part, if I was a farmer, I would get a man for as little as I could. (Hear, and laughter.) If he would work to me for 1½d a day, I would give him no more, and I would work the poor devil as long as he could stand. (Hear, and loud laughter.) I would make him work the whole year if he would do it for 1½d; but that is not expected on their side. We must have fair play for both, and we must just get as much as we can. (Hear, hear, and cheers.) It is every man for himself; and we must all stand out. (Hear, hear.) Then as to the bondage, I would have no bondage women. If they want women, let them hire them. (Hear, hear.) If a man has women within himself, it is all very well for them to work, but let them be hired and paid for their work. (Hear, and applause.) Lads, let us hire none for the farmer. If you hire a bondager, and the farmer gives you a shilling a day for her, why she takes it all out of you here (patting his stomach, causing loud laughter by the significant action)—at dinner time, and then you have to find her breakfast and supper for nothing. (Hear, hear.) The consequence is that perhaps you have to go to your old father if you want anything. You see my coat. Now, I have no wide (great) coat; and if I wanted one, I should have to go to my father to get money for one, as the bondager takes all my wide coats. (Hear, hear, and applause.) Mind, now, lads, none of you hire to-day to find a bondager. If you do, I hope when you come to hire your bondager at Mayday, she may ask you £12 for the half-year. (Hear, hear, and applause.) Let us hire none. What sort of life have we now? You have to be up at half-past four o'clock in the morning, and if you are ten minutes late you will have a skinflint of a master asking "What's the matter this morning you are so long?" (Hear, hear.) You go on working until six o'clock at night, then you come in, and are kept rubbing their poor skins (the horses) until nine o'clock at night. (Hear, hear.) Then you have to go home to bed, and up again at half-past four. Let us stand like men together, and ring the knell of the bondage system this day in Alnwick.

William Campbell, hind with Mr John Dand, Shankhall, near North Sunderland, next addressed the meeting. He was listened to with great attention. He said: Men, our brothers acted like men at Wooler on Thursday, for they stood out and got 15d a day, and I hope that the Alnwick men will stand out and do the same. (Hear, hear, and loud applause.) You see that I have no wide coat, but have only a plaid. That is because the bondage system makes me unable to afford one. (Hear, hear.) The time has now come when every man must look out for himself. This day we are the masters, and if we only stand together they will have to yield to us. (Hear, hear, and cheers.) We have the ball at our feet, and I hope that every man will assist in keeping it rolling. (Loud applause.) If any man hires to-day for the bondage, we hope he will be whipped out of the town. (Applause.) There is one thing I wish particularly to tell you. Some of you are asking what you are to have a week. Some say 15s. Now, when you go to be hired the farmers tell you they will give the best of wages. Don't believe it. Let me ask you to name the child first, and you will know what to call it afterwards. (Laughter and loud cheers.) Mind what you are about, and hire none by the week. (Hear, hear.) Suppose you hire for 15s a week and you go out and get yourselves wet through and through, and you are laid up, your master will then say "Oh, your 15s a week was for when you were out at work, not when you were idle." (Hear, hear.) Have nothing by the week. Hire by the year, and then if you are sick you will have your wages going on; for who is so fit to pay a man when sick as the man who gets his work when well. (Hear, hear, and applause.) You get sick working for a man, let that man pay then when you are not able to work from sickness. (Hear, hear.) It is a complete delusion, about week's work, and I hope you will not fall into it. (Hear, hear, and applause.) Then let us to-day ring the knell of the bondage system, and every man give a strong pull at the ropes.

A collection of a penny a piece was then raised to defray the expense of intimating to those who had not attended the meeting, through the bellman, the resolution come to, and the meeting broke up.

The proceedings throughout were characterised by a praisworthy spirit of moderation, and, we doubt not, will go a great way to bring about the desired change. Owing to the resolution come to by the men not to engage to find a bondager, those farmers who persisted in making that a stipulation in their agreement found some difficulty in coming to terms. We believe, however, that some of them succeeded in inducing the hinds to give in, although the large majority of the engagements effected were on the new system, which guarantees to the servant a rise from 10d, to 1s a day throughout the year, and 2s 6d at harvest. A great number of the men kept aloof, and did not seem inclined to engage, choosing rather to wait till a future day, when they expect to find masters at their own terms.

Figure 59. Alnwick. Alnwick Mercury, 10 March 1866

The reporter in the Berwick Warder (9 March 1866) gives a clear description of the farm workers' history and situation. He mentions a previous unsuccessful attempt, about twenty years ago, to get rid of "the bondage", which probably refers to the dispute in 1837.

Gilbert Turnbull is quoted in this account and he is again using humour to make his point to the crowd. He is scathing about the earnings of the bondager. He thinks at just 1d. per hour the pay rate is only suitable for a small boy.

William Campbell also uses humour to make a point about the women workers. He says, *'If a master came to a hind who had no grown up family and wanted him to engage in bondage, let him tell him he had no woman but his wife, and that he could not afford to keep another. That was plenty and sometimes more than enough for one man.'*

A collection of 'a penny a-piece' raised 'half-a-sovereign' to pay the bellman so that the decision of the meeting could be announced around the town for the benefit of those not at the meeting.

It was also noted that farmers were there in unprecedented numbers with their vehicles filling the yards of the Swan and Star. Unfortunately, pickpockets were also in evidence and many people lost money which they could ill afford.

THE NORTHUMBELAND HIRINGS FOR FARM LABOURERS.

The Northumberland farm labourers, or hinds, as they are locally called, which is derived from the Anglo-Saxon word *hina*, a servant, are paid in a peculiar way. The usual items which constitute his year's wages, are six bolls of oats, four bolls of barley, two bolls of peas, and one boll of wheat. The boll is what is called the old boll, consisting of six imperial bushels. The cash varies from £4 to £6, according to the modifications in the other terms. He has 1,000 yards of potatoes planted, a cow's keep provided, a cottage found, and coals led, which, if valued at current prices, amount to about fifteen shillings a week. But, besides this, the hind's cow, on an average throughout the year, after supplying his family with an ample supply of milk, produces eight pounds of butter, which is never sold now at less than a shilling in the pound; and with his spare corn, potatoes, and milk he feeds two good pigs, which produce not less than thirty-six stones of the very best bacon; but there is attached to the hind's conditions, the following one—he agrees to find a sufficient woman to work when called upon for one shilling per day from Mayday to Martinmas, and tenpence per day from Martinmas to Mayday, and one and sixpence per day during the time of harvest. These terms were formerly eightpence and tenpence, but the amount for some years past has been as stated above. This condition is what is called the "bondage," and presses very severely upon a hind when his wife and grown-up family cannot do the work required. Then, indeed, the provision is beneficial, as it provides his family with regular employment; but, when he has a young family, and the cares of his wife are all required at home, and he is obliged to engage a stout woman at perhaps £12 per year, to work the bondage, it is felt to be a great grievance, for his cottage affords no decent accommodation for her; and her food makes a great inroad upon the means for supporting his family, at a time when it is required. This has always been a great heart-sore with the Northumberland peasantry, which the hateful name of bondage has greatly exaggerated; and calling the kind of work to which these women are sometimes put, to loading manure-carts and turning over manure heaps, is most degrading. A great attempt was made about twenty years ago to get rid of the bondage, but it did not succeed. Since then, in individual cases, it has been dispensed with; but in general the system has been strictly carried out, because, in this country, towns and villages being situated considerably apart, the farmer requires to have a permanent body of labourers resident on his farm, and bound to serve him at all lawful times. This year, another, and successful effort has been made. At Wooler and Rothbury they have stood out against it, and at the great hiring at Alnwick on Saturday last, the same determination was stuck to. It had been announced that a meeting of hinds would be held in Bailiffgate in the morning before the hiring, and by ten o'clock a considerable crowd of them had assembled in front of the railing at the entance of the street. They were exceedingly orderly, and a most

becoming spirit prevailed amongst them, Gilbert Turnbull, a hind at Christon Bank, was the first to address them, which he did in a humorous strain, commenting upon the poverty of the hinds, the impossibility of their getting a "wide coat" to their back, the miserable pittance of a penny an hour which the bondager got for service—why, a boy not so high (measuring his height with his hand) with a coalrake could rake as much "glar" together in the hour—and so on in a strain which created much laughter and raised many a cheer. The other speaker, Wm. Campbell, also a hind, from Shank Hall, spoke in a fluent, vigorous, and sensible manner, and urged his fellow labourers to act in union to resolve like men to rid themselves of the hateful bondage, and their prosperity would thank the men of Northumberland of 1866 for their determination. If a master came to a hind who had no grown up family and wanted him to engage in bondage, let him tell him he had no woman but his wife, and that he could not afford to keep another. That was plenty and sometimes more than enough for one man. He advised them not to hire by the week, but as hitherto, by the year; and not to be put of by a promise of getting the best wages going; name the child and you'll know how to call him; get the wages fixed, not less than 15d. a day for the woman, and 3s. in harvest; that day *they* were the masters; and if they stuck together they would succeed. Men, he concluded, let us this day ring the knell of the bondage, and let every man present give a strong and stout pull to the ropes. A collection of a penny a-piece which amounted to half-a-sovereign, was raised, and given to the bellman to proclaim in the market at various times during the day the result of the meeting. So large an assemblage of hinds was never seen in Alnwick before; about 2,000 came by rail alone; and crowds poured in from all quarters. There was also a large gathering of farmers. The Swan and Star yards were full of vehicles, and the ordinary at Mr. Pike's was numerous beyond all precedent. Young married men hired, and a great many without the bondage, and hardly any with it. The wages have been advanced from 10d. to 1s. a day throughout the year, and 2s. 6d. at harvest. Many were left unhired, but there seems to be little doubt that the men have succeeded, and the farmers do not show much reluctance in acceding to the demands. The system will soon right itself; the farmers at a distance from towns and villages will engage those cheifly who have adult or adolescent families, and the younger men will find masters in the neighbourhood of towns where a supply of female labour is always to be had. The manner in which the hinds have conducted themselves has been very praiseworthy, and those amongst them who have taken the lead in the matter have been temperate in their language and demands. We are sorry to say that pickpockets had too rich a harvest. One hind was robbed of £10, and many others of sums of less amount—but far too much for a poor man to lose—were lost. Everything passed off very well. Some of them, perhaps, finding, like Tam O'Shanter, that

"Aye the ale was growing better,"

might linger too late in the town; but at a good hour of the evening all was quiet as usual.

Figure 60. Alnwick. Berwick Warder, 9 March 1866

A week later a further hiring market was held and again reported fully in both the Alnwick Mercury 17 March 1866 and the Berwick Warder 16 March 1866. There is some repetition in the accounts, word for word, but otherwise the accounts give interesting and different information.

MARCH HIRINGS.—On Saturday last, our usually quiet little town presented a busy appearance on the occasion of the holding of the second hirings, and the renewal of the determination of doing away with the bondage system. A week ago, we adverted to the resolution which had been arrived at by the hinds in this respect, and set forth the altered system upon which they wished to enter. It was expected by many persons that a second demonstration upon this moot point would be made here on the day above mentioned, but there were no indications of the sort. Many hinds had been privately engaged during the intervening week, and the attendance at the hirings were not so numerous. This fact seemed to strengthen the hands of those who were in favour of the movement. Men were eagerly sought after and readily engaged, the prices being varied, dependent upon merit, and, owing to the demand, rather in advance. No speeches were made, and the business done was limited, quiet, and apparently satisfactory. There seemed to be a disposition to gradually conform with the wish expressed the previous week of abandoning the obnoxious bondage system, and of improving the terms offered where the men or women were able and experienced ; and from the steady resolution of the hinds to do away with the system it may safely be assumed that after the mortal blow it received here, it will, in a year or two, have entirely ceased to disgrace Northumberland. It is creditable both to the hinds and the farmers, that the former have been firm but temperate in their demands, and that the latter have met these in a considerate spirit. No farm labourers in the land have been better off than the Northumberland peasantry, and now that a considerable rise has been made in their wages, there is little doubt that they will continue to maintain their reputation as the best conditioned peasantry in England ; as the illustrious Cobden, when agitating for the repeal of the corn laws, in the Town Hall at Alnwick, said he had found them to be. The cow club supplies them with the means of replacing their cow when they are so unfortunate as to lose one ; education is cheaply provided for their children in the parish schools ; almost every parish is now supplied with a lending library, and several with a news room. With these advantages, and a supply of the necessaries of life from year's end to year's end, as their engagement with their masters provides them, few labourers will be found with so many means of substantial happiness.

Figure 61. Alnwick's 2ⁿᵈ Hiring. Alnwick Mercury, 17 March 1866

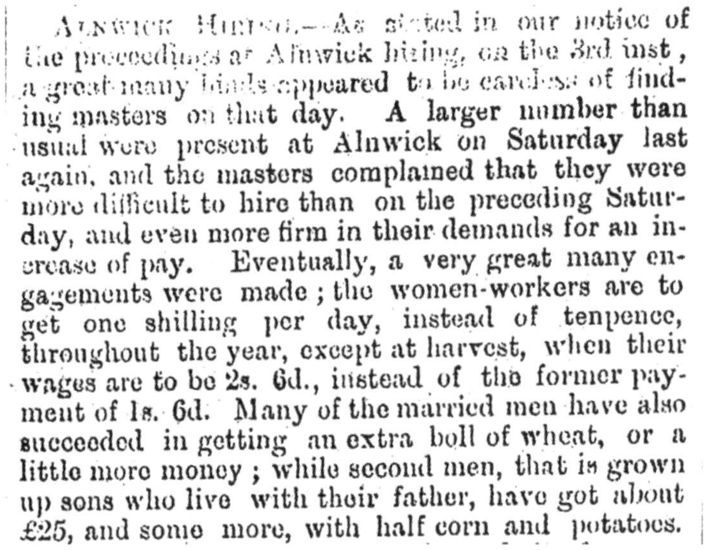

ALNWICK HIRING.—As stated in our notice of
the proceedings at Alnwick hiring, on the 3rd inst ,
a great many hinds appeared to be careless of finding masters on that day. A larger number than
usual were present at Alnwick on Saturday last
again, and the masters complained that they were
more difficult to hire than on the preceding Saturday, and even more firm in their demands for an increase of pay. Eventually, a very great many engagements were made ; the women-workers are to
get one shilling per day, instead of tenpence,
throughout the year, except at harvest, when their
wages are to be 2s. 6d., instead of the former payment of 1s. 6d. Many of the married men have also
succeeded in getting an extra boll of wheat, or a
little more money ; while second men, that is grown
up sons who live with their father, have got about
£25, and some more, with half corn and potatoes.

Figure 62. Alnwick's 2ⁿᵈ Hiring. Berwick Warder, 16 March 1866

These last two reports praise the way the dispute had been conducted, by the hinds and farmers, and that the *'temperate demands'* and *'considerate spirit'* had led to a satisfactory conclusion. The reports also enumerate the many benefits now available to the hind and his family such as cow clubs, schools, lending libraries and news or reading rooms.

The Alnwick Mercury includes a sad little footnote to the report of the Kelso Horse Fair where it notes *'A few hinds were present who had stood out for such high wages at the hiring market a fortnight ago, that they could not obtain places. Finding it impossible to carry their point, the employers all refusing their rates, they ultimately accepted arrangements on the terms ruling the previous market.'*

A final letter, for this time of dispute, appeared in the Berwick Warder of 30 March 1866. Here P. H. Hume of Lawfield, Cockburnspath (writing on the 12 March 1866) takes the opportunity to review the situation now that *'the excitement'* is over. He condemns combinations and states that he *'never countenanced the "bondage"'* and also that *'it does not belong to East Lothian.'* This is confirmed by William Fairbairn who mentions *'that in the county of Haddington the bondage system is now comparatively rare'*. He does, however, point out that Irish workers are used instead. East Lothian was noted for its use of seasonal workers, from Ireland and the Highlands, which helped to meet labour requirements. Alastair Orr notes that *'about half the female labour force in the Lothians in the 1860s were immigrants'* and these girls were housed together in cottages or bothies. [Orr 1984].

HINDS, OR PLOUGHMEN—THEIR LATE
AND PRESENT POSITION.

Lawfield, Cockburnspath, March 12, 1866.

Sir,—Now that the hiring-markets for the season are nearly over, and the "bondage" grievance adjusted by its practical abolition, while the demand for an increase of wages on the part of the hinds has been granted, by an addition of from £2 to £4, according to circumstances, it behoves us calmly and dispassionately to review the whole subject, in order, first (the excitement being over), to see if the case for the hinds was justified by facts ; second, to see if the concession will be a final measure ; and, thirdly, for the purpose, should this not prove to be the case on the part of the hinds, whether the farmer will be able at the next agitation, which I am sorry to see is threatened, to keep his ground, and refuse further augmentation.

First, The "bondage" being out of court, were the premises, as laid down by the hinds, true, when based upon the argument of increased cost of living *solely?* I humbly think not, and refer you to the following table in support of my averments. For simple and clear arrangemen, I shall put the case under "Now" and "Then" :—

"NOW"

1 Sugar, 4½d, per lb.
2 Tea, good, 2s, 6d, per lb.
3 Pot barley, 1½d, per lb.
4 Soap, 5d, per lb.
5 Bread, 6d to 7d, per 4-lb. loaf.
6 Pork, 6s, to 7s, per stone.
7 Oatmeal, 10d, to 1s. per peck of 7 lb.
8 Potatoes, 10s, per boll of 4 cwt, to 20s.
9 Milk (sweet), 4d. per pint of 4 mutchkins, to 6d.
10 Butter, 1s, to 1s, 4d, per lb, ; sweet, to 1s, 6d.
11 Boots, strong, 12s, to 14s, per pair.
12 Flannel, stout, 2s, per yard.
13 Cotton shirting, strong, 9d, per yard.
14 Worsted, strong, 10d, per cut.
15 Hats, bonnets, ribbons, "veils," cheaper,
16 Prints, 9d, to 10d, per yard.
17 School fees, 30 per cent. up, but education all the difference better.
18 Coals, cheaper 7d. per cwt.
19 Light, much cheaper, and very superior.
20 Houses much improved ; neither night night-work nor extra hours. In many cases, no work whatever required in the stable. Harvest hours, two hours shorter, and wages double, with more holidays.
21 Free house, and every article of consumption brought weekly to their door free of charge.

"THEN."

1 Sugar, 8d, per lb.
2 Tea, 6s to 8s, per lb.
3 Pot barley, 1½d per lb.
4 Soap, 7d per lb.
5 Bread, to 1s per 4-lb. loaf.
6 Pork, 8s per stone.
7 Oatmeal, 1s to 1 4d per peck of 8lb.
8 Potatoes, 6s to 8s per boll of 4 cwt.
9 Milk, 3d, per pint—sweet.
10 Butter, 7d to 10d per lb—sweet.
11 Boots, 12s to 15s per pair.
12 Flannel, 1s 6d to 2s per yard.
13 Cotton shirting, stout, 6d per yard.
14 Hats, bonnets, ribbons, "veils," much higher.
15 Prints, 6d to 7d per yard.
16 School fees less, but teaching not so good.
17 Light much, very much, dearer, and not so good by one-half at least.
18 Every article had almost to be bought from towns, and had to "shear" for their house.
19 Worsted, 6d to 7d per cut.
20 Had to feed, clean, and dress horses.
21 Night-work, longer hours and far distances.

By a careful perusal of the above tables, it will be found that in times gone by ploughmen or hinds were not socially so well off as now, while the cost of living, everything taken into account, was actually dearer than now ; for it will be observed that, with very few exceptions, what they had to *purchase then* was dearer, and to sell cheaper ; and what they have to *sell now* is very much dearer, and to buy cheaper. I literally never countenanced the "bondage ;" and it is indeed a name which I hate, and does not belong to *East-Lothian.* Now, then, since it has gone, let it go ; but I respectfully urge that with its exit the tenantry should be free from agitation and combinations on the part of the hinds, seeing, as I have endeavoured to prove, that they have no *primâ-facie* case on the ground of increased expense of living ; while the fair and honest way, according to Free-trade economy, is just openly and honourably to sell their labour in the dearest market, and never to resort to coercion by combination, which sooner or later, being against the principle of fair-play, recoils on themselves. I am delighted to see them rise in the social scale, their hours of labour shortened, and their comforts increased ; but I firmly believe they will never gain these desirable objects permanently by resting their case on false premises.—I am, &c.

P. H. HUME.

Figure 63. P. H. Hume. Berwick Warder, 30 March 1866

P. H. Hume gives long lists of figures for the cost of living and from these concludes that the hinds have no 'prima-facie case' for the further action that he fears is threatened. He lists commodities under two headings 'then' and 'now' but does not indicate the date of 'then' which is not helpful. These lists also contain subjective valuations such as quality of schooling, lighting, feeding and grooming the horses, night work and the condition of the houses, which could, I am sure, begin a long debate.

Three items stand out. The cost of bread and tea are now much reduced and the value of butter increased. Butter was a commodity made and sold by the hind's wife to help the family income, so these changes represent a plus for the hind.

Although the hinds complained about not being able to live on their income, the reason for this was not expressed as being due to the cost of living but due to the cost of the bondager who was able to demand a high wage. She cost the hind, board included, more than she could earn.

Life After 1866

In 1872 Dr. R. Shirra Gibb visited Earlston hiring market immediately on taking over the *'large Lauderdale farm of Boon'*. He comments that farming was prosperous and wages *'ruled high'*. *'At Earlston hiring – in 1872 at any rate – there was no agitation for shorter hours, and by hiring a good family one was assured of full time for full pay.'* [Gibb 1927].

This shows that the issue of shorter hours of work was still to be dealt with and illustrates the new system mentioned in the Rutherfurd's Directory (1866). This new system was essentially a 'family hiring' with a chance for the daughters, in some cases, to be treated as independent workers. Their father was not paid a gratuity with regard to their work and they received a correspondingly higher daily wage.

The family contracts were not approved of by everyone and even in 1850 Stuart wrote *'rather than be teased with them* (bondagers from outside the family), *the hinds often keep their own daughters at home as bondagers, when either they ought to have been earning better wages as principal servants or at some other occupation'*. [Devine 1984 chap 6].

The family contract did, however, become the norm.

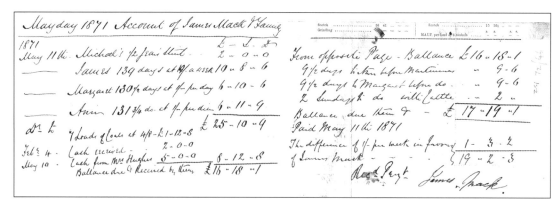

Figure 64. The account of James Mack and family.

The account is dated 11 May 1871 so this indicates this is the final settlement for that year. The family members, Michael, James, Margaret and Ann are named on the account and the number of days recorded with the rate of pay. Deducted from this is the cost of seven loads of coal and two advances of cash. Margaret has worked, caring for the cattle, for two Sundays. Michael's stint money probably represents a cash allowance in place of pasture for sheep. The document is signed by James Mack and the money at this point is just part of a joint family income and how it might be shared we can only guess. Some families would be very democratic and in others the father or even the mother might 'hold the purse strings'.

Dr. R. Shirra Gibb goes into great detail about wages over the years and the gradual decline of the gains system. He noted that payment for harvest work was changed as harvesting changed with the 'introduction and more efficient working of the "Reapers", and later of "Binders".

He also notes – *'For about ten years, 1880 to 1890, wages for men were on what was called the "Lauderdale, or small Boll Wage". This worked out as things were then, thus:*

	£
Free house and garden	*4*
Coals, driven	*2*
Money, according to the qualifications of the man, and the number of outworkers he could supply, £18 to £22, average	*20*
1200 to 1600 yards of potato drills, 35s. to 45s. average	*2*
A cow's "keep," or a "put-on" cow and keep	*9*
65 stones of oatmeal	*8*
18 bushels of barley	*4*
In lieu of dinner in harvest	*1*
In all, say	*50*

Notice the use of the term *'outworkers'* for the women workers who are part of the man's contract, and therefore, strictly speaking bondagers.

Prior to the above, in 1875, I had hired a "Double Hind" (two ploughmen in one home), one, the father, at the "Big Boll," or "Kelso Boll" wage – that is, 100 stones of oatmeal and 4 bolls of barley (instead of, as above, 65 stones and 18 bushels respectively), which at average prices would be about £50; the son was also at £50. In the following year another man got a "Boll" which worked out then at £53.'

He also notes in detail the wages he paid from 1900 to 1910. *'Between 1900 and 1910 all wages rose, and were paid monthly; the gains or perquisites, except the potato-ground and occasionally the cow, having been abandoned. An odd servant would bargain for 10 stones of oatmeal for porridge for the family, and it was difficult to refuse this. A house and garden with potato-ground and 18s. per week became the common wage, or 12s. for outworkers, who were, generally speaking, very inferior to the old class. The harvest wage and harvest meat were also given up.'* His comment about the *'inferior'* outworkers is interesting but unfortunately he gives no explanation of why he reaches this conclusion.

'Harvest meat' was an important part of this crucial time in the farming year and had a long history. The *'beer and bap'* of Mary Rutherford's time (1908 – 1948) had been *'Ale and Rowles'* in 1724 (an old farm account – Ford Estate papers). *'Brantins, girdle scones with cheese sandwiched between'* were once *'prepared for women in the hay harvest and carried to them in the field.'* [Balfour 1904].

Minnie Bell (née Wilhelmina Brown), working in the first half of the 20th century, remembers that her mother put up hot meals for the harvest time. A cart came round and collected the meals, from the cottages, which were wrapped in towels, to retain the heat. This was much appreciated as she said, *'It wasn't just a flask of tea, it was a real dinner!'* So in this case the food was prepared by the mother for her family and not provided by the farmer. [Bell].

Tom Wilson of Wooler and others also mentioned oatmeal water for the harvest time. A few handfuls of oatmeal were thrown into a milk can or churn of water and the water ladled out as required. Tom said this was very refreshing!

Dr. Shirra Gibb continues to note the level of wages:

From 1910 to 1913 *'the rise in wages would be equal to 3s. per week and 1s. for outworkers'*. *'In 1915 the current wages for ploughmen and spademen were: potato-ground and 28s. to 32s. per week, with a deduction of 5s. per week if a cow were kept; the outworkers 24s. to 25s.'*

'In 1917, under the same conditions, wages were up to 34s., outworkers 21s.; and in 1919 they rose again to 40s. for men less 7s. per week for a cow's keep, and for outworkers 24s. to 25s.'

'In 1920–1921 wages again rose to 44s.6d. per week for men, less 9s. cow's keep; outworkers 30s. Now, in 1923, the normal wage is about 10s. per week below the maximum'

Throughout, the outworker or the woman worker was earning about two-thirds of that of the men.

7. Memories and Details

Memories of Hiring Markets

One of the earliest comments on the hiring markets is from north of the Tay, by a Stonehaven Farmer. This is from an entry in the Diary of J. Badenach – a Stonehaven Farmer 1789-1797. He writes *'cutting Hay till breakfast after, all Persons Male and Female at the ACCURSED market of Garvock for Hiring Servants which should be abolished.'* Obviously this is highly frustrating for the farmer who wanted to get on with his hay-time.

In 1827 Alexander Somerville attended Duns hiring market hoping to be hired as a carter. He says he stood there *'with a piece of whipcord in the ribbon of my hat, and a piece of straw in my mouth as a signal I wanted to be hired'.* He was unlucky and did not find a place. There were more men than masters. [Robson 1984].

Hastings Neville also mentions that at a hiring fair hinds would put '*a sprig of hawthorn in their hat,*' and *'a shepherd a tuft of wool'.* Besides wearing an emblem of his craft the worker would turn himself out smartly. [Neville 1909].

Walter White remembers (in 1858) his '*first sight of bondagers; it was soon after sunrise one morning in Alnwick, when I saw thirty or forty washing their hands and faces in the pant – a public fountain in the market place;'* [White 1859].

Perhaps this was not an unusual sight, for 1858, as these were large gatherings.

The Peebleshire Advertiser (25 October 1879) gave voice to the negative aspects of the fairs when it stated that *'the fairs were a positive disgrace to our boasted civilisation.'* Michael Robson also mentions that *'ministers' 'denounced'* them (the fairs) for *'drunkenness and immorality'.* [Robson 1984].

Thirty years later in 1913, Joseph R. Duncan, who was the general secretary of the Scottish Farm Servants' Union, wrote about the hiring fairs. He thought they were '*simply a relic of barbarism*' and noted that *'the farmers went through the men pretty much the same way as they did their cattle. They perhaps did not run their hands along the men but they sized them up'.* [MacDougall 2000].

May Douglas records a similar experience when she writes *'My old aunt was a bondager. She said they used to stand on the cobbles at Alnwick and the farmers used to look them up and down as if they were horses'.* [Porteous 2004].

Annie Guthrie, tells of her experiences of the hiring fairs: *'The farm workers didn't approach the farmers, you didn't do that. That wasn't the done thing. The farmers had to approach the workers.'* Usually asking *'Are you to hire?'* Jean Leid adds more information. After the initial enquiry the farmer might say *'Ah'll see you when ah come back'* Later he might say *'oh well, ah've seen so-and-so fermer and ee hevnae got a very guid character'.* *'Oh, well,'* some o' them, the ferm workers, yaist tae say, *'oo've gotten yours, tae, so we're no' comin'.* [MacDougall 2000].

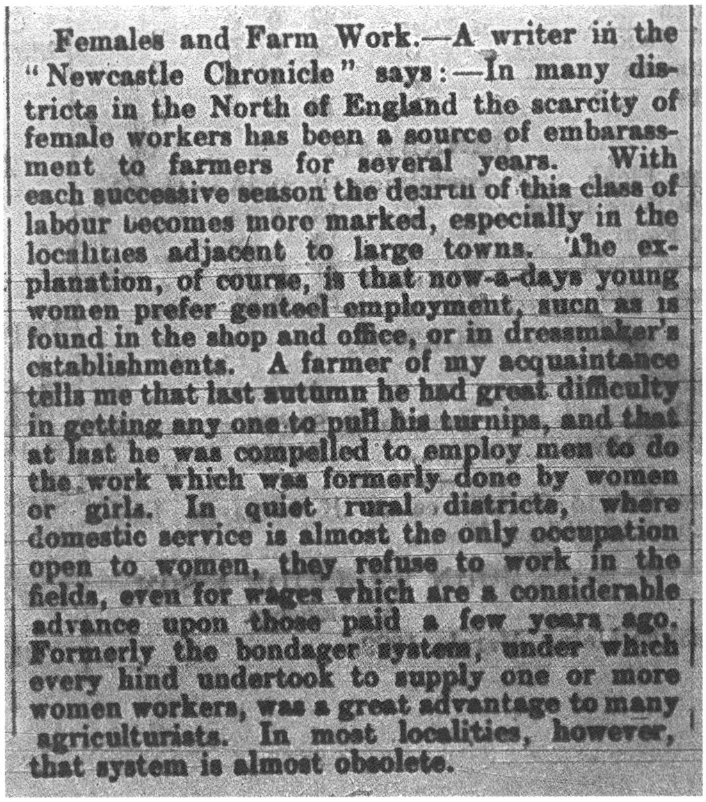

Females and Farm Work.—A writer in the "Newcastle Chronicle" says:—In many districts in the North of England the scarcity of female workers has been a source of embarassment to farmers for several years. With each successive season the dearth of this class of labour becomes more marked, especially in the localities adjacent to large towns. The explanation, of course, is that now-a-days young women prefer genteel employment, such as is found in the shop and office, or in dressmaker's establishments. A farmer of my acquaintance tells me that last autumn he had great difficulty in getting any one to pull his turnips, and that at last he was compelled to employ men to do the work which was formerly done by women or girls. In quiet rural districts, where domestic service is almost the only occupation open to women, they refuse to work in the fields, even for wages which are a considerable advance upon those paid a few years ago. Formerly the bondager system, under which every hind undertook to supply one or more women workers, was a great advantage to many agriculturists. In most localities, however, that system is almost obsolete.

Figure 65. Females and Farm Work. Berwick Advertiser, 10 March 1899

This news item in the Berwick Advertiser, initially printed in the Newcastle Chronicle, shows how times and attitudes are changing. Girls were beginning to learn of new opportunities and their choices were not limited to farm work or work in service.

Compare this with Mary and Agnes Black, daughters of the farm steward at Ilderton and farm workers who said in 1893 *"We would both rather go to service than work in the fields"* which shows they felt there was only one alternative to farm work for them. Their attitude to the hiring fairs was that they *" go to the hirings for sport".* Their mother said, *"The girls go to the hirings, and like it. They wear their best clothes, and their white veils and bonnets. They often look a lump better than the gentry, for they look fresher like".* [Fox 1893].

Ada Mary Howarth writes of her memories of attending a Jedburgh Hiring with her father in 1926 as a little girl. *'In 1926, as a slip of a child of ten dressed in a pale blue shift, I attended the Jedburgh Hiring with my father. It was a fine Spring day and the market place was a hive of activity, crowded with people enjoying themselves. There was a sense of excitement in the air, as when it is "all change" in a game of musical chairs. In those days, only the Mercat Cross occupied the middle of the square and no obtrusive motor traffic demanded priority for its passage through the town – people had the square to themselves.'* [Howarth 1998].

Wat Thomson speaking in 1974 said it was a *'Good thing this old custom was done away with now'. 'Kin' o like sellin' cattle.'* He also said it was *'a starving[2] job to stand in the street'.* [Thomson 1974].

'Mrs Hazel Pettigrew, the Kelso baker's daughter, remembers farm workers standing in groups in the square waiting to be hired.' 'It was awful, very shaming for them. The first year we were up at the shop in Bridge Street, it was a very wet day and the farm workers were waiting at the door. They came to town in open carts and they hadn't the oilskins then.' [Wager].

---

[2] (archaic) = cold.

The fairs were eventually held indoors but not till the middle of the 1920s.

Hiring fairs disappeared after *'the passing of the Agricultural Wages (Regulations) (Scotland) Act in 1937'*. Also, shortly after W.W.II broke out farm workers were not allowed to move. Mary King said *'there wis what they ca'ed a stand-still order: if ye had a job ye'd tae stay in it till the war wis finished'*. Two Orders were passed in 1940 and 1941. [MacDougall 2000].

Even before these changes and restrictions, the hiring fair was no longer the only way of acquiring employment. In fact hiring fairs had been gradually diminishing in importance for a number of years. The Wooler and District Advertiser notes in 1927 that despite an average attendance *'Very little business was done,'* and this was due to men making arrangements prior to the hiring fair. Eight years later the fair was even smaller and although *'there was a fairly large number of workers present' 'few farmers attended'*. The March Hirings in 1936 were remarkably quiet and it was not until mid-day that *'there was a good number of farm-workers and farmers'* but even then *'little hiring was done. The demand was 'for ploughmen and women workers, but these were scarce.'* Registry Offices and newspaper advertisements had gradually replaced the hiring fairs. Remember the young man who advertised in the Newcastle Courant in 1837.

Barbara Robertson includes the footnote from *'The Berwickshire News, March 10th 1908. The Hiring Market Report ends: "Year by Year more hiring is done through the medium of newspapers or registry offices, and the day is becoming more of an annual holiday for the purpose of meeting friends".'* [Robertson 2005].

Bookkeeping

Payment in kind and casual labour required careful accounting to ensure everyone felt confident that they were being treated correctly and could check back to settle any disputes. Examples of this accounting make interesting reading and give a valuable insight into aspects of life at this time. Payment in kind was not paid in a one-off transaction but grain was given at regular intervals when required.

Figure 66. Isable Chrinklaw's account for the year 1789 to 1790

An early record in the late 18th century shows the account of an Isable Chrinklaw. (Middleton Hall Archive) Her role is not clear, but she is hired for the year, and receives wages of £3.5s.0d plus a stone of wool. Isable receives cash, wool and cow's cheese through the year. Her account finally adds up to £3.6s.8d.

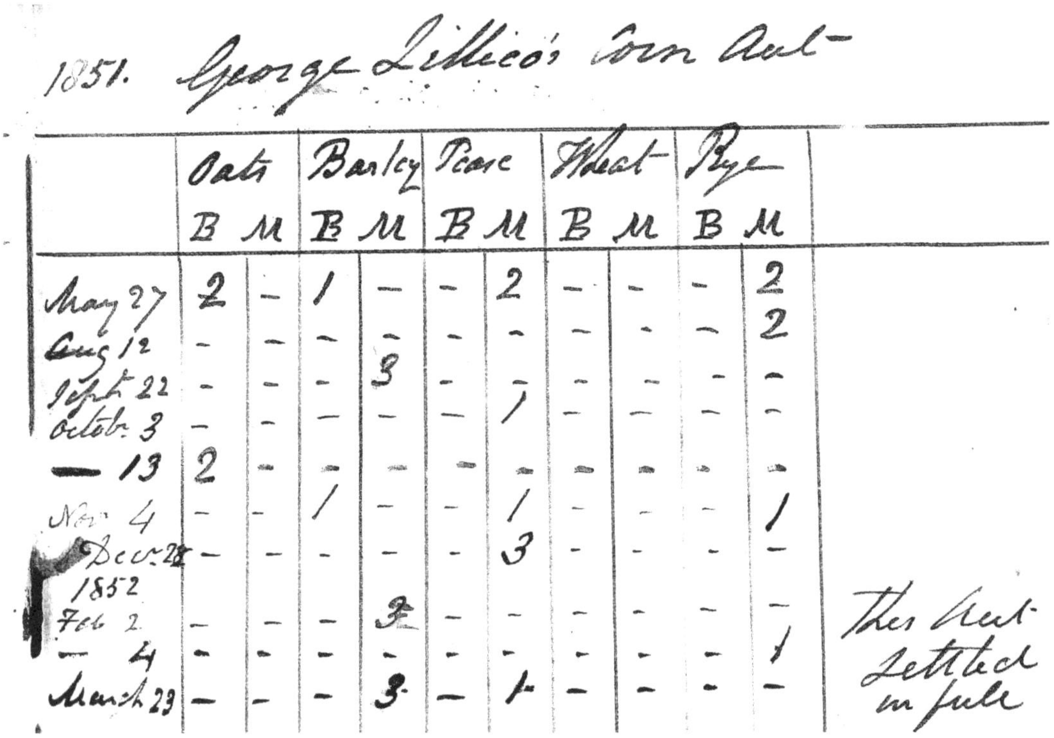

1851. George Lillico's Corn Acct

	Oats B	Oats M	Barley B	Barley M	Pease B	Pease M	Wheat B	Wheat M	Rye B	Rye M
May 27	2	–	1	–	–	2	–	–	–	2
Aug 12	–	–	–	–	–	–	–	–	–	2
Sept 22	–	–	–	3	–	–	–	–	–	–
Octob 3	–	–	–	–	–	1	–	–	–	–
— 13	2	–	–	–	–	–	–	–	–	–
Nov 4	–	–	1	–	–	1	–	–	–	1
Decr 28	–	–	–	–	–	3	–	–	–	–
1852 Feb 2	–	–	–	2	–	–	–	–	–	–
— 4	–	–	–	–	–	–	–	–	–	1
March 23	–	–	–	3	–	1	–	–	–	–

This Acct settled in full

Figure 67. Hinds' Corn Book

The farm servants' corn accounts are another example of careful accounting. This page is from a book, entitled the 'Hinds Corn Book', and is part of the Middleton Estate archives. George Lillico receives oats, barley, pease and rye. These 'gains' are handed out in measures or bolls. The largest amounts issued at one time are of oats and barley. The account is signed off as settled in full.

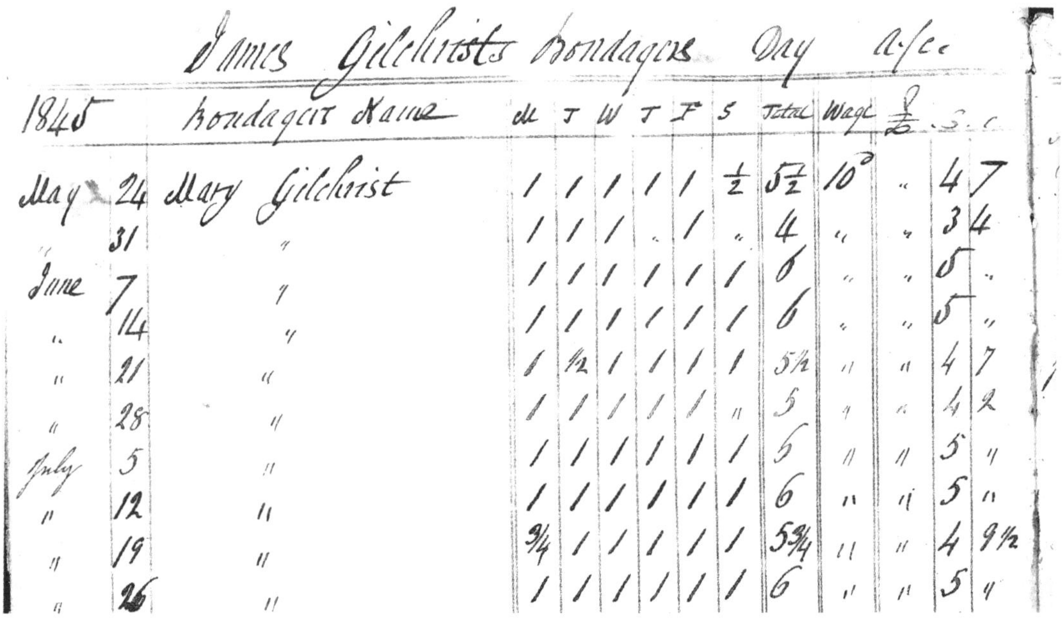

James Gilchrists Bondagers Day a/cc

1845		Bondager Name	M	T	W	T	F	S	Total	Wage		s	d
May	24	Mary Gilchrist	1	1	1	1	1	½	5½	10d	"	4	7
"	31	"	1	1	1	.	1	"	4	"	"	3	4
June	7	"	1	1	1	1	1	1	6	"	"	5	"
"	14	"	1	1	1	1	1	1	6	"	"	5	"
"	21	"	1	½	1	1	1	1	5½	"	"	4	7
"	28	"	1	1	1	1	1	"	5	"	"	4	2
July	5	"	1	1	1	1	1	1	6	"	"	5	"
"	12	"	1	1	1	1	1	1	6	"	"	5	"
"	19	"	¾	1	1	1	1	1	5¾	"	"	4	9½
"	26	"	1	1	1	1	1	1	6	"	"	5	"

Figure 68. Bondager's Day Account

James Gilchrist's Bondagers Day Account records the days worked and money earned by Mary Gilchrist for three months in 1845. Here we see a careful record of the days Mary worked. In this section she earns 10d per day but from the middle of November (possibly Martinmas) until 25 April she earns only 8d a day. The time worked is not only counted in days and half days but also quarter days and three-quarter days. The busiest time for Mary is from May through to the middle of September.

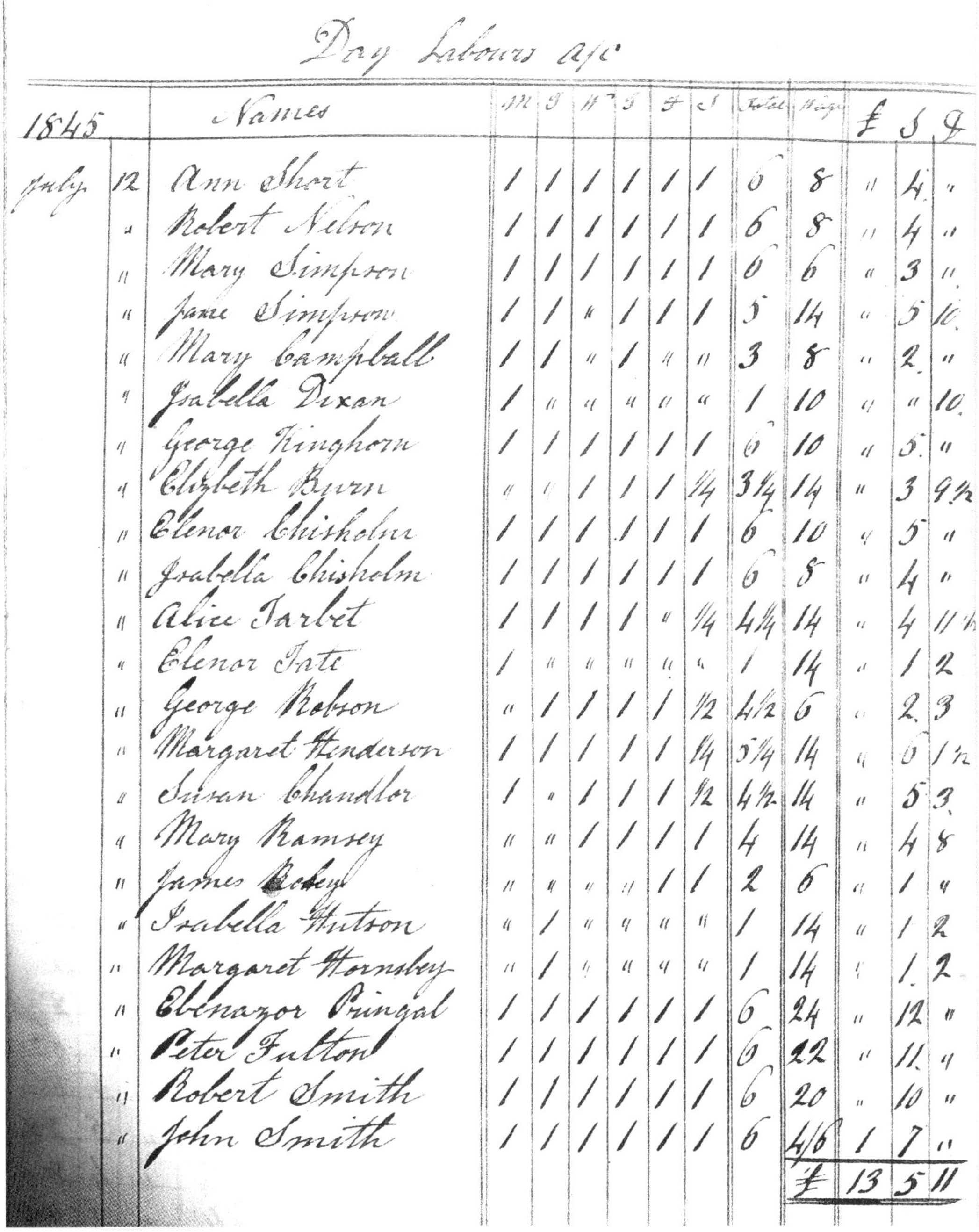

1845		Names							Total	Wage	£	s	d
July	12	Ann Short	1	1	1	1	1	1	6	8	"	4	"
"	"	Robert Nelson	1	1	1	1	1	1	6	8	"	4	"
"	"	Mary Simpson	1	1	1	1	1	1	6	6	"	3	"
"	"	Jane Simpson	1	1	"	1	1	1	5	14	"	5	10
"	"	Mary Campbell	1	1	"	1	"	"	3	8	"	2	"
"	"	Isabella Dixon	1	"	"	"	"	"	1	10	"	"	10
"	"	George Kinghorn	1	1	1	1	1	1	6	10	"	5	"
"	"	Elizabeth Burn	"	"	1	1	1	1/4	3 1/4	14	"	3	9 1/2
"	"	Elenor Chisholm	1	1	1	1	1	1	6	10	"	5	"
"	"	Isabella Chisholm	1	1	1	1	1	1	6	8	"	4	"
"	"	Alice Tarbet	1	1	1	1	"	1/4	4 1/4	14	"	4	11 1/2
"	"	Elenor Inte	1	"	"	"	"	"	1	14	"	1	2
"	"	George Robson	"	1	1	1	1	1/2	4 1/2	6	"	2	3
"	"	Margaret Henderson	1	1	1	1	1	1/4	5 1/4	14	"	6	1 1/2
"	"	Susan Chandler	1	"	1	1	1	1/2	4 1/2	14	"	5	3
"	"	Mary Ramsey	"	"	1	1	1	1	4	14	"	4	8
"	"	James Boley	"	"	"	"	1	1	2	6	"	1	"
"	"	Isabella Hutson	"	1	"	"	"	"	1	14	"	1	2
"	"	Margaret Hornsby	"	1	"	"	"	"	1	14	"	1	2
"	"	Ebenezer Pringal	1	1	1	1	1	1	6	24	"	12	"
"	"	Peter Fulton	1	1	1	1	1	1	6	22	"	11	"
"	"	Robert Smith	1	1	1	1	1	1	6	20	"	10	"
"	"	John Smith	1	1	1	1	1	1	6	4/6	1	7	"
										£ 13	5	11	

Figure 69. Day Labourers' Account

The Day Labourers Account for July 1845 shows how many extra workers were needed at Lilburn Hill for the busiest times in the farming year. These workers are also employed for quarter days, half days, three-quarter days as well as whole days. They are generally paid from 6d to 14d per day with four men receiving the much greater sums of 20d to 54d (4s.6d.) a day. Obviously some of these workers are children and their pay ranges from 6d to 10d a day. Pay for an experienced adult seems to be 14d per day. Day labourers were often paid at a higher rate than those on a yearly contract, but of course, their work was not constant.

Mrs Thomas Hepple remembers her mother telling her about going to work in harvest time near Cambo. She says that *'at harvest time the farmers used to drive in to Cambo in carts to get workers, and the labourers' wives, my mother amongst them, would jump out of one cart into another to go with the farmer who offered them the most money.'* [Bosanquet 1989].

Another interesting comparison between the bondagers and the day labourers was made in the 1867 Royal Commission. Mr. Henley commented favourably on the bondagers' clothes as *'admirably adapted for their work'* but he thought that *'women who only work in the fields occasionally'* had a *'draggled appearance'*. [Henley 1867].

It is intriguing to wonder what the bondagers felt about the day labourers but unfortunately I have not discovered any information about this. Did the bondagers play a leading role when they worked in the fields with the day labourers?

Disputes

Disputes arose between the employer and employee and sometimes these cases went to court to be settled.

One early record of a dispute is in the Cotesworth Papers – William Cotesworth of Gateshead and Shipcote. Here the noted pay is men 8d. a day, women 4d. a day with additional 2d. to 4d. a day for harvest time. The problem is that the men are unwilling to accept a practice which has gone on for a number of years.

The steward wrote in 1722 – *'We have had a sore struggle among our workmen upon our keeping off a week's wages as we have usually done in former years to oblige them to stay with us in hay and corn harvest.'* Later *'Thos. Leighton and Wm. Dockwray(?) left without reason, but that they had hired themselves by the year which is false for now in mowing time they are seeking mowing in their neighbourhood.........'.* No further action appears but the power of the steward may have led to the two men being blacklisted.

Mr. Robinson, when talking about 'Harvest customs in Northumberland', noted a restriction placed on pitmen and their families by Sir John Hussey Delaval. *'It was an old custom for all the country apprentices to assist in harvest operations but in colliery districts there was a most curious restriction as to the freedom of pitmen and their wives with respect to harvest work. In an old yearly bond between Sir John Hussey Delaval and his workmen at Ford Colliery in 1766, there was the following remarkable clause:- "and we the said putters and pitmen, doth further agree to and with Sir John Hussey Delaval, that if any of our wives or selves do shear at all, to do it at no place but Flodden and Westfield during harvest".'*

Almost a hundred years later, a court case in October 1836 deals with what seems to be a dispute about whether the girls had worked for 6 full days or for only part of the days as the farmer stated.

The Berwick and Kelso Warder, 22 October 1836:

Wages of Labour.
Two girls complained that a gentleman had refused to pay them their wages for working six days on his farm in the neighbourhood of Berwick. The defendant said he had not employed them but for part of the six days, and that his farm-steward had not seen them on the ground: besides he had desired the girls not to return to the field on which they said they had been latterly working. After a good deal of conversation, the Magistrate recommended the defendant to halve the difference with the complainants, which he consented to.'

The magistrate's compromise seems to be a fair judgement. Perhaps the fault lay in the farm steward and his supervision of the workers.

A year later in the Berwick Advertiser 11 November 1837, there is a case brought before the Justice of the Peace by three men – James Waite, Francis Dodds, and Robert Craig from

Chirnside - against Alexander Bird the tenant farmer at Fogorig. The dispute was about the payment of *'arles'*[3]. The men considered they were still hired and wanted to work as arranged. This short-term arrangement for harvest was perhaps not so carefully noted as the longer hirings. It seems the Justice of the Peace again worked hard to get a workable compromise. The men got their 16 days' work but only three from Mr. Bird. The men would probably have liked to have achieved 29 days' pay. 13 days they had worked elsewhere and 16 days due to them from Mr. Bird.

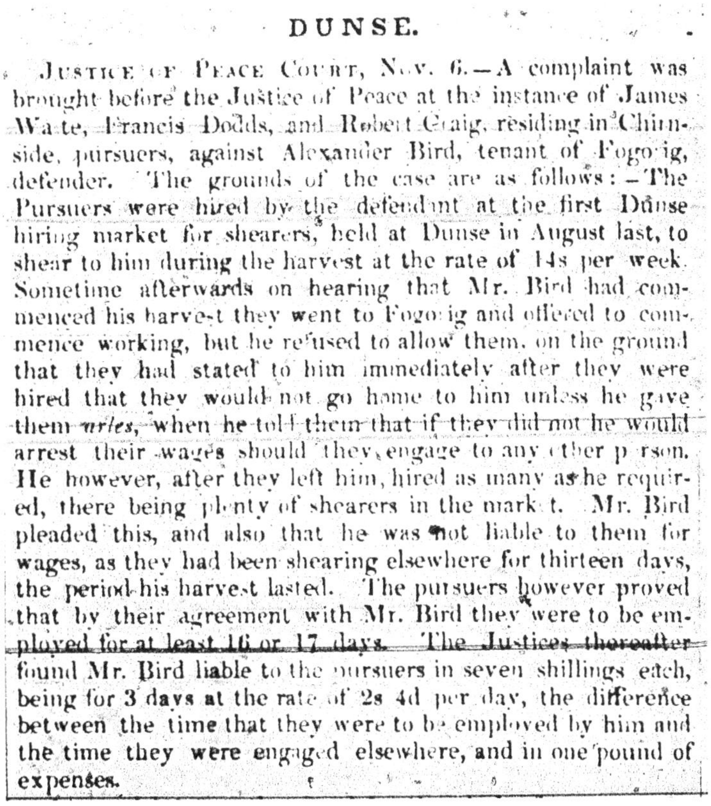

> **DUNSE.**
>
> JUSTICE OF PEACE COURT, Nov. 6.—A complaint was brought before the Justice of Peace at the instance of James Waite, Francis Dodds, and Robert Craig, residing in Chirnside, pursuers, against Alexander Bird, tenant of Fogorig, defender. The grounds of the case are as follows:—The Pursuers were hired by the defendant at the first Dunse hiring market for shearers, held at Dunse in August last, to shear to him during the harvest at the rate of 14s per week. Sometime afterwards on hearing that Mr. Bird had commenced his harvest they went to Fogorig and offered to commence working, but he refused to allow them, on the ground that they had stated to him immediately after they were hired that they would not go home to him unless he gave them *arles*, when he told them that if they did not he would arrest their wages should they engage to any other person. He however, after they left him, hired as many as he required, there being plenty of shearers in the market. Mr. Bird pleaded this, and also that he was not liable to them for wages, as they had been shearing elsewhere for thirteen days, the period his harvest lasted. The pursuers however proved that by their agreement with Mr. Bird they were to be employed for at least 16 or 17 days. The Justices thereafter found Mr. Bird liable to the pursuers in seven shillings each, being for 3 days at the rate of 2s 4d per day, the difference between the time that they were to be employed by him and the time they were engaged elsewhere, and in one pound of expenses.

Figure 70. Dunse Justice of Peace Court. Berwick Advertiser, 11 November 1837

Perhaps the next case, of an unattended horse travelling on the public highway, shows the sort of short cuts that might be tried by some hinds, or was it more to do with carelessness?

Berwick Advertiser 11 May 1844:

At Dunse.
George Trotter, hind at Kennetsideheads, was find 5s. for allowing his horse to travel on a public road unattended; and John Wilson and George Pilmuir, both hinds at Swinton Bridge End were find 6s. each for the same offence.'

In the J. Bailey and G. Culley report of 1794 they state that *'Three single-horse carts are driven, without any difficulty, by a man, or a boy, or even women and girls'*!

Another case: *'in November 1900 the Berwickshire News reported that Alexander Purves successfully sued Arthur Hardy, the farmer at Dowlaw in the Small Debt Court at Greenlaw for £2.18s.9d. "being wages unpaid for a period of one week in February last, when pursuer was laid off work by influenza, and for a further period of about 6 weeks in April and May, when he was again laid off work while suffering from ringworm. Witnesses were adduced to*

---

[3] Money given in confirmation of a bargain; especially, that given, when a servant is hired, in confirmation of the engagement.

prove that this was the custom of the district – that servants in the position of the pursuer were not paid any wages when off through illness. The sheriff said that no matter what the custom was, the law was that where a servant was off through illness for a short period the employers were liable for wages".

Percy Robson of Lowshieldgreen (Birtley, Northumberland) writes in his Day Book for 31 March 1838, on the hiring of Thomas Hall as herd for the period May Day 1838 to May Day 1839. The agreement has the clause *'and should Thos. Hall Break down in sickness not being able to do his work Messrs Percy and Thos. Robson reserve the Power of paying to Thoms Hall, any of the weekly allowance in cash'.* The exact significance of this payment in cash is unclear but it is an arrangement to cover sickness.

Annual contracts, stated Alastair Orr, *'not only afforded farm servants security of employment but also entitled them to sick pay. "By law we are obliged to give him food and wages for six successive weeks, if ill health does not keep him away longer than that from working". However, this provision did not apply to female servants.'* [Orr 1984]. Alastair Orr's information comes from a select committee report entitled 'Agriculture and persons employed in Agriculture in the UK 1833' and also the Wilson Fox's 1893 Royal Commission report on 'The Agricultural Labourer.' [Fox 1893]. Further protection against the financial problems, caused by ill health and accidents, led to Friendly Societies being established and this will be included in the next section.

The next case was for wrongful dismissal in 1909 between James Wight, farmer, of Greenwood and his employee William Plenderleith. The sheriff-Substitute, Macaulay-Smith, lays out the facts of the case, which make interesting reading. [Crosbie 2002].

'1. William Plenderleith was engaged by James Wight as a farm servant for the year to Whitsunday 1909 and he was to bring with him a male worker. Plenderleith's wages were to be 18 shillings per week, with free house and 1800 yards of potatoes. The wages of the said male worker were to be 13 shillings per week.

2. Plenderleith, under said engagement, supplied his brother Alexander as said male worker.

3. About 7.00pm on Monday 1 February Plenderleith informed the farm manager that he desired to go to Dunbar Hirings on the following day (Tuesday) along with his brother.

4. The farmer at this time had already engaged the services of a steam threshing mill for operations on his farm on the said following day, this fact having been known to Plenderleith for about a week previously.

5. The said operations required the attention, not only of all the regular farm hands, but also a number of extra workers whom the farmer had already engaged, this also being known to Plenderleith.

6. The farm manager informed Plenderleith that only in the event of the said mill failing to arrive in time to begin operations next morning could he and his brother be allowed away.

7. The said mill arrived at the farm the same night (Monday) shortly after 9 o'clock, and during a period of more than half an hour was located in circumstances of easy observation.

8. Plenderleith either knew, or could by exercise of ordinary attention have known, of its arrival.

9. Notwithstanding the said arrival, Plenderleith on the following morning (Tuesday) went off to Dunbar with his brother.

10. About 7 o'clock that evening (Tuesday), after the return of Plenderleith and his brother, the farmer sent for them and dismissed them from his employment, on the grounds of disobedience of his orders.

11. Shortly after the date of the Dunbar Hirings, two other Hiring Markets were held – Duns and Berwick respectively.'

The Sheriff-Substitute ruled that, in accordance with custom, a farm servant was legally entitled to offer himself for a new situation and that right involved access to a hiring market. He also ruled, however *"that the servant's rights must be reasonably exercised and that in that exercise, the interest of the master as well as that of the servant, must be fairly considered".* His judgement was:

"1. Plenderleith's request, at the time and in the circumstances in which it was made, was not a reasonable one and leave of absence, in such circumstances, could not be demanded as a legal right.

2. Plenderleith's conduct on Tuesday 2 February in going to Dunbar was, in effect, in the circumstances stated, insubordination, on account of which the farmer was justified in dismissing him."

The result of the case seems to suggest a strong need for reasonableness from both parties. The communication on the side of the farmer seems to have been clearly made but perhaps the timing of the threshing day was misjudged. The legal right and common practice of workers having the right to attend the fairs (a bone of contention even in the 18th century – see the comment by J. Badenoch the Stonehaven farmer in the section "Memories of Hiring Markets") must have weighed heavily with William Plenderleith. We could speculate that there were other things at work which had not been aired – disagreement between the farmer James Wight and his employee or some disagreement between the steward and William Plenderleith. Nothing is mentioned about whether William and Alexander had been offered another year of work.

Wat Thomson, a shepherd, says *'It cut both ways – a farmer had to put up with the worker – the worker had to put up with the farmer who was not so good.'* [Thomson 1974].

Many agreements would be made purely by word of mouth and then the bargain sealed by the giving of a coin by the employer – the arles. A story is recorded of a girl at a hiring fair who took advantage of this way of making a bargain. She *'went round giving different names and engaging herself to several people, and made quite a lot!'* There is no record of whether she was found out and any repercussions that resulted. Evidently the rule was that if the bargain was broken the employee was *' supposed to send back the arles.'* [Bosenquet 1989].

Friendly Societies and Cow Clubs

At a time before the Welfare State workers could make provision for times of hardship by paying into Friendly societies. Michael Robson in "The Border Farm Worker" mentions that *'In addition to banks, (savings banks) most parts of the Borders in the early nineteenth century had a Friendly Society, into which workers paid in a small contribution of about 5s. or 6s. a year to insure themselves against sickness or similar disaster. In some places a further form of insurance existed in the form of a Cow Club, which was a means of covering the loss of a labourer's cow. Those living in upper Lauderdale must have had a rather grander notions of such a club since theirs was called the Oxton Bovial Society'.* [Robson 1984].

The Berwick Advertiser 28 November 1840 includes an article from a Doncaster Paper which sets out the purpose of Cow Clubs and how beneficial they can be.

The Berwick Advertiser Saturday 28 November 1840:

The societies named 'Cow Clubs', whose principle is to defray to a-member the loss he sustains from the death of his cow, are highly deserving of commendation. They are established in several of our villages, and our banks, or the savings bank, often perform the duties of treasurer. The establishment of the "Doncaster Cow Club" has effected highly beneficial results. It comprises 20 members, who for each insured cow, pay each 4s. per annum. When a member's cow dies three-fourths of the value of it are awarded to the owner by the club. - Doncaster Paper

The Lilburn farm apprentice writes with feeling at Lilburn Grange in 1842, about the importance of cows to the hinds. *'The greatest comfort to the Hinds is having a cow kept for them but the Hind has to buy the cow and they often give as much as £15 for them and if the cow dies all will be up with them'.* [NRO 851].

Dr. R. Shirra Gibb (writing of his farming experiences from the 1870s) also thought *'the farm-servant's cow'* was *'one of his greatest assets, whether from the money point of view or that of the family's health and well-being'.* He calculates the cost to the farmer of the cow as £10 to £12 when grass, straw, linseed cake and attendance are taken into consideration. He points out that *'£9 was the amount counted at hiring time'.* Making butter and selling it could earn the hind's family an extra £10.

For this to be successful he says *'it needed ideal servants, ideal masters, ideal cows, and ideal management'.* He laments the dying out of this practise and says he knows of *'a farm with five servants' cottages, the school children from which carry out every afternoon a tin of milk from a dairy in a neighbouring town for the use of the farmer and his family'.* An enormous responsibility for the children and hopefully it arrived safely without any mishaps! I can remember, as a child, testing the theory or fact of centrifugal force with a milk pail – not always successfully!

A shepherd hired by Dr. R. Shirra Gibb from the east side of the county when asked *'why he wished to leave, he replied: "Oh, for nae other reason than that we canna keep a cow and canna get milk. Believe me," he said, "that the milk used, and there's no' much o'd, comes out the seven miles in a milk-cart from Berwick!"*

Bovine tuberculosis could be a serious problem and a newspaper item from the Berwick Advertiser 7 January 1907 records a meeting where five claims out of eight had been due to tuberculosis. This also had serious implications for human health.

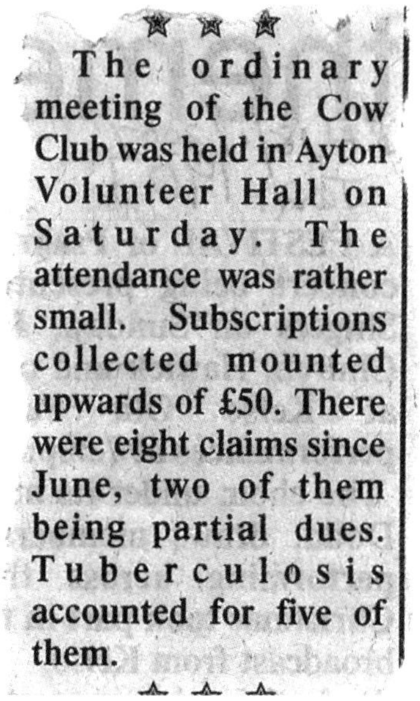
The ordinary meeting of the Cow Club was held in Ayton Volunteer Hall on Saturday. The attendance was rather small. Subscriptions collected mounted upwards of £50. There were eight claims since June, two of them being partial dues. Tuberculosis accounted for five of them.

Figure 71. Cow Club. Berwick Advertiser, 7 January 1907

On a lighter note Walter White writes about cottage life in 1858. *'In some cottages, the beds serve as a partition between the family and the cow-stall; and there is a story of a cow being seized with the gad and butting a bed over on the floor in the night'.* [White 1859]. Hopefully no one was badly injured. (Gadfly is a blood-sucking fly that distresses cattle.)

8. Flitting

Flitting day was on 12 May in Northumberland but in the Scottish Borders and the Lothians it was on 26 May. Rutherfurd's Directory (1866) refers to 26 May as the *'old Scotch Whitsunday term'* and that this was *'when houses are changed, leases of farms are entered upon, and hinds and shepherds change their service; unmarried ploughmen, and domestic servants change places at both the Whitsun day and Martinmas (22 November) old Scotch terms. The new Scotch terms of Whitsunday (15th May) and Martinmas (11 November) prevail in some of the gentlemen's houses, and are the rule on the English Border'.*

Moving from Scotland to England or from England to Scotland must have been more difficult due to the different *'term'* dates. I have only discovered one reference to this problem. Andrew Purves, in "A Shepherd Remembers", mentions this in relation to his family's move to Doddington. The outgoing shepherd was retiring and stayed on to bridge the gap. [Purves 2001].

Hastings Neville, writing in 1909 [Neville 1909], about the *'flitting'* and how the local people call 12 May *'The May'*, bemoans the fact that though referred to as *'The May'* it bears no resemblance to the celebrations in other parts of England with their special days on 1 May (May Day) or oak apple day on 29 May. No maypoles, processions, bands or May Queen. Instead, he says we see *'our roads from morning to evening thronged with carts piled with the furniture and bedding of a large portion of our population'*. Hastings Neville would be pleased to see the village of Ford now celebrating May Day in the *'proper'* way, with a May Queen, Isabelle Maxwell, this year (2007), processions and maypole dancing.

Later he describes the carts, two per family, very vividly, *'the furniture in one cart piled to a dangerous height, with the grandfather clock lying lengthwise and risking its life on the top'. 'In the second cart are the women and children seated on the bedding, caring for the caged canary, and the cherished pelargonium which grew at the cottage window, and the arum lily, now disconsolate with its glossy leaves drooping and waving a sad farewell.'*

Figure 72. Flitting Day in the Parish of Ford.

Mr. Jim Mallen of Yetholm remembers flitting using two carts. He said the good furniture went in one cart and the rougher outdoor things, coal, potatoes, tools, tin bath etc., went in the second. Sometimes you had to put some of the indoor things in the second cart but as little as possible.

Rev. W. S. Gilly wrote in 1841 that *'the Northumbrian cottager can scarcely be said to have a home'* because *'It is too much his custom to change his dwelling place; or, in the language of this region, "to flit"'*. There are he says *'a combination of causes'* for this constant moving but one big reason is the family agreement which means as circumstances within the family change their employment requirements also change. He notes that *'We, therefore, frequently observe an industrious and well-conducted hind quitting the service of a farmer, under whom he has been living with mutual satisfaction, as soon as his children begin to grow up'*. [Gilly 2001].

Ada Mary Howarth (born 1916) remembers witnessing *'the flittings'* at the family farm, Gatehousecote, when she was young. *'All was excitement, as the time was one of general posts, and the local roads would be dotted with horses and carts piled high with household goods, the younger children riding on top with the older ones and adults walking beside the cart.'* She also mentions *'The moonlight flit'* which *'was an occasional moment of high drama to the daily round, when a family would disappear from their cottage overnight, having moved lock, stock and barrel without giving notice to the farmer, and their absence would not be discovered until daylight next morning'*. How was this achieved? She speculates; unofficial horse and cart or perhaps – *'handcart, wheelbarrow or pram'*. Of course this *'flit'* was not necessarily connected with the official flitting day!

Dr. R. Shirra Gibb (born about 1850) remembers as a boy watching the events involved with flitting because *'About Term Day there was usually a school holiday'*.

The big problem caused by the constant movement of families, which is aired over and over again, is the detrimental affect on the children's education. School Log Books are full of complaints about the movement of pupils. On one occasion the difficulty was that new pupils arrived in May followed very closely by a school inspection, therefore giving an invalid impression of the teaching at that school to the advantage or disadvantage of that particular teacher.

Wark Primary School 1905 Log Book:

5th May Children leaving at the May Term, are gone now – as is usually the case, with few exceptions, attendance therefore reduced.

12th May Holiday today Friday being flitting day, and attendance – would have been small.

19th May Admit six newcomers – making number on registers 66. More may be expected at Scotch Term – 28th May.

More recently, Mrs Nancy Taylor (born 1929) married to Willie Taylor, a shepherd and very talented musician (fiddle player) lived up on Chatton Moor at Chatton Sandyford. They moved from there to make getting to school easier for their son. The lack of a road made things difficult for the little boy who sometimes rode on the pony. They moved to Southernknowe in the College Valley and there the school was next door! Many children had extremely long walks to school. These journeys became impossible in bad weather.

Walter White touches on education when he writes in 1858 *'As a class the hinds are industrious and well-conducted; not slow to see the advantages of education or to send their children to school. But they are migratory and obstinate to maintain their rights'*. (White 1859]. The idea that the migratory instinct is thoroughly ingrained is repeated frequently. So much so that *'nomadic'* or *'semi nomadic'* was also used. A. Geddes writes that in 1938-39 *'On average, throughout the south-east, a quarter of the younger pupils in country schools left for other places, to be replaced by others coming from elsewhere'*. [Robertson 2005].

An unnamed ploughman who was born in 1911 echoes the assertion by Walter White of the hinds maintaining their rights although he would more probably say it showed his father's independent spirit. *'Oh ma faither jist liked tae move when he wanted to: it let the fermer ken he didna own him.'*

R. W. Bosanquet of Rock, Alnwick reported to the 1867 Royal Commission and expressed a similar opinion . He said that *'The power of limiting their agreement strictly to a year, and of the changing if they pleased without any reason assigned, is at the foundation of the independence and respectability of our north country peasantry.'* [Robertson 2005].

There are many stories about flitting which give an insight into life and enlarges our view of times past. Mary King was born in 1905 at Bellshiel near Swinton. She describes a flitting in about 1916 from Northfield, between Coldingham and St. Abbs, to Temple Hall about 2 miles away:

'Well, there were usually three carts, Oo got a' the furniture on the three carts. Usually the third yin wis what they ca'ed a short cart, that wis a sma' yin. And the mother usually went in that wi' the youngest bairns and the cat, if ye had yin, or the pig in a bag. It wid lie squealin' among the straw. The pig lay in the bag till ee got there and then – it wid be a wee pig likely – ye wid pit it intae the sty efter ye arrived. Well, often if the pig wisnae too big ye'd take it wi' ye – if ma fither could carry it. Oh, if it had been a big pig, well, it would jist have been killed before that, or sold. So ma sisters and me walked tae Temple Hall, well, behind the carts likely. The wee-est yins would be in a cart but us bigger yins would walk. Ma mother would go in a cart, ma father would be leadin' yin o' two horses.' [MacDougall 2000].

Another lady remembers a flitting where the cat had been placed in a bag and she nursed it – *'holding the sack with puss in it on her lap, and no doubt speaking away to her from time to time'*. She describes how she was seated on the sofa on the back of a lorry whereas her mother had memories of moves by horse and cart. She recalls the *'cat would be one o' the first things to be 'packed' on flitting morning, in case she (it) disappeared during the flurry'*. [Robertson 2005].

Mrs Isabel Barrie of Milfield remarked on the custom of always packing the carts or lorries so that the sofa could be safely used as a seat.

Mrs Laura Coe from Rothbury has many anecdotes to tell although she did not work in agriculture herself. Her husband remembered seeing many bondagers working at Haggerston and she remembers two at Outchester Farm near Waren Mill. She recounted a story that, she felt sure, some people would find hard to believe. At Outchester a family was due to flit on the usual flitting day (12 May). During the night granny had died but due to the prevailing circumstances (one family moved out by midday to let the new family in) the family had no option but to place granny in the cart with their belongings and move as planned.

Hastings Neville writes further about flitting in "Under a Border Tower". *'There is, of course, the excitement which comes with the expectation of a change of place, and the children are happy if they are well. But there are pitiful sights to be seen sometimes on those piled up carts. There are sick children - we have seen a cart full, all with the measles – and then there are the old and infirm – the grandmother of eighty-six, she is often a difficult problem to "flit", but she gets hoisted sometimes to a dangerous perch, but seems quite comfortable on the soft chaff bed, how she is got down again it is painful to imagine.'* [Neville 1896].

Mrs Coe mentioned that once the move was made the question asked was *'did you get a clean house?'* Sometimes a lot of cleaning and papering had to be done.

Barbara Robertson also writes about arriving at a new house and what was desirable. Hopefully *'the efficient housewife-cum-kindly neighbour would sweep out the house just prior to departing, and would also usually leave the kitchen fire either burning ready for the new folk or at least ready laid with sticks and coal so as to give them a good start. At the same time she would be hoping that the same reception would meet her at the other end of the journey, though there was no certainty of this.'*

There are a few further stories about flitting of a light-hearted nature.

The first is from the Bolton Parish Description (Bolton near East Saltoun in East Lothian) written by the Scottish Women's Rural Institute in 1974:

'About the year 1910 an old man of 80 took service at Under Bolton. When the next Hiring Day came round a neighbour said to him "Aiblins ye'll no' be movin' on the noo; its likely ye'll be for settlin' doon". The reply was "I've nivver been ony mair than a year in ony place an' I'm no' gain tae begin in my auld age" – and off he went.' [Bolton 1974].

Ellingham Women's Institute (Ellingham is near Alnwick in Northumberland) records an incident which took place in 1904. [Ellingham 1904]:

'A story is told of a man who flitted every May Day for twenty years. Then, for once, he was stopping on another year. As May Day approached he became more and more restless till at last on the 12th he went to the farmer and asked if he might have a couple of carts for a short time. He was asked why he wanted them, "Just to tak' the furniture a bit doon the road," he answered.'

Another story on a similar vein blamed the wife for the restlessness. *'Ye'll hae heard the story O' the hind telling the master at Speaking Time that he'd no be bidin'? No? Oh weill, it gangs this wey that the maister then asked the man what for was he leavin', as he hadna expected that kind O' answer. Weill says the hind, it's like this: the wife's a bit weary o' the place an' never getting away onywhere, and wanted a bit o' a change, and a flittin' ye ken aye lets ye see another bit o' the country. Weill if that's the only reason says the fermer, take a horse and cairt some effernoon next week and gie ye're wife a bit o' a hurl rooned by some o' the ferms but be shair and come back by lousin time.'* [Robertson 2005]. Note that this was from a man born in 1910 – oral evidence from recordings made in the 1970s.

Mary Rutherford, a bondager for forty years in the Mellerstain area near Kelso said *'I tell you what I like best? Not having to flit every year. It was awful, thon flittin' I remember driving a horse and cart through the Square in Kelso with all the furniture and my mother sitting up at the back. I'm glad to be settled here and not to have to flit anymore.'* Mary was interviewed by Liz Taylor for The Scotsman, Wednesday 5 July 1978.

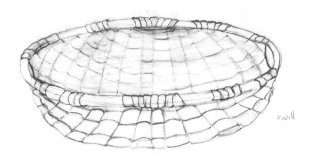

Figure 73. Swill. (Dinah Iredale)

9. Housing

The state of housing in the Scottish Borders, East Lothian and Northumberland was very poor - so poor, in fact, that many people felt compelled to comment. Bulmers Directory 1886 records a very early comment made *'in 1734 by George Mark'* *'Doddington parish comprehends 202 families and 7 villages. It is remarkable for the largeness and badness of its houses'*.

An even earlier comment in the 17th century by *'the naturalist John Ray, described those in East Lothian as "pitiful cots, built of Stone and covered with Turves, having in them but one room, many of them no chimneys, the windows very small Holes, and not glazed".* [Fenton 1987].

A description of cottages in the mid 18th century states that the cottars houses *'were still only mean hovels with walls no more than 5 feet high'* and these *'were made of alternate courses of turf and field stones.'* There was only one room and this was *'about 12 foot square'.* [Whyte 1991].

Figure 74. A Farm Worker's Cottage by Rev. W. S. Gilly

Ian and Kathleen Whyte say that 'The standard house layout throughout Scotland before the Agricultural Revolution was one in which human beings and livestock were accommodated under a single roof, using a common entrance with only a flimsy partition separating them'. They also mention some excavations at Springburn Park near Kelso where 'three simple stone-walled, cruck-timbered houses were discovered. These houses had cobbled areas at one end which appear to have been occupied by livestock and were dated to the late twelfth and thirteenth centuries.'

Houses like these are sometimes called *'byre-dwellings'* or *'long houses'.* A long house for poor people *'a cottar family and their single cow was not necessarily very long.'* When describing the interior of these cottages Ian and Kathleen Whyte mention that *'in the poorest dwellings the division between man and beast was only a low wooden partition. It was reckoned to be beneficial to "let the coo see the fire"'.*

At the end of the 18th century the report by John Bailey and George Culley [Bailey 1805] mentions building work. It notes how farm buildings, farm-houses, offices etc., have improved:

'Buildings, for the use and convenience of farms were formerly very shabby and ill-contrived; but those that have been erected of late years, are better adapted to the various purposes wanted on extensive farms and improved cultivation.'

They also comment on the cottages and say *'such cottages as have been erected a number of years, are built with stone and clay, and covered with thatch; those that have been built of late years, are of stone and lime, covered with tiles, and mostly a floor of lime and sand: they consist of one apartment, 15 feet by 16, to dwell in, with a small one at the entrance, for a cow, coals, working tools, etc. 9 feet by 16, and are only one storey high: very few of them want the accommodation of a garden.'* These small improvements by the early 19th century are a start, but not the beginning of rapid renovation or replacement, as there are further complaints and comments about conditions in the middle of the 19th century.

W. S. Gilly, the vicar of Norham, is very prominent in the condemnation of the housing for farm workers. He writes in 1841 that a great deal of thought and attention has been given to improving cow-byres, pig-styes and sheep-folds to house the improved livestock brought about by the *'advancement of agriculture as a science'*. He then pleads for similar consideration to be given to the provision of cottages for the farm workers – *'let us take care to lodge our peasants as well as we lodge our beasts'*. [Gilly 2001].

Figure 75. A Row of Cottages by Rev. W. S. Gilly

W. S. Gilly describes the cottages as *'miserable hovels'*, *'the walls look as if they will scarcely hold together'*, *'the chimneys' 'lean on the roof' 'the rafters are evidently rotten'* and *'the thatch yawning to admit the wind and wet'*. He blames the constant flitting as a reason for farmers not having much incentive to improve the cottages and the hind not much incentive to *'bargain as he otherwise would, for the condition of his cottage'*. He does acknowledge the improvements made by some owners of estates such as the Earl of Rosebery a few years earlier. The plans and specifications for these cottages were made available through the transactions of the Highland and Agricultural Society and the Society offered medals to those who built *'cottages of a good construction'*. He was pleased to note that *'these medals are already in demand'*. [Gilly 2001].

Figure 76. Doddington about 1900. The thatched cottages on the right are now double storey. Notice the buildings in the background. The school and school house on the left and the mill on the right. (Anne & Derek Fairnington, Wooler)

Alexander Fenton quotes from R. Kerr's General View of the Agriculture of Berwick 1809 where cottages had been built in long rows – *'the hinds' row'*. *'They were single storey buildings in long rows, built in such a way that they had alternately a thick and a thin partition wall. The thick wall contained the fireplace. Examples in Berwickshire, in existence by 1809, had roofs of pantiles, slates or thatch, and floors of clay, hard rammed earth, or bricks. Internally they measured 21ft x 16ft, and were divided by the placing of box-beds into a chamber, a closet for storing milk, meal and potatoes, and a lobby with a coal-hole.'* It is also noted that *'It was, of course, cheaper to build in rows, since walls, and roofs were shared'*. [Fenton 1987].

Figure 77. Cottages at Hay Farm, Ford. Notice the bondagers with the shorter skirts and a standpipe for water in the centre of the square. (Anne & Derek Fairnington, Wooler)

Figure 78. Cottages at Riffington Farm (now Tillmouth Farm). June 1905. Notice the tools etc., hanging on the walls. One tool is a square metal gird for carrying buckets of water or milk. (Mrs Jane Cook, Hetton Law)

The *'hinds' rows'* can still be seen all over the region of Northumberland, Selkirkshire, Roxburghshire, Berwickshire and East Lothian. Also notice that some cottages are built in a square, not a row, with a central yard area. Some are still single storey with two or three cottages having been made into one, while some have had dormer windows added to the loft area. In some cases a complete upper storey has been built up and the original height of the gable is often clearly visible.

W. S. Gilly mentions improved cottages at Duddo with *'single room only, but this of a good size,'* and with separate *'byre and pig sty'*. At Grindon *'each cottage has two rooms, and also a cow byre, pig sty and that other convenience, the want of which is too general in every village in the North'*. The lack of ceilings (the rooms are open to the rafters) is a minus here and would, if put in place, *'add materially to the warmth and comfort'*. Those at Thornton Park he holds up as especially praiseworthy. There are six cottages *'each has two rooms ceiled,' 'ventilated by a window which opens'* and also *'a grate, an oven, and furnace-pot as fixtures'*. There was a *'small dairy, pantry, and coal-house to each cottage'*. Finally, *'a cow-byre, pig-sty, a convenience of another kind, and an ashe or dung-pit and a front garden'*. He also mentions improvements at Ford, Cresswell, Bewick and Holy Island. [Gilly 2001]

Over the border *'The Duke of Buccleuch was a leading landlord in the drive to improve farm-buildings and cottages and thus provide more civilised living conditions for farm workers. With himself as Chairman and the Rev. Harry Stuart as Honorary Secretary they founded an "Association for Promoting Improvement in the Dwellings and Domestic Conditions of Agricultural Labourers in Scotland".'* [Howarth 1998].

Whilst the Rev. Gilly deplored the state of many cottages he praises the efforts made by the families who make these *'hovels'* into a home. He contrasts the outside with the inside. *'To look at the exterior, you would suppose that they were inhabited by a tribe of savages. Enter the doors and you will behold an apartment amply supplied with household chattels, and smiling with content. The cotter and the housewife have done all for themselves which good management can devise.'*

Improvements were definitely underway. F. H. Doyle in his report in 1843 notes that *'Sir Walter Riddell, a practising barrister in London, has found leisure to think of the comfort and morals of his tenantry in Northumberland, and has built some cottages near Rothbury, of which, though I did not see them, I heard the people of that town speak in terms of high, and I doubt not, well-merited praise'*. Looking at the situation with optimism, the minister of Aberlady thought, in 1845, that there was *'ground to hope, that the cottages on every farm will, at no distant period, have two apartments instead of one'*. Further in his report F. H. Doyle felt that landowners were *'becoming every day more deeply impressed with the feeling, that some sacrifice of time and thought, and even amusement, in order to promote the general well-being of their dependents, is not a charity, but a duty'*.

In 1858 Walter White writes *'an association was formed for the building of improved cottages and the Duke of Northumberland, Earl Grey on his estate at Howick and the Commissioners of Greenwich Hospital have had cottages built with an upper floor and with due regard to light, air and cheerfulness, as well as decency'*. He also adds *'Such, however, is the force of habit, that some families still preferred sleeping all together in the kitchen, to going to bed upstairs'*. This attitude is remarked on by many writers and will reappear later in the chapter.

About ten years, later in 1864, a report by the Medical Officer to the Privy Council, Dr. Hunter, considers that housing in *'rustic parts of Northumberland'* is very much what it should be – *'a ground floor with a windowless loft'*. After expressing this opinion he gives more detail. *'Often there is but one room, a good kitchen with a bedstead, which has seen many generations, placed in one corner. These cots are not un-suited to couples without children; far better than two miserable rooms, one above another. They too frequently have but one window. There is often a little screen or inside porch. Other cots, for larger families, have a back room and a back door or window; in this case, both rooms contain a bed. Some cots have the further luxury of a passage through to the back door, and into it the door of each room opens. In nearly every case there was all the comfort which fixtures and furniture can give. In this climate the smallness of the gardens is no great loss, and generally there was at least yard room and conveniences.'*

Matthew Tewart Culley, landowner, Coupland Castle replied to the 1867 Royal Commission about poor housing. *'Health no doubt suffered too, but less than might have been expected, from the salubrity of the climate and the short time which the labouring population actually spent in their houses.'* [Henley 1867].

The Medical Officer, Dr. Hunter, later remarks on the bondage system and its advantages to hind and farmer but remarking in a later paragraph that *'It is curious to observe that the very dung of the hind and bondsman is the perquisite of the calculating lord. A thrifty race of farmers on a poor soil have long understood this matter, and the lord will allow no privy but his own to exist in the neighbourhood, and will rather give a bit of manure here and there for a garden, than bate any part of this seigniorial right'*.

Berwick Hill, near Morpeth, is given as an example where *'no privies were allowed, except at the farmhouses, to which people might go'!* This mention of privies and the lack of them leads into the related problem of drainage or lack of it, also dung heaps and the water supply.

W. S. Gilly thought that, whilst draining the land for agriculture had been undertaken, little attention had been given to the *'ground on which cottages stand, and the paths which lead to them'*. He describes the areas around the cottages – *'While nuisances of all kinds – pools of fetid water and sloughs – convey their noisome vapours to the very threshold of our labouring population, the lanes and paths by which they should be approached are rendered almost impassable by mud and mire'*. [Gilly 2001].

J. Sinclair in the early 19th century (The General Report of the Agricultural State, and the Political Circumstances of Scotland – Edinburgh 1814) cited by Alexander Fenton had also mentioned privies, *'the cottager should be taught the value as well as the comfort, of a necessary house; though in some parts of the country, it will take some time before they learn the truth'*. [Fenton 1987]. He is very well aware of the difficulties of changing longstanding habits and customs.

Fifty years later (1864) the Medical Officer expresses the unkind opinion that *'I suspect they do not really feel the want of privies; some like to affect a higher civilization than they possess, others like to have a grievance;'*. He then looks back in time and explains the historical situation with regards to privies and echoes J. Sinclair's opinion saying *'but privies except as a means to storing valuable dung have hitherto been a failure among them'*. [Hunter 1864].

There were interesting reports on housing to the 1867 Royal Commission. [Henley 1867]. Sometimes the individual reports are very brief and sometimes they are very detailed:

'Mr. Patrick Baker is the overseer to the poor of the parish of Lowick, and has known it all his life'. He states *'The cottages are very bad, generally one room and mostly bad thatch, very few necessaries'*.

Rev P. G. McDouall, vicar of Kirknewton in Northumberland, states that *'With regard to the cottages provided for the labouring classes, the accommodation is sadly deficient; it is necessarily prejudicial to morality, and fosters in a sad degree that want of self-respect and of consciousness of responsibility which too generally prevails, and without which true morality cannot exist'*. Later in this report to Mr. Henley the Rev. McDouall states that he thinks *'no improvement can be looked for till the system of free labour is established, a suitable class of houses built provided with out-houses, gardens, proper water supply, drainage, and such like necessaries and comfort'*.

In the same report, Mrs Maclean, a shepherd's wife at Lanton, states, *'We have only two rooms for five children, maid servant, my husband, and myself. The hired girl sleeps in the room we occupy'*.

Mrs Ewart, a hind's wife also at Lanton, says about her house, *'There is nothing but one room; the coals lie at the door. There are no out-door necessaries, but there is a pigsty and a place for a cow'.* Mrs Telfer whose *'husband works "at his own hand" because he does not like the bondage, as he would then have a stranger to lodge in the* house' says *'she rents her house off the farmer and pays £3 a year for it. It is a very poor place only one room; no convenience of any kind'.*

When John Bailey and George Culley wrote about manure (1794–1805) they included this account of how hill farms dealt with the problem of dunghills! *'Upon the hill farms around Cheviot we have been often surprised to see, at the doors of the shepherds' houses, such immense dunghills, the accumulation of unnumbered years, probably centuries: to avoid this increasing nuisance, many of them have ingeniously contrived to build their houses near a "burn-side", for the 'convenience' of having it 'taken away by every flood!'* This, the writers say, results in the unnecessary buying of hay from the lowlands. They reason that the dung could have been spread on the land, and the grass would then have grown much more thickly, so giving an increased crop of hay.

Mr. Isaac Percival, (78) retired gamekeeper, Angerton Mill shares his memories in 1929. *'"I've seen a house myself where you went in here, and there was the cow, and here was the cuddy, and the living-room was there" (And the hens would be in the passage, put in his housekeeper). "I've been there often for my grandfather was born there." (You had to pass through the byre, past the heels of the cow and the cuddy to reach the living room.)'* [Bosanquet 1989].

Mr. George Handyside can remember at Cambo *'When there was at least one house where the cow and people went in and out the same door.'* [Bosanquet 1989].

Water supply was not mentioned a great deal in these early reports. W. S. Gilly when describing the old cottages says *'No pumps or wells, nothing to promote cleanliness and comfort'.* [Gilly 2001]. Later accounts in more recent times suggest long distances to standpipes and photographs show one standpipe for a number of cottages.

A steward's wife, Mary Johnson, told the 1867 Royal Commission that they had lived at New Bewick for 49 years and reared 11 children. Despite her husband's position as steward and the fact they had been faithful employees their living conditions are difficult. She comments that there is no water near her cottage and that, *' It is hard work to carry it so far on her head.'* [Henley 1867].

The farm cottages were still in need of improvement in the early 20th century.

Alexander Fenton notes that in the 19th Century the housing provision was *'a disgrace to the country'.* Also that *'It is still the rule to find no proper water supply convenient, and to find sanitary conveniences non-existent'. 'Sculleries and outhouses are the exception'.* He also notes that *'There was no regulation to enforce the erection of privies, though the 1897 act laid down that the local authority may require the owner of a house to provide a proper supply of wholesome water at, or reasonably near, the house'.* [Fenton 1987].

Ada Mary Howarth describes her memories of life on the family farm, Gatehousecote, in the Scottish Borders in the 1920s and 1930s. She says *'in the late Twenties, Parliament passed the Rural Housing (Scotland) Act to encourage landowners to make improvements, in sanitation and living space.'* Grants were available and *'during the thirties, nearly all the Border landowners and owner occupier farmers took advantage of this Government largesse and, where only a skylight in the roof pitch had lighted and ventilated the attic rooms below it, "out-shot windows" now sprouted from every cottage roof, giving extra space, light and air to the bare-boarded attics which might provide sleeping accommodation for up to five or six children'.* [Howarth 1998].

Ada's father had great *'zeal for modernising'* and in 1930 added *'a bedroom, bathroom and flush W.C.'* to *'the row'* at Gatehousecote. *'A great advance on 'the offy' or hut at the bottom of the cabbage patch, with a commode seat over a hole in the ground'.* [Howarth 1998]. Bathrooms and a W.C. inside was a great change. A lady from Akeld recounted how two bondagers, who lived in The Square at Akeld, responded to the improvements. *'They wrapped the toilet in brown paper'.*

Born in 1945 and brought up in rural North Yorkshire I can remember many cottages with outside privies with dry toilets, or Elsan (chemical toilets) and sometimes a flush toilet but still outside. This was common well into my teens. I can also remember visiting a house in Gateshead in the late 1960s where the W.C. was down steps into the yard outside. My maternal grandparents retired to a cottage, which they bought when their son took over the running of the family farm, where rainwater was collected for washing etc., and drinking water was carried in pails from the village pump, a hundred yards or so away. Collecting the drinking water with granddad was a great treat for us children who lived in a house *'with a tap'* and we had to be reprimanded by mum for asking too often for a drink of this delicious and new-fangled water. This is just to set the situation in Northumberland, Scottish Borders and East Lothian in the context of what was happening in other rural areas.

Jean Willis from the Alnwick area has also written about farm life in the 1920s and 1930s. Her mother was widowed and became a bondager in order to get a cottage to live in. *'By the time mother needed a cottage some farmers had begun to advertise for workers, and papers were brought in that both the farmer and the woman had to sign and then there were no more handshakes or lucky silver sixpences.'*

Later she describes the cottage in great detail. *'The cottage that we got was very small, one bedroom for five, and the kitchen which my brother had to sleep in. When the two beds were in the bedroom there wasn't much room for anything else.'* She describes a chimney that smoked dreadfully and range with *'an oven on one side and a set pot for hot-water on the other'.* For a water supply they had a rain barrel outside the *'one'* door to the property and the *'water tap'* or standpipe which *'served seven families and was a good distance from the house. We had to walk past four houses and carry the water back'.* The sanitary arrangements are also given in detail. *'The netty (loo) was outside. It had a wooden seat and frame. The wooden seat had two holes, a high one and a low one for a child. There was an ash pit at the back and when you did a 'job' a shovel full of ashes was put down the hole and it was all pushed into the ash pit. When the ash pit was full farm workers came with a horse and cart to take all the "goods" out of the ash pit and spread it on the land. It made good manure and the ashes helped to lighten heavy soil. The one netty had to serve three families (about 15 people). It was no use if you were in a hurry and someone else was in. There was no sink to wash your hands after.'*

As noted earlier the cottages with all their lack of space and amenities were made into surprisingly comfortable homes. W. S. Gilly writes in 1841. *'In justice to this excellent class of persons the hinds of the Border, I must describe the interior of a cottage, when it is fairly "put to rights", after the occupant has taken possession.'* He asks us to imagine it is December when we visit the hind and his family. *'At first (in many cases, not all) we are put a little out of humour at finding that a cow is tenant of the space, through which we pass into his "parlour and kitchen and all", but though a smell reaches our nostril which tells us that all cannot always be clean, where a large animal is stalled, yet it is evident that he takes care to "red up" the place, and keep the cowhouse as distinct as he can from his own part of the house, though no partition wall divides them. It is but a slight wainscot work of his own contrivance, which separates Richard from his cow; but as soon as we have entered within his own domicile the general aspect within will gladden our hearts.'* He goes on to describe the box-beds which are, of course, a prominent feature of the room. Another feature of the room is the dresser with its pretty crockery – *'large blue dishes and plates, some of Staffordshire ware, and others of Delf, intermixed with old china or porcelain tea-pots, cups, and saucers'.* The *'handsome clock in the tall case and chest of drawers'* are mentioned together with barrels of meal and herrings as well as flitches of bacon. There are books in most households. Pride of place is given to the family bible *"the big ha' bible, ance his father's pride".* With this are further small bibles and *'prayer books'*, *'books of devotion, of history or of useful knowledge, are ranged by side of the bible – and* (most importantly) *they all show that they have been frequently read'.* [Gillie 2001].

So how did these families *'convert'* the shed into a *'tidy chamber'*? What did *'put to rights' and to 'red up' entail?* In contrast to the opinion expressed by W. S. Gilly in 1841 that due to constant *'flitting'* *'the hind'* *'does not bargain, as he otherwise would for the condition of his cottage'* [Gilly 2001], the 1867 Royal Commission shows a different attitude. Mr. R. S. Bainbridge, occupier, Woodhorn, said *'at the yearly hirings one of the first questions asked by our hinds is, "What sort of cottages have you?"'* [Henley 1867]. Forty or so years later, when Minnie Bell's father went to hirings in the late 19th to early 20th century, he was concerned about the accommodation he would be getting for his family. Minnie said that *'family came first'* with him and that his opinion was that *'a good house was worth a £1 a week in the wage'*. Minnie and family had worked on Sisterpath Farm near Marchmont and later at Charterhall near Duns. [Bell].

Mr. Isaac Percival says, in 1929, *'about ninety years ago when there were no ovens and no windows; when people shifted they had to take their windows and fireplaces with them. No, the houses weren't all alike, the windows were different sizes, and they had to be made right with boards, - and cow dung.'* [Bosanquet 1989].

Dr. R. Shirra Gibb remembers the cottages of Roxburghshire in about 1857 (he took up farming as a young man in 1872) and he says *'to make the house habitable lay entirely with the occupants'*. The cottage had *'one fairly large room with a door and two windows, the walls merely plastered and not lathed, while the open joists and rafters had nothing above but sarking to which the slates were fastened'*. The hind had to bring *'with him posts, doors, and some boarding with which he partitioned off a small porch at the entrance; he then put up two box beds, with their doors to the kitchen-end their backs forming the partition between the kitchen and what was to be the room-end. If there were any space left, between the beds and the back wall of the house, that became the milkhouse or pantry. Sometimes there was a small window of one or two panes to the back, which was made use of to light and ventilate this pantry. Having finished the joiner work of his house he had to turn blacksmith and mason and adjust the bars and swey, which he had also brought, for the barless kitchen grate'*. He goes on to write how the ceilings were added using rushes. *'Next he produced his "Bennells". These consisted of large rolls of dried, blackheaded bulrushes (scirpus locustrus) sewed and strung together so as to form light and fairly impervious sheets. These were put up as a ceiling for the two rooms, being tied to or hung from the rafters as was more convenient. The "Bennells" made wonderfully tough sheets, and a wonderful house altogether the man had made. Starting with the bare walls in the early morning and followed up by the goodwife as painter and paperhanger they brought light out of darkness and comparative comfort out of nothing. The floor, which was generally of dry, beaten clay had to be levelled up in many parts.'* [Gibb 1927].

Dr. R. Shirra Gibb remembers as a boy *'going to the top of a loch near my old home and seeing men with scythes wading in the water among the "Blackheads". At the time, I took them to be gypsies. And perhaps they were, but later I found out that they were cutting the rushes for "Bennells"; or, it might be more correct to say that they were cutting "Bennells" for making rush mats and rolls. Was the word "Bennells" the common, local name of the rush, or was it the manufactured product ready to put up as a ceiling or screen where required? The name "Bennell Moss," which occurs in various parts of the country where these fine, tall rushes grow, does not help much, as it was undoubtedly a common practice for farm-servants to get a holiday during dry weather to go to a "Bennell Moss" and cut "Bennells." After they were taken out of the water they were set up in stooks, and later carted home. I have not been able to find out if there were ever any right inherent to an estate to cut Bennells, or not. On many estates the servants have a right to cut peats on mosses many miles away.'* [Gibb 1927].

Miss Richardson speaking in 1929 said, *'She used to visit Mrs Waitte, at Harwood House, on the moor, there was a canvas ceiling; probably the house wasn't ceiled.'* [Bosanquet 1989]. Barbara Robertson notes *'the organisational abilities or otherwise of the housewife would undoubtedly show up'* and *'a good planner would make all the difference'*. [Robertson 2005].

Dr. R. Shirra Gibb states that the cottages at Boon (his farm near Lauder) dated to about 1854. They were larger than many having two rooms and a loft which was reached by a stepladder. Later they were improved by the addition of *'a porch', 'a milkhouse', 'coal-cellar'* and a *'good stair'* and *'two large skylights'*. *'In his Report to the Local Authority on Farm Servants cottages, the Sanitary Inspector gave a plan of a Boon Cottage'* as an example of good housing. [Gibb 1927].

The papering previously mentioned was not always easy to achieve. Mrs Jean Willis's mother had problems when she papered their small cottage. Jean describes it as follows: *'These two rooms had originally been one room, which had been divided using planks of wood, which were very uneven and full of knot holes and uneven gaps. When mother papered over this it wasn't long before holes showed through and the paper split where the slats did not join. On the bedroom side, the wood stanchions were planks nailed to the stanchions from the kitchen side. The posts on the bedroom side were just like a garden fence, posts on one side and rails on the other. The back kitchen had been large but a pantry had been fashioned out of slats on boards built inside. (Would this be modernising?) There was no ceiling as such in the back kitchen, only bare slates.'*

A mother in the Whalton area of Northumberland who lived in *'one of these unilocular houses'* had told the medical officer Dr. Hunter, *'that the loft was useless'* as a sleeping – room, though he thought that *'it only wanted a window to make it an average cottage bedroom'*. He did admit that, *'Sometimes the ceiling of the cottage and floor of the loft is continued only halfway across the room, the other half of the room being open to the roof. A few steps made this half loft or large shelf a convenient cupboard or little dormitory, though perhaps hardly safe from dangers of rolling over. It is, however, warm enough.'* but *'to sleep in the dark out of reach altogether of the fire is considered the depth of human misery.'* [Hunter 1864].

The dislike of sleeping upstairs is frequently referred to by commentators, such as the Rev. P. G. McDouall, vicar of Kirknewton. He replied to Mr. Henley in 1867 that *'where upper rooms exist the inhabitants will not use them;'* and that this had been used as an excuse for not *'increasing the accommodation'*. He rather condescendingly states that *'it must be remembered that to effect any change among the lower orders is necessarily a work of time'* but then takes the landlords to task by saying that *'such objection (to the upstairs rooms) in no way removes the landlord's responsibility for allowing the existing evil state of things to continue'*. [Henley 1867]. Rather perverse arguments against the enlargement of cottages was the lack of furniture to furnish a larger premises, and that more furniture would cause problems at flitting time.

Mr. Thomas Tait, a shepherd at Paston and 70 years old in 1867, expressed his views about the use of upstairs rooms. *'The ground floor cottages are the most convenient. How is the mother to cook the dinner and look after a sick bairn when it is upstairs; she is always on the stairs. Some people would say that the upstairs rooms are more healthy. They would nae say so if they try them here in the cold of winter.'* [Henley 1867].

Ada Mary Howarth (1920s-30s) relates how she visited Mrs Cairns in the middle cottage of *'the row'* where she *'can remember seeing the trap-hole to the attic, reached by a ladder, lined like cherubs with four or five children's faces'*. [Howarth 1998]. Barbara Robertson, also writing about the first half of the 20th century, includes the childhood memories of how pleasant it was, when ill, to be amongst the family and not isolated upstairs. *'I mind when I had croup once or maybe it was chickenpox, and was off school for a week or so. But I seem to remember that I quite enjoyed being in bed for I was allowed to lie in the box bed in the kitchen, which was cosy and of course not lonely. And one of the most pleasant memories is in fact of dozing off to sleep with the firelight flickering and the quiet talk of the family all around. Very comforting I'm sure it must have been.'* [Robertson 1990]. This leads into the subject of box beds, which were considered to be a real problem by many reformers.

W. S. Gilly tried to encourage *'the peasantry'* to substitute curtains for the *'sliding pannel'* which normally close the box beds. The problems he says are *'confined air'* and *'the difficulty of approaching an invalid, particularly when surgical aid is necessary'*. He also includes a letter from Mungo Park, Esq., Surgeon, &c. who is *'medical officer to the district of Norhamshire'*, who states that if cottages were of more than one room *'the very objectionable use of close beds might be discontinued'*. He feels these beds are *'detrimental to health'* and *'a very great inconvenience to medical men'*. The *'hind and his family'* Rev. Gilly says *'plead truly'* that the beds are a warm place to sleep in a cold cottage and they help to maintain decency. [Gilly 2001].

Revd. P. G. McDouall is also concerned about *'when contagious or infectious diseases or fevers break out; few, if any, of the inhabitants'* escape because they are living and sleeping in such confined spaces. [Henley 1867].

Mrs Hetha Bruce of Lowick remembers that the cottages at Lowick Northfield in the early 20th century had floors of beaten earth and pole beds. The poles were at each corner of the bed and supported curtains. Beds were placed head to head or toe to toe with a curtain between. These might be the curtains that W. S. Gilly had advocated in 1841 but beds were still in the living space.

The campaign for better housing was spread over almost a hundred years which can be summarised by four more quotations.

Walter White writes in 1858 *'See an empty cottage before the hind has brought in his lumbering box-beds, his press, his chairs and table, before he has set up his grate in the empty fireplace, or fitted his window to the empty hole in the wall and you will think it not good enough to be a stable.'* [White 1859].

The 1893 Royal Commission reported that *'Cottages have steadily improved, although much remains to be done in this direction.'* [Fox 1893].

The Report of a Medical Officer in November 1898 on the cottages at Hay Farm, near Ford: The cottages in January had been *'in a dangerously wet condition'* and *'overcrowded'*. *'Nearly all have been enlarged, additional rooms have been built, with boarded, instead of cement floors, new windows have been put in, made to open at both top and bottom, the ground outside the houses has been lowered in several places and ventilating bricks have been built into walls below the floor line.'* The cottages had been changed from places *'unfit for human habitation'* to *'light, airy, dry, comfortable and healthy dwellings'*.

Andrew Purves noted that *'In the 1920s a scheme to upgrade rural housing in Scotland was set afoot by the Government and Local Authorities. Landowners were to be compelled to bring the cottages on their estates up to a certain standard, chiefly regarding sanitation and water supply.'* Later, he notes, that *'It was not until after the Second World War, however, that both hot and cold water, baths and electricity was installed in most farm cottages.'* [Purves 2001]. Some very isolated cottages were without modern conveniences until the 1960s.

10. The Work

The bondagers were renowned for the speed at which they worked and their deftness in carrying out the tasks. John Bailey and George Culley wrote in detail about working practice with regard to the *'new'* crop turnips and concluded that *'women in the northern parts of the country excel'* in hoeing turnips. They had *'at different times visited Norfolk, Suffolk, and all the principal turnip districts in the island; but never saw turnips so well hoed and completely cleaned, or kept in such garden-like culture, as on these borders'*. [Bailey 1972]. Mr. Henley in his report in 1867 says *'the women who work in the field in Northumberland are physically a splendid race'*. [Henley 1867].

Wat Thomson speaks about the women workers in more recent times. Interviewed in 1974 he remembers a farmer praising the women workers saying they kept everything tidy when filling the muck carts or feeding the stock. If a man did the same work *'it was just a slaister!'* Wat Thomson also said women were sought after. They could turn their hand to anything. *'They were a terrible handy thing on a farm!'* He said this at least twice. [Thomson 1974].

The following is a list of the work undertaken by the bondagers. This list, with one or two additions, was compiled in 1976 by Mr. and Mrs. Cockburn, who were retired agricultural workers:

1. Turnips – singling, hoeing, lifting and shawing (Many references were made to not carelessly stabbing the turnips when using a fork or a shawing hook. This damage might cause the turnip to rot when stored. The hook was to lift the turnip out of the ground. It was hooked round the root.)

2. Potatoes – planting, gathering, dressing and sorting.

3. Hay – turning, making the hay into kyles and then pikes, leading and stacking.

4. Corn – lifting and tying sheaves to make way for the binder, stooking, leading and stacking.

5. Threshing – cutting sheaves, carrying chaff (this was the lowliest job on threshing day. One of the uses for chaff was as filling for mattresses so this was the time when it was changed), carrying straw – before balers the straw was carried by the bondagers in large bundles. Mr. William Tait talked about the use of the *back rope*. This was a length of rope with a metal loop at one end. The loop was hooked on the thresher to catch the straw and the end pulled through the loop and tightened. The bundle was then carried to the cattle closes.

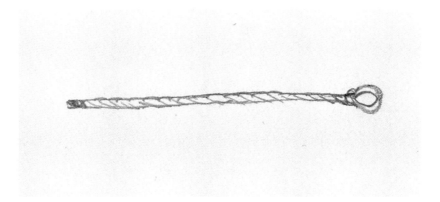

Figure 79. Each bondager had her own back rope. (Dinah Iredale).

Each bondager had her own back rope and there was *'hell to pay'* if someone took your back rope instead of their own. Joan Pringle (Joan was a Land Army girl who worked alongside a bondager at West Fenton Farm near Wooler during the Second World War) also talked about the back rope, as did Mr and Mrs Cockburn. They explained that the women carried the bundles of straw like carrying a creel – the rope went round the head. Joan in contrast took the rope over her shoulder. She said the back rope made a manageable bundle but *'we looked like a walking hay stack'*.

6. Hedging – clearing up after the hedger.

7. Manure – filling the carts, spreading the heaps in the fields. The frequent comment was that this was very heavy dirty work! Mr. William Tait of Duns said *'The bondagers handled the straw, then they handled the manure when mucking out the sheds to the midden. Then from the midden to the carts; from the carts to the heaps. Every 5 yards were marked length ways and across a field to make 5 yard squares. One heap of manure to each square. This manure was handled again as it was spread.'*

Mrs Hetha Bruce of Lowick mentioned clearing stones from the fields before sowing and collecting up wickens or couch grass as the fields were harrowed. The wickens were then burnt. Mrs Purvis of Wooler talked about living at Grindon near Norham, where her father was the cattleman and had a bondager to help him. Irish cattle were bought in to finish and be sold as beef. As a little girl Mrs Purvis (born 1916) remembers visiting the large shed where the cattle were housed, and in some way looking down on the backs of hundreds of cattle. This made a big and memorable impression. Mrs Bella Moffat recounted to Mrs Sybil Straughan how the bondagers took turns to work with the shepherd, cowman etc. and worked the same hours as the men.

Figure 80. A bondager helping the shepherd at shearing time. Riffington Farm (now Tillmouth Farm), 1905. (Mrs Jane Cook, Hetton Law)

Mr Jim Mallen, speaking about the early 20th century, said that although the bondagers were no longer true bondagers in the sense that they were not hired by the hind but directly by the farmer, they did work alongside one particular man. If the hind needed some help *'his bondager'* worked with him and at other times she worked with the group of bondagers.

The work listed in the Labourers Time Book for the Swinburne Estates (Aug. 1872/ Mar.1874) include haymaking, levelling a road, cutting thistles, cleaning grass from around young trees, spreading manure, taking cattle from Capheaton to Cowstand, scaling grass parks, beating guano, assisting in sowing guano, assisting in carting firewood to the hall, scaling and spreading soil in grass parks, breaking clods, stoning drains in the grass parks, cleaning the hedge at a young plantation in Bonny Riggs, scaling lime in grass parks (handling lime could be dangerous, making lips bleed and eyes sore - Mr. Tait said his wife Janet protected her eyes by using home-made goggles), cleaning the cottage at Burn Hill, cleaning manure out of the Hemmels, 1 person and 1 day cleaning the school (23 May), hoeing turnips, rooting docks, gathering corn at Cowstand Farm, cutting whins. Two days' holiday are mentioned. One was Christmas Day and the other 7 March, when "No work done" was recorded, so perhaps this was the hiring day. There seems to have been up to 11 women/girls and 2 men/boys included in this daybook and they worked between 2½ to 5¼ days per week.

Nancy Clark (born 1917) talking to Fred Kennington about her work on the land said she spread muck for weeks!

Auty Series, G.H., W.B.

Wooler.

Figure 81. Wooler – notice the heaps of muck in the foreground.
(Anne & Derek Fairnington, Wooler).

This was from little heaps set out in a regular pattern all over the field, or in this case fields! She was very fed up and did not get any praise. One day Mr. Barr, the farmer, gave a 5/- a week rise. She was so pleased. Mr. Barr said to her father, *"she never stopped!"* Her hard work had been noticed! [Clark].

Jean Kinghorn (born on 10 March 1904), talking to Fred Kennington in 1999, said she started working at 14 as *'an half-un'*. She helped a bondager look after the cattle which was a 7 day job. Jean remarked that, *'You didn't carry corn till you were a full worker at 16'*. She particularly hated sowing slag (basic slag). It was black like lead and came from the manure works. At the end of the day you were black and washed in cold water. I am not sure whether this was what was advised or if hot water was not available. She mentions lifting heavy sacks using a lifting stick which involved two people lifting the bag together. She said of this heavy work, it was *'No bother!'* She didn't remember any injuries and said *'it just came naturally'*.

She said the women lifted 12 stone and the men lifted 16 stone. *'You were'*, she admitted, *'ready for bed at night'*. [Kinghorn 1999].

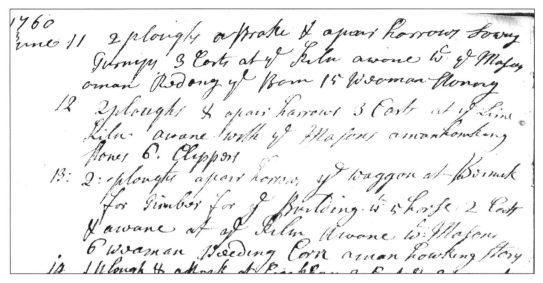

Figure 82. A record of the work undertaken each day. Notice the use of 'ye' for 'the' and the 15 women hoeing on the 11 June 1760. (Simpson Papers, Middleton Hall).

The Working Hours

The formidable list of work demanded strength and staying power to complete the long working day. The day started early at 6am, and sometimes getting up was not left to chance. At Kimmerston near Ford in Northumberland Margie Dixon can remember a horn being blown to get the workers up in time to have their horses ready for 6 am. She lived there from about 10 years of age and can remember hearing the horn being blown three times and wondering what it was. She thought this was an unusual practice and would be the responsibility of the steward or ploughman steward. The Second World War brought this custom to an end.

Margie's experience may have been rather unusual for the 1930s but historically it may have been quite common. The 1867 Royal Commission recorded that a horn was blown at 4.30am at Lanton for a 5.30am start. Over the border in 1845 Jamie Riddell had to *'Ring Wemen up every morning at 5'*. So again time keeping was not left to chance. [Robson 1984].

In the novel *'The Adventures of Mr. Verdant Green'* by Cuthbert Bede the visitors to Northumberland experience being woken up at sunrise by someone blowing a cow's horn. *'In the morning at sunrise, when our Warwickshire friends were yet in bed, such of them as were light sleepers would hear a not very melodious fanfare from a cow's horn – the signal to the village that the day's work was begun, which signal was repeated at sunset. This old custom possessed uncommon charms for Mr. Bouncer.'* [Bede 1877].

Bella Moffat speaking to Sybil Straughan describes how the morning's work began. *'At 6am the men stood at one side, the women at the other side, to hear instructions.'* The steward was the head farm worker and he issued the instructions.

Glen Aln also notes how the farming day got underway and writes about the farm stewards. *'Stewards differed in their ways and mannerisms. One near the Border had a peculiar habit of making each man sit immediately behind his horses when giving orders. He commenced at the ploughman steward, but instead of facing or looking at him he looked at the horses and pair by pair told them what they were going to do that day.'* The second steward he says *'stood at the door of the stable and shouted out the orders, all the while bending up and down with his hands dug deep in his trouser pockets. When he had finished he would say, "Aye, aa think that's aa; anyway that'll dae th' noo."'* Unfortunately we are not told how the orders were given to the women workers. Perhaps this was left to the ploughman steward. We can be sure that these interesting mannerisms would be a good source of amusement amongst the workers and I wonder how many tasks were finished with the words *'That'll dae th' noo!'* [Aln 1945].

Figure 83. Farm workers, in Berwickshire, assembled in the farmyard at Whitsome Laws. (Mrs Betty McLain, Ramrig, Duns).

Work got underway and then about 9 o'clock there was a short break. George Lumsden, steward to Mr. Charles Rea, Doddington, describes the routine to the 1867 Royal Commission in the following way: They have *'breakfast before they start'* but *'they generally carry something out with them (a piece and a tin bottle of tea perhaps), and they have about 15 minutes at 9 o'clock, working till quarter past 11, when they break off for two hours and a quarter; then continue to work till 6. In the harvest time they have 20 minutes in the forenoon, and 15 minutes in the afternoon.'* [Henley 1867]. Harvest days were extra long days – working often till dark.

Figure 84.   Metal bottles for carrying tea out to the fields.   Notice the sock and newspaper which helped to keep the tea warm.   (Mrs S. Armstrong,   The Armstrong Household and Farming Museum, North Charlton Farm, Alnwick).

The length of day and breaks varies a little in these personal accounts but the general routine is very similar.   The time of starting and stopping would be ruled to a certain extent by the daylight available.   Certainly winter days were shorter hence the reduction in the payment given to bondagers for their winter work.   Dinner hours were sometimes 1½ hours rather than two.   The Lilburn farm apprentice (see chapter 3) makes alterations in his diary about the dinner break – from 11.30am to 12 noon and starting again at 1.30pm and making this an hour-long rest.   [NRO 851].   Perhaps he was making allowance for the work of caring for the horses after their morning's work, which would take up some of the 1½ hour break.   Certainly the rest was for the horses not for the people although it did allow most workers time to go home for dinner.   This was an important point in the 1867 Royal Commission.   Mr. Henley reports *'The bulk of the evidence I have received does not bear out the opinion that fieldwork is one of the great causes of immorality.'*   One reason being that *'Women and children do not remain in the field (at mid-day rest) but return home together for their dinner.'*   [Henley 1867].

Nessie Burns (Interviewed in the Southern Reporter – Thursday 17 December 1998) started work, at 14, as a bondager in the 1930s.   *'I would walk to work in the morning to start at 8am, carrying a piece and a tin bottle with something to drink.   We would work until 11am, then would walk home again for dinner.   Then it was walk back to the farm to start again at 1pm and we worked until 5pm.'*

Mr. Henley in the 1867 Royal Commission reported that the dinner hour could be from 12 noon for 1½ hours (from work to work), or it could be 2 hours. They go and return in the masters' hours.   [Henley 1867].   In the 1893 Royal Commission Mr. Hindmarsh says, *"If my men and women are working 1½ miles from home my steward lets them off earlier. I say that walking means working."*   [Fox 1893].   Another variation given by Mr. Thompson, Chillingham Barns and Alan Scott, in 2006, was *'home in your own time and back in the bosses'.*

Evelyn Pendleton of Kirknewton remembers seeing bondagers sitting under the hedge at about 9 o'clock having their breakfast (second breakfast) when she was on her way to school.

They would chaff her about her white socks and new summer sandals and tell her she would make it rain!

Walter White writes in 1858) *'They work from six in the morning till six in the evening and during their dinner hour you may sometimes see them romping, but commonly they betake themselves to the nearest path or road-side and there lie down to look at the passers-by.'* [White 1859].

Another writer expands on this characteristic habit of the bondagers. He writes *'In fine weather, as you go along at noon, you find them lying in groups on the grassy borders of the high-road. The men you seldom or never see in such a place; they throw themselves down under a wall or hedge in the fields during their hour of rest after dinner; but the women get out whenever they can to the roadside. On asking a lady what was the reason of this, she replied, with a significant smile – "Female curiosity to be sure! The men are apathetic, and throw themselves down anywhere; but the women like to be where they have a chance of seeing what passes."* And no doubt this is the true solution of the mystery; for as you go by – though from their perfect stillness you might suppose them to be asleep – yet you generally catch the glitter of several eyes, peeping from beneath the apron or shawl that they have thrown over their heads.'* [Howitt 1856].

Beatrix Potter stayed at Lennel House, near Coldstream, in 1894 and wrote about the fieldworkers in her diary. On one particular day she and her father came across some workers near Wark Common. She noted they were on their way to work with the men in front forming one group, and the women walking behind forming another. The workers were very quiet before strangers but showed great curiosity. The women stared with gentle, benign interest rather in the way of cows. [Potter 1986].

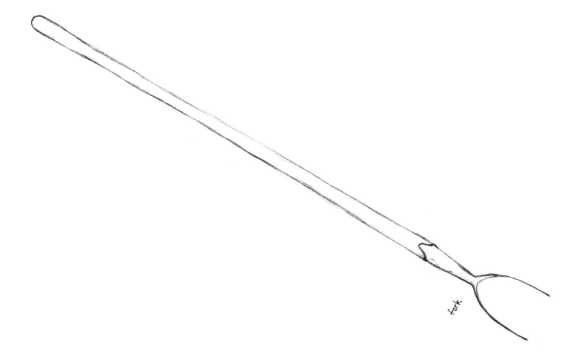

Figure 85. Fork. (Dinah Iredale)

Children

Children often worked on the land and were able in this way to earn something towards the family finances. This caused some concern and opinions were expressed through various commissions. School Log Books also noted absences due to fieldwork.

**Figure 86. Young bondagers helping to sort and weigh up potatoes.
(Mrs Catherine Johnston, Ladykirk).**

Wednesday 1 August 1894 near Swinton.

Beatrix Potter wrote in her diary that it was impossible to tell whether the bondager, in her all-encompassing costume, was young or old. Her father, passing a worker on the road, had called a greeting and had been very surprised to see, that the figure he had supposed a woman, was in fact a child. [Potter 1986]

Sir F. H. Doyle found in 1843 that children went out into the fields to work sometimes as young as 10 years old. The children usually work during the summer months and go back to school during the winter. [Doyle 1843]. John Fenwick Esq., of Netherton, said the children assist their mothers and earn 5d to 6d a day. He put the age for this as 12 or 13 and adds *'those of the pitmen much earlier'*. Messrs Hindmarsh, Nelson, etc., from Alnwick thought the age was more 11 to 12 and they *'earn from 4d to 6d a day'* Mr. Hindmarsh of West Horton near Wooler says *'The children go out occasionally at 12 or 13 and earn about 5d a day at first'*. Mr. Jobson, Practical Farmer, Chillingham writes he has 6 *'girls above 8 and under 16 years of age employed at light work such as collecting couch, weeding corn, hoeing corn, and turnips'*.

Later in 1867 George Lumsden, steward to Mr. Charles Rea, Doddington, reports that *'The youngest boy now working on this farm is 9 years of age. He is weeding potatoes.'* The other boys (3) *'are about two years older'*. *'The youngest girl is 11'*. *'He has never known any injury to be done to either women or children by field work.'*

Mr. Thomas Tait, shepherd at Paston and 70 years old said *'School in winter, work in summer, is what ought to be Boys and girls should go out to work at 10 years of age. The latter end of April to the fore part of May is the time that children come out to work upon the land. They do not go back to school till the potatoes are taken up.'* *'Most people wish to make their bairns as good scholars as they can afford; anyway it is a duty'*.

Emma Bell of Mindrum had *'seven children; they went to work at 10 years old'*. She said *'What would the poor do if they had seven or eight children and could not send the eldest to work to help the youngers, to pay for school and shoes; they could nae do.'* Anne Mills, wife of a hind, Downham Farm, Carham parish who *'has 10 children'*, had the opinion that *'No child should leave school for work before going on to 12.'*

Over the Border parents were also keen for their children to receive *'at least a little schooling'* and in some very remote areas families were known *'to unite in hiring a teacher for the winter half year'*. It is thought that this kind of arrangement had been made in the Breamish Valley in Northumberland. So winter was the time when most schooling took place for many children. Mr. Anthony Dagg, a shepherd at Linbriggs, valued education and *'about 20 years ago he hired a schoolmaster, and took a chance of getting other scholars'*. [Henley 1867]. There are a number of examples of education taking place in remote areas, in the report of the 1893 Royal Commission. A shepherd's daughter teaches *'at the end of the Cheviot Hills'* and *'at Langleeford, under the Cheviots, perhaps 10 or 12 children are taught in a shepherd's cottage by a lad who is boarded, and the other shepherds help to pay.'* [Fox 1893].

James Hogg, the Ettrick Shepherd, born 1770, started work herding cattle aged 8. For half a year's wages he got a pair of shoes and a ewe lamb, his first step to becoming a shepherd.

School Log Books gave various reasons for absence but many were due to the seasonal work on the farms. *'These books show that children were absent regularly each year for hay-making, potato-lifting, clipping, peat work, lambing, winter foddering, driving sheep, keeping house, beating for shooters, pig killings and for such reasons as illness, lack of boots, watching a ploughing match, floods, and being afraid of the bull. Country life and the needs of the farm had always overruled the teacher, whatever timetable he tried to enforce.'* [Robson 1984].

Branxton and Cornhill – School Log Book – 9 August 1901:

'Some of the children reminded me at the close of school today that their mothers wanted them at home or rather to carry food into the harvest field, and the parents had said "It was time they had their holidays now".'

It is easy to imagine the children anxiously plucking up the courage to give the message, as directed by their parents, and, at the last minute before going home, blurting out exactly what had been said at home!

Education Acts brought a more uniform level of education for all, whereas previously the provision for education was very ad hoc. The problem for children living in very scattered and remote farms was still very real and education was often missed when the weather dictated that a journey on foot of a few miles was just too much for a small child, or just plain foolhardy.

The Work Throughout the Year

Jean Willis describes the work of a bondager throughout the year:

The winter months with stock inside meant a lot of work. Cattle were fed on hay and turnips. The turnips had to be cut into slices and the turnip cutter required two workers *'One dropped the baggies into the (hopper) cutter and the other turned the handle.'* This was like an old – fashioned mangle with the large wheel and handle and a hopper like a very large mincer!

Hard work, as I know having done this kind of work after school and struggled through the cattle to their troughs as they eagerly sought the turnips. Jean talks about preparing 30 baskets or swills and feeding the cattle about 5pm using hurricane lamps.

Stock inside meant hemels to bed up with straw and, of course, lots of muck to deal with. Clearing muck was a big part of winter work – keeping the doors to the hemels clear of muck so they would shut and not break with the strain put on them by the growing manure in the hemel. Jean mentions *'glar'*- *'The glar (mud) came from the iron trimmed wheels'* or *'from the straw'* and was scraped from the yard using a harl – which was a *'long handled tool with a flat blade, which clanked'*. *'The glar was cleared into heaps to be led back into the fields.'*

The men at this time were ploughing or feeding the cattle and sheep outside. Many teams of horses were needed to plough a field which, these days, can be ploughed by one man, a large tractor and a large plough in four hours. The gentleman who mentioned this remembered seeing teams of horses ploughing on Whitsunbank at Wooler. The work would go on for days.

Another winter job was mending pokes (bags or sacks) with large packing needles – twice the size of darning needles. The sacks were *'hung on hemp rope lines to keep them clear of mice and rats'*. Dirty sacks were washed in the horse trow (trough) which then had to be *'scrubbed out or the horses would not drink from it'*. Chaff sheets, were made by sewing two sacks (opened out) side by side.

Threshing was another winter occupation. There might be a *'built in thrasher'* or a machine might visit the farm.

Figure 87. Threshing Day.

'The women got one of three jobs to do. Either they had to stand on top of the thrasher and cut the bands on the sheaves of corn, to let the thrasher man feed the sheaves in slowly as the thrasher would not do the job properly' if the sheaves went in too quickly. *'Then the drum affair shook the corn from the stalks, the corn went one way, the straw (stalks without the corn) went another, the small corn and dirt another and the chaff (husks) another.'* The other two jobs were carrying straw or carrying chaff. The chaff mostly went to the hemels but some was used as mattress filling.

The work continued for days because the corn in the granary in *'mountainous heaps'* had to be turned by the women to help dry it and prevent mildew. After that it was dytered or cleaned. The dyter was a large wooden box 4ft high x 6ft wide with riddles. *'there was a handle attached that turned to make the riddles shake'* and so removed dust, dirt and annes. Annes were the *'spiky things on the ears of corn'*. *'The person filling the dyter had to measure the corn with a bushel. This was a large round wooden box with two handles when it was full a stick was rolled over the top to make a level bushel and tally (weight and quantity) were marked down.'*

Earlier, measuring quantities was difficult because different areas had different standards so that even using the same term might still mean you were talking about different amounts. John Bailey and George Culley spoke about this in their report of 1794 where they said *'Weights and Measures are in a sad state of confusion: a pound, a stone, a bushel, a boll, are rarely the same in different markets, and frequently vary in the same market for different articles.'* Later they state that *'The Board of agriculture could not do the public a greater service, than by bringing forward a regulation of weights and measures. One weight, and one measure, derived from the same root, and increasing or decreasing in a ten-fold ratio, would introduce simplicity, ease, and perspicuity, into all transactions of business (where calculations are necessary), as would prevent the numberless mistakes and errors which are daily happening.'* [Bailey 1972].

Jean Willis recalls that 20 stone bags (approx a hundred kilos) were loaded by men onto carts to go to the station, and Jean Kinghorn mentioned that there were 4 bushels for a bag of 18 stones. Grain when measured in bushels is complex because a bushel of wheat is heavier than a bushel of barley and oats are the lightest of all. Moisture content could also affect the weight of a sack of grain. Generally, two women working together filled the bag using a bushel measure, and a man carried these sacks after the two women had lifted it up for him. [Kinghorn 1999]. The 1867 Royal Commission reported that the women *'can vie with the men in carrying sacks of corn'* and that they *'carry upstairs to the granary 8 stone of wheat, 8 stone of barley and 9 stone of oats.'* [Henley 1867]. These weights are considerably less than those of 12 stone, 16 stone, 18 stone and 20 stone already mentioned. Jean Willis said that corn went away to the station about every week, so this measuring, lifting and carrying was constantly undertaken.

Another cold winter job was sorting potatoes. They were *'whaled and sorted'*. *'The whale was a machine to help sort potatoes. It was a griddle (riddle) with large and small holes. One person filled the griddle and the second shook it and watched for rotten ones.'*

A little later in March mangolds were cleaned for the lambing ewes which meant getting them out of the pit where the mangolds had been stored (just the same as potatoes) and then they were topped and tailed.

Picking stones off the fields was another important job as this prevented damage to the reaper or binder blades. Stones were carried in a bucket or sling made of a bag (with one corner pushed into the other and then fastened round the woman's neck) and left in heaps to be collected by horse and cart. Big stones were broken with a hammer. Stones were used to level up gateways to stop accidents to carts or animals.

Figure 88. Bondagers and Hinds at West Fenton, Wooler. The women are carrying geebolds or whankies which were long handled sickles. These were used to cut down thistles. (Johnny Moore, Wooler).

Jean Willis mentions April and May being a time for cutting thistles in the growing corn and, the ubiquitous mucking out and muck spreading. Potatoes were planted and she comments *'Who planted the potatoes? Bondagers of course!'* Hedge trimmings were tidied up and burnt and hen houses cleaned out at this time.

June and July was very much the time for making hay but there were also turnips, bagies and mangolds to single. Jean said this was one or two weeks' work but sometimes more.

Figure 89. Workers singling at Scremerston.

Later these crops had to be hoed to rid them of weeds and the potatoes also had to be hoed to remove weeds. The grass was cut, to make hay, using two horses pulling a reaper. The hay was turned to help dry it and then when dry enough it was made into kyles (small heaps). These kyles were raked smooth to *'let the rain run off'*.

John Bailey and George Culley detail how hay is gathered and the methods are very interesting but very risky. *'For the purpose of drawing it (the hay) together to be put into pikes, or ricklets, it is either cocked or put into large heaps, which are trailed in by one horse, yoked to the ends of a large rope put round the bottoms of those cocks or heaps; upon the hind part of which a boy gets with his feet, to keep it down, and prevent its slipping over the top of the hay; when arrived at the place wanted, one end of rope is taken off the hook at the horse's shoulder, and being thus loosened at one end, the horse moves forward, when the rope draws through under the hay, and leaves it.*

Figure 90. Building Pikes – The man at the front is using his weight to help gather a kyle. The horse and rope will pull the kyle to the pike. (Anne & Derek Fairnington, Wooler)

When the hay is neither put into cocks nor large heaps, but remains in a thick row, it is then necessary to use two horses, viz. one yoked to each end of a strong sweeping rope, and two persons to get upon the rope with their feet, one on each side of the row, who rest with their arm upon the hay, and step forward on the rope as the hay gathers. To prevent the hay from slipping off behind, a small cord is fastened to the hind part of the sweeping rope, and extended to each person's hand, which they let out as they step forward, or find otherwise necessary. By either of the above modes, the hay grown upon a field of eight or ten acres may be drawn together in a few hours, and is much more expeditious than either sledges or carts.' [Bailey 1972].

Miss R. E. Bosanquet and Mrs Handyside remember that *'When most of us were children the kiles of hay used to be drawn together by two horses with a rope between them, and the heaviest man, and all the children riding on the hay; there was a delicious fear that next moment might land us all in a heap amongst the great horse hoofs, but it never did, the heaviest man was always able to keep us safe.* [Bosanquet 1989]. Jean Willis, writing about the early 20th century, mentioned how hay was gathered, by sledge and the hay rake, to make pikes, which were large heaps. A number of people mentioned the implement 'tumbling tam' which was also used to gather hay. Mr. Jim Mallen from Yetholm describes 'tumbling tam' in the following way. It was a wooden implement with wooden tines to scoop up a kyle and it was pulled by a horse. When the 'scooped up' kyle was close to the place where the pike or ruck was to be built the operator tipped up 'tumbling tam' by the handles. The implement went right over, 'tumbled' right over and then it was ready to collect the next kyle. The rounded handles helped with this tumbling action.

The bondagers helped the men to make these pikes. The pikes were raked down and the *'bottom pulled out to help the hay to settle and to stop the wet getting in from the bottom'*. After this they were roped down. *'The ropes used were made of hay that had been pulled out of the bottom of the pikes. You twisted a little bit of hay on a fork then you kept up the same motion on top of the pile of hay till the rope was twisted. They had to be tied in tight and the end of the rope was then pushed into the hay.'* There were two ropes per pike. The photograph used as the cover of *'Herrings and Hiring Fairs'* by Maureen Brook shows a completed pike with a man twisting out a rope from the pike. Just off the picture to the right someone is twisting the hay with a hay rake – the wooden crosspiece and teeth are just visible. Rope making was an important skill and more about this will be included later.

The bogie is mentioned by many people and Ada Mary Howarth, in *'Life in a Scottish Border Farmhouse in the Twenties and Thirties,'* includes a picture from a catalogue and gives the dimensions as 10ft x 8ft wide. [Howarth 1998]. A bogie first appeared in 1887 at the Royal show at Newcastle.

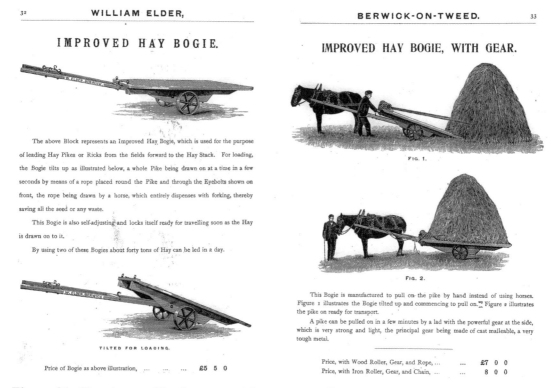

Figure 91. Two types of bogie – one with gear, to pull the pike onto the bogie, and one without which would require a second horse and a rope. (W. Elder catalogue, late 19th Century).

John Bailey and George Culley describe a method of moving a pike before bogies were introduced. *'When the large stack is made in the field, the "pikes" are drawn to it, by putting a strong rope round the bottom, the two ends of which are fastened to the hind part of a cart, in which are yoked three or four horses. This saves the trouble of forking and loading them in carts, and is done in much less time.'* [Bailey 1972]. Mrs Hetha Bruce of Lowick liked moving the pikes using the bogie. A horse towed the bogie, which is low and would tip up. Another spare horse was used to take the pike onto the bogie. This spare horse had a rope attached and this rope was taken around the pike and then used to pull the pike onto the tipped up bogie.

Jean Willis comments that when stacking hay in a building *'up to the rafters'* it was *'very hot for the women up next to the roof'*.

Mrs Isabel Barrie of Milfield said it was important to work as a team when stacking either hay or corn. Passing on a sheaf of corn or forkful of hay at the right moment for the stacker and not just tossing them forward without thought. Some Land Army girls did this till they got the hang of it. There had to be a rhythm to the work.

She remembered stacking with a rather grumpy, silent man who forked up regardless of the speed she, as stack header, could pass it on to the stacker – even prodding her with the fork at times. The stacker said the way to put him in his place was to just shuffle any excess hay onto the floor, just push it off unobtrusively with your feet. This was to teach him to slow down and work in rhythm with the other two workers. No one would want to fork the hay up more than once!

**Figure 92. Workers stacking hay or straw in the stack yard at Way-to-Wooler Farm.
(Mrs Craigie, Wooler).**

Another ingenious device used at hay time was the hay pole. This was used, as the stack grew too tall to just fork the hay up. This seems to have been quite a difficult piece of apparatus to position. Jean Willis said *'It took a lot of man power and strength to manoeuvre into position.'* The ropes, which had been used to help guide the pole into the hole in the ground, were pegged down. A metal grab was attached and it was *'worked by a horse roped to a swingle-bar'*. About half a pike could be lifted up onto the stack.

Figure 93. The hay pole in use. Notice the large stack and the bogies.

Bondagers were up on the stack to help the stacker. The hay had to be spread evenly as a lopsided stack could fall over. When the stack was complete the bottom was pulled out and ropes were made to tie it down. About 100 ropes to each stack and as the stack settled the ropes had to be tightened (re-tied). Jean Willis said about tying down *'you went along and about halfway up the stack you pushed your hand into the firm hay and pulled a handful and tied the rope to that'*.

August for Jean Willis was *'corn time'*. When cutting the corn by binder the field had to be opened up. The *'dyke back'* was cut by men, with scythes, so the binder and horses could get in, without trampling good corn. This corn was gathered up into sheaves by the bondagers. They tied them with straw twisted into a rope and fastened round the sheaf. Once the binder was working the sheaves had to be stooked. It was important to get them at the correct angle so the sun could reach all sides through the day. The bondagers took care to get the stooking right as it was often a wet miserable job to put stooks up again if they had fallen down. (Rainwater sprayed up from the stubble stalks and the sheaves themselves could be soaking wet.) After such a miserable experience *'They used to say they were soaked to the bum (or words meaning that)'*. The stooks were led on large carts which were extended by the addition of a harvest frame. *'The bondagers forked sheaves on to the cart for the men to load.'* This was the usual working arrangement. Mr. Mallen from Yetholm confirmed this was usually the way the men and women worked together.

**Figure 94. Mrs Janet Tait on a load of corn with the little boy George Dougal and
Jim the horse. (Mr. W. Tait, Duns).**

However, Jean Willis also said *'Sometimes they (the bondagers) even loaded and drove
carts'*. There is a photograph (1940 approx.) of Mrs Janet Tait which shows her loading a cart
with a man forking up to her. In the 1867 Royal Commission many contributors thought
women should not drive or lead horses but the women said *'We fight to drive carts, it is easier
work than loading.'* [Henley 1867].   Mary Black in the 1893 Royal Commission said
'Forking up corn is hard work, and they feel it in their sides next day.' [Fox 1893].

In the stackyard the bondager was usually the stack-header or striddler which entailed
standing on the edge of the stack, catching the sheaves and handing them on to the stacker.
Mrs. Mallen of Yetholm said when *'striddling'* it was important to pass the sheaf head first to
the stacker not foot first. The *'foot'* or stalk end was liable to scratch the stacker. Jean Willis
also gives details about stacking. She says that the head of the sheaf was stacked pointing
inwards in order to be kept dry. *'When the stack got to the easing, the point where the roof of
the stack begins, the middle of the stack is filled with extra sheaves'*. This ensures that the
roof is constructed at a suitable angle. The stack was thatched and sometimes *'a figure in the
shape of a cockerel would be mounted on the top'*. *'The farmer nearly always threshed some
of the corn stacks at this time as it saved having to thatch them, and also gave straw to thatch
the seed corn stacks that were kept for spring.'* *'Most farmers also liked chaff poured down
first in the fad or hemel.'* This chaff made the manure more easily lifted in the spring. The
stacks once thatched were clipped to tidy them, and roped down.

**Figure 95. Model Stacks showing the thatching, ropes and corn dollies.
(Mrs Maisie Campbell, Wooler).**

George Mole (1923-1988) says *'Stacking, like many other jobs on the farm, was an art, with a right way and a wrong way of doing it. It gave the farm worker some considerable pleasure and satisfaction to see very tidy, upright, and smart looking corn stacks when the job was completed. Much of the credit for my first stack (Harvest at Nesbit near Fenton, Wooler in 1943) must go to Miss Meg Lea, the woman who was on the stack with me until very near the top, when the final sheaves were tied in.'* [Mole 2002]. Joan Pringle, a Land Army girl at Fenton near Wooler during the Second World War, admits that her first attempt at stacking ended with a stack that needed a prop to hold it upright but it still had a corn dolly on the top!

The work continued with potato picking, pulling turnips, mangolds and then bagies. Minnie Bell particularly disliked potato picking because she says *'I'd a long back'* and all that bending did not suit her. [Bell].

**Figure 96. Workers lifting turnips. Notice the shawing hooks.
(Mrs Catherine Johnston, Ladykirk).**

Figure 97. Workers sorting potatoes.

November and December meant the cattle were once more back in the fads and had to be fed twice a day and of course bedded and mucked out. The additional work running up to Christmas was the plucking of turkeys, geese, ducks and chickens.

Straw rope making was another task undertaken on a wet day or during the winter. Many ropes were needed and new ones made to replace old worn out ropes. John Dixon, Wooler, gave details, even including a little sketch, about this process of rope making. The sketch shows a straw rope maker, which had a number of local names.

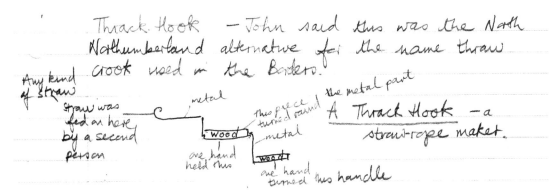

Figure 98. John Dixon's sketch of a Thrack Hook.

In East Lothian, where I first saw a straw rope maker in the 1970s, it was called a thraw-crook but in Northumberland Tom Wilson of Wooler called it a thrack-hook and Margaret Marshall called it a wylie. The technique was the same – straw was fed on to the hook by one person and the other turned the handle which twisted the straw into a rope whilst at the same time moving back as the rope grew in length. Straw rope makers varied in style and there were even double ones with two hooks.

Bill Davidson of Duddo remembered stacks tied down with straw ropes. These ropes were put on the stack so they crossed diagonally to keep the thatch secure. He also remembered the pride taken in making a good stack. One steward, he says, at Crookham Westfield Farm, went round the stacks of corn shearing back any stalks that stuck out making the stacks look ragged. This steward, Bill said, was a perfectionist and as the stacks were by the roadside to Cornhill he did not want anyone to go by and say his stacks were less than perfect. This was a common comment about stacking and photographs show some beautiful stacks.

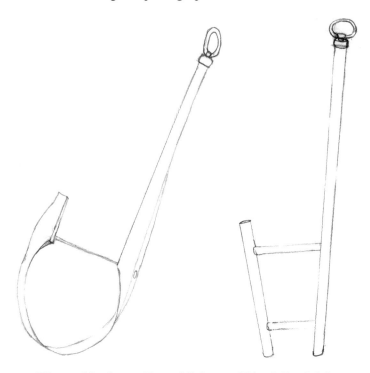

Figure 99. Straw Rope Makers. (Dinah Iredale)

Figure 100. Well-made stacks on the Way-to-Wooler Farm. The stacker is wearing protection for his knees. (Mrs Craigie, Wooler).

Threshing machines were one of the earliest forms of mechanization on the farm and they made a big difference – particularly in the use of manpower. Previously, threshing had been undertaken by men using flails which required greater man power, and so the work was more spread out through the winter months. Andrew Meikle of East Lothian introduced his *'perfected' 'threshing mill'* in 1788. The power for this machine could be either horsepower in a gin-gang (the horse walked round and round turning the mechanism for the mill) or a waterwheel. Hastings Neville wrote about the threshing mills and quotes from the 1794 report by John Bailey and George Culley, saying that *'Threshing machines were first adopted in Northumberland in 1763.'* One of the first to install a machine was a Mr. Oxley at East Flodden. Hastings Neville also noted that *'There is still a building in our village (Ford), now a joiner's shop, which was allowed to be the thrashing floor of the villagers'.* [Neville 1909].

Accidents

In 1790 in the Burial Register of St. Mary's Church Belford there is a note which is in addition to the usual entries. *'Several Threshing Machines during this and the last two or three years have been erected in this and neighbouring parish. Muckle an ingenious mechanic from Scotland who built Waren Mill about 6 or 7 years ago was (if not the original inventor) the first that brought them to any degree of perfection. Improvements I am told have been made upon his plan by Mr. Bailey of Chillingham and Mr. Raistrick of Morpeth. The contrivance is very ingenious, but threatens to hurt the poor; three or four men or women in this way being able to thresh as much corn as twelve in the common way.'* So the skilled worker with the flail was becoming redundant but it was a gradual change. Hastings Neville could say *'Some of the best of these men continued their use of the flail for some time after the threshing machines were generally used'.*

There is a sad entry in the same Belford Burial Register for 1798. *'Margaret Mather, of Fenwick East Steads in the parish of Kyloe – Daughter of Andrew Mather, Hind and Margaret his wife (late Reed) Died 9 April - Buried 11 April – 8 years Kill'd by a threshing machine.'*

Accidents did happen in agriculture where serious injury or death occurred.

Jane Glass talking to Alnwick Local History Society in May 1999 mentions another accident with a threshing machine. *'A young girl of 15 named Isabella Clark was working at a threshing machine when she opened the hatch, fell in and was crushed. She subsequently died of her injuries and was buried at Doddington.'*

Another accident with a threshing machine or mill was recorded in the Berwick Advertiser 23 March 1844 at Lamberton near Berwick. Again a girl is injured but on this occasion escapes death.

ACCIDENT. On Wednesday morning, about eight o'clock, Robert Johnston, steward to Mr. Eliot, Lamberton, went in to mend the belt of the threshing mill, accompanied by a young woman of the name of Ellen Yule, daughter of James Yule, hind at Lamberton, who was holding a light. Johnston came out to give some necessary orders, at same time desiring her to remain until he returned. The engineman, meanwhile, set the engine agoing, and the young woman, being afraid to remain, attempted to get over the wheels, which caught hold of her clothes, and she was drawn in amongst the machinery. An alarm was immediately given, the engine stopped, and she was extricated from the machinery, with her clothes literally torn to pieces. Fortunately one of the wheels broke, and to this circumstance the preservation of her life in all probability may be ascribed. Medical aid was immediately procured; and although much bruised, she seems now in a fair way of recovery.

Figure 101. Accident at Lamberton. Berwick Advertiser, 23 March 1844.

Tragedy was also occasionally reported after a hiring fair. In the Berwick Advertiser (10 March 1899) the death of Robert Aitchison was reported. He had attended the hiring fair from Milne Graden West Mains and was later found drowned in the Tweed. The farmer William Mather said Robert was a sober hard working man of 68 who was staying on. The inquest into his death appears in the Berwick Advertiser of 10 March 1899, where an open verdict of found drowned was returned. The report of the inquest shows a thorough examination of all the evidence, but the mystery remained of what Robert had done after he had left the White Horse at 5.20 pm.

SAD DEATH OF A FARM SERVANT

DROWNED AFTER THE HIRING MARKET.

On Monday evening an inquest was held in the Board Room of the Workhouse at Berwick before Mr W. Weatherhead, borough coroner, and a jury, touching the death of Robert Aitchison, farm servant, belonging to Milne Graden West Mains, whose dead body was on the Shad at Berwick that morning. The following was the evidence adduced:

William Mather, farmer, Milne Graden West Mains, said—The body viewed by the Coroner and Jury is that of Robert Aitchison agricultural labourer, aged 68 years. I believe. He worked with me and left Milne Graden West Mains on Saturday morning last to attend the hiring market at Berwick. Deceased was a sober industrious man. He was not leaving my employment.

Catherine ...., wife of Peter Robson, innkeeper, Castlegate, Berwick, said—The back door of our house the White Horse Inn—opens almost immediately opposite the Station gates. I have known the deceased for many years. When he came into the town on Saturday morning a little after nine o'clock, he called at our house. He only stayed a few minutes. Deceased returned again about five o'clock in the afternoon. He had evidently had some drink, and appeared dazed. He asked me for a half a glass of whiskey, but I refused to serve him. He sat down in the parlour, and about twenty minutes past five I told him it was time to go to catch the train, which left at twenty past five. Deceased left by the back door, and went in the direction of the station. He did not buy a bottle of whiskey in my house. There was nobody in his company in the afternoon.

Robert Henderson, labourer, Berwick, said— About ten o'clock this morning I was walking on the Walls, and when near Bay View House, a man named John Byrne whom I met said there was a body lying on the Shad. I looked over the Walls towards the Shad and saw a man's body in the water. I went down to the riverside at the Shad and found the body of deceased in the river about ten yards from the shore. The body was lying face downwards. The tide was ebbing at the time. The police ambulance was sent for and the body was taken out of the river and conveyed to the Workhouse. There was no hat on the head of deceased.

Sergeant Tough said—I assisted this morning to convey the body of the deceased from the Shad to the Workhouse. I afterwards searched the clothing of deceased, and in the

left pocket of the vest found a watch attached to a chain fastened to a button hole. The watch had stopped at 2.23. In the left pocket of the trousers I found a leather purse containing 16s 6d in silver, and loose in the right hand pocket there was threepence in copper. In the same pocket there were two pocket knives. I also found in the purse half of a return ticket from Tweedmouth to Twizel dated 4th March inst.; also a single ticket from Berwick to Tweedmouth dated the 4th inst. Deceased had a topcoat on. In the inside pocket of his coat I found a pint bottle full of whiskey. The cork had not been drawn. The body was fully clothed, but the hat was amissing. I was present when the body was put on the ambulance. The skirts of the overcoat were turned over the head, which was quite hid. Enquiries have been made, but no trace of deceased can be discovered after he left the White Horse Inn.

Dr George Alexander Dickson presently acting as "locum tenens" for Dr Maclagan, said— I examined the body of the deceased in the Workhouse to-day. I found no marks of violence. I found the skin over the nose, cheeks, eye brows and forehead had been grazed by the action of sand or gravel. These marks were "post mortem". The "post mortem" lividity was slight, but rigidity was well marked all over the body. The skin had the roughened appearance usually seen in cases of drowning. The hands were clenched and had a bluish grey colour, and the nails contained sand. In my opinion death was caused by drowning. There are no appearances of any violence having been used against deceased. I think life had been extinct from 36 to 48 hours.

The Coroner briefly reviewed the evidence and said the doctor told them no violence had been used against deceased, and all his property had been found in his possession. It was clear after leaving the White Horse that deceased had gone to the station, because he had a third class railway ticket dated Saturday from Berwick to Tweedmouth, and also a return half ticket from Tweedmouth to Twizel which was the station for Milne Graden. Therefore, there was no doubt when deceased left the White Horse he had gone to the station and had purchased the ticket. At least everything pointed to that. He might have purchased the ticket earlier in the day, but that was not very probable. It was quite clear deceased did not get into the Kelso train because these tickets were found in his possession, and no more was known of him. It was a mere matter of speculation where the deceased went after he left the White Horse. He might have missed his train and gone to sleep somewhere, and on awaking wandered to the New Road or the Quay or anywhere. However, that was mere speculation.

An open verdict of found drowned was returned.

Figure 102. Drowned after the Hiring Market. Berwick Advertiser, 10 March 1899

The report of the inquest is very lengthy and this suggests that such an occurrence is rare and the newspaper made a feature of the tragedy. We learn that Robert had not been attacked or robbed. He had purchased a railway ticket, for his homeward journey, to Twizel Station but had somehow got into a situation which led to him drowning in the River Tweed. There is no mention of Robert's family, but perhaps in the background are the women who rely on Robert as the householder to provide a home for them. Perhaps there is a daughter still at home who works as a bondager although by this time she would, officially, be called a woman worker. At sixty eight, he must have been getting to the end of his working life with all the uncertainties of a period when there was little or no help for the old and often the only place left to them was the poor house.

Other More Recent Accidents

Mary Anderson from Yetholm recounts two accidents that she remembers, one involving herself, and one involving a friend.

She remembers Sir Alfred Goodson of Kilham being very angry over an incident with a hay bogie. Mary was stealing a ride, a treat many children enjoyed, and she fell off and got her foot caught in a rope. She did not want to call out because the man driving the bogie would really tell her off as riding on the bogie was strictly forbidden. Luckily, she managed to get herself free.

Another accident, again when she was young, was with a reaper. She and her friend were in the hay field and too close to the reaper driven by Mary's brother. Her friend stepped out of the way, but the wrong way, and was badly cut by the reaper. Mary's brother tied up the injured ankle and carried the child home (quite some distance) from where she was rushed to hospital. Luckily the surgeon was able to save her foot. Mary's brother always remarked with amazement that the horses had stayed where he had left them – they had not moved at all.

Walter A. Ramage in *'An Auld Herd's Memories'* recounts an accident he had when carting hay from Ruletownhead to Hownam. *'I got a bit of a fright when I went in for the next load. I got yoked up and made off to climb Swinnie Heights when about a mile along the road, there was a tree with its branches hanging out which caught on the front of the cart and it gave such a tug it lifted the front of the cart up. The belly-band broke and the cart lifted the horse up in the air. He was hanging by the shoulder chains which were choking him when he gave one great loup and down he came with both trams (cart shafts) broken right off and the hay and cart upside down. I just had to go back to the farm and get another cart and the men to come and load the hay for me. It was pretty late or I got home that night.'*

George Mole also experiences an accident, which stays in his memory. *'Nearly every year someone would have what was called a "couped load" and it happened to me at Fenton (near Wooler). After loading the sheaves high on your cart, you set off for the stack or stackyard, sitting high up on the front of the loaded cart, driving your horse. Everything would be going fine then, all of a sudden, you would find yourself yards away from the horse and cart, with sheaves of corn all around you. The horse was down on its side between the shafts of the cart and all the ropes broken. All the nearby workers come running across and got the horse free first, then put the cart back on to its wheels. After checking that the horse was okay and not injured, and that the cart wasn't broken they finally turned to me to ask if I was okay.'* [Mole 2002].

The final account of an accident is by Greta Elliot:

'When Greta's mother was 14 (in about 1914) she went out in the fields with her sister who was five years older cutting thistles before they had a chance to seed. This was Greta's aunt Lizzie. Greta's grandfather had died at 36 so her grandmother had to work as did Aunt Lizzie as she grew up. She was a bondager and wore the traditional dress including a large straw hat, a watch on a chain, metal stays and metal toe caps in her boots. There was a huge storm and the two girls sheltered under a tree. There was a flash and the tree was split from top to bottom and had a large chunk missing. Aunt Lizzie was struck and fell to the ground unconscious. The straw hat was never found, the watch was broken in pieces and burnt, the leather of her boots had gone and only the metal plates remained. Lizzie's clothes had been torn off. Greta's poor mother ran home to raise the alarm shouting 'Lizzie is dead, Lizzie is

dead'. She had to be carried home on a gate and was unconscious for three weeks. She was burned on the chest from the metal stays and watch chain and on her feet. The doctor said that she would not have survived if she had not been well fed and with a strong constitution.'

The result of this accident was that Greta's mother *'was petrified by storms'* and *'would hide in a cupboard in an empty bedroom'*. Lizzie, who *'remembered nothing'*, did not fear storms and it was she who met the children from school on stormy days.

Due to an exceptionally violent storm in 1932 which resulted in the death of three cattle near Kypie, 2 horses at Howtel and 5 sheep at Crookhouse, the children sheltered in the Keeper's Cottage which was half way between Howtel and Kypie. From here *'they saw Aunt Lizzie coming down the road from Kypie calmly carrying an umbrella!'* [Sharpe 2007].

Hierarchy

Farm workers worked within a hierarchy.

Andrew Purves in *'A Shepherd Remembers'* gives a detailed description of the various types of farmers from large land owners to the more modest owners, and finally, the smallest landowners and tenant farmers large and small. After this came the farm steward who, depending on the size of the farm, took responsibility in varying degrees for the day to day running of the farm. The shepherd was an independent worker often working away from the farmstead and needing to use his own initiative and take full responsibility for the sheep, which usually included his own pack.

The steward, grieve or manager organised the day's work from strategies he had planned with the farmer or sometimes he had sole responsibility. Beneath him would be a ploughman steward or a first ploughman, who could deputise for him if necessary. Other workers would be the hinds, the cattleman and the halflings, turnip dick or odd laddies. The steward was also in charge of the women workers who were led by a first woman or forewoman. Sometimes there would be a second woman to help or deputise for the first woman. Mrs Violet Brown mentioned that her brother's wife was a bondager at East Lilburn. She was first woman and her sister was second woman.

Those taking extra responsibility were paid a little extra and this included the cattleman for his extra work at weekends. Mary King says her father, as first ploughman, got a little extra *'maybe a shillin' or twae a week'* and *'when the work began my father would lead the wey'*. [MacDougall 2000].

The first woman had to make sure the bondagers were smartly turned-out, and would send a bondager home to smarten-up if necessary. Mrs Mona Thompson of Wooler said *'We turned ourselves out very well, at least on a Monday morning'*. The first woman also ensured good time-keeping, set the pace of work, and decided when breaks were taken. Mrs Sally Dunn, Seton Hall, Berwick, said she did not carry a watch but the first woman did.

Mr. William Tait of Duns said his wife Janet worked at Marygold near Duns and eventually became the forewoman and had a dozen people working under her.

Minnie Bell, who worked at Sisterpath near Marchmont in the Scottish Borders, loved singing turnips and particularly liked it when she was fore-woman and led the team. [Bell].

Mrs Gladys Mole and her sister Mrs Nan Watson tell how when the first woman was getting on a bit, and could no longer keep up a good pace, the other bondagers would quietly step across and do a bit of her row. Gladys and Nan worked in one of the cooperative stores in Wooler as office worker and cashier and both married farm workers.

Mr. Bill Davidson of Duddo remembered that when work such as singling was going on there would be quite a lot of conversation among the workers. The men might talk about football but the conversation could be much deeper and quite philosophical in nature.

Mr. William Tait of Duns commented, on the well-known Kirknewton photograph of bondagers, that 'the boss or steward is in the middle and the workers did not stretch across the field but were *'boxed'*. Each did a row, but stayed close together. He said the women were paid less but they led the field.

Mr. Jim Mallen of Yetholm did not recognise the *'boxed'* method of working but felt the photograph of the workers at Scremerston was more representative of the way he remembers working. He, like Mr. Tait, said the women led the field. The men always worked behind the women. This was the custom and no man passed the women. As a very young man he and another young man had raced ahead and got a good telling off. He said the women could be nasty if you stepped out of line. He also said that he and his friend may have had a laugh about it later but it was a serious telling off. Later, he said, he and his friend might try it on a bit just to get a reaction – taking a rise out of the women!

Mrs Margie Dixon of Wooler remembers working in this *'boxed'* pattern with the steward coming up behind the workers where he supervised and helped (Mr. Mallen said the steward would take out any doubles – take them down to a single plant). Margie, who worked on the land but did not dress as a bondager, also remembers that if the younger girls, like herself, chatted too much he'd say *'Come on lasses, down to work!'* Glen Aln recalls another steward who would say stop your *'havering'* if *'the bondagers were enjoying themselves and laughing heartily'* [Aln 1944].

Discipline was obviously needed at times but this was understood and it was also appreciated that the steward would always do some hoeing or singling to help the youngsters keep up. Sometimes two young girls worked together on one row until they had acquired more skill. Another way of helping a young unskilled girl was to let her work both ways on one row – doing what she had not managed to do one way on the return journey. This ensured the gang stayed together. Margie said young lads were treated in the same way as they learnt the job.

Mrs Violet Smith of Wooler mentioned that older bondagers would work a bit of the younger bondager's row so, although slow, the younger bondagers could stay in the group and not get left behind. It was a lovely gesture and much appreciated by Violet and Mona (Mrs Mona Thompson of Wooler). They said, *'It was lovely to come to a stretch of row already done!'* Mr. Alan Scott said the pace of work had to be one that could be kept up all day. *'We kept together. If one worker raced ahead the farmer might expect everyone to work as quickly! It would become too exhausting.'*

Mrs Mary Anderson of Yetholm, who was born in 1928, worked on the land but did not dress as a bondager. Her sister who was 13½ years older than Mary did dress as a bondager. Mary remembers that there was sometimes a bit of sly banter about the first woman. Whilst singling turnips the other workers remarked, as the first woman pulled away ahead, *'Take no notice of her, she's mad!'* Mary remembers the workers in the turnip field would be arranged as follows – first woman (sometimes forging away ahead) second woman (Mary's sister) keeping up a good pace, then Mary (quite slowly) and then the men. When Mary felt the men put on a spurt and catch up with her, close enough to jostle her, she'd ask *'Where is he?'* meaning the boss must be somewhere about or they would not be hurrying. Sure enough the boss would be coming over the field!

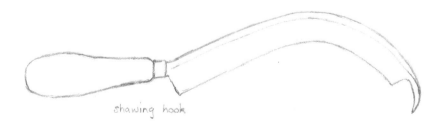

Figure 103. Shawing Hook for lifting turnips. (Dinah Iredale)

Appendix to Chapter 10. Harvesting.

The corn harvest was critically important, so the problems of cutting corn efficiently and quickly, naturally stimulated new ideas.

The very early tool was the toothed hook. Using this involved bending, grasping the corn stems and using a sawing action to cut them. The scythe hook followed the toothed hook and working with it involved a more slashing motion. This was not favoured by some farmers, who felt very strongly, that the toothed hook or heuk was the better tool. Both these tools were used by men and women. T.M. Devine notes that women were considered to be *'physiologically better adapted to bending than men'*. [Devine 1984 chap 6].

The scythe needed a larger, more sweeping, cutting motion and was used initially for cutting grass and only later for cutting corn. Generally this was a tool used by men only as they had the necessary upper body strength.

The reaper (1850 onwards) with sails was the first successful horse-drawn method of cutting corn. This made cutting the corn considerably more speedy but binding the sheaves was still by hand.

The binder was the next step – a reaper with a means of gathering the corn into bundles which were then tied and thrown down ready for stooking. The binder, which is within my memory, was an excellent machine when working well. The satisfying clicking and clacking of the tying mechanism was very audible and reassured that all was well.

Finally, the combine harvester came along and encompassed the work of binder and thresher.

The Lilburn farm apprentice (1842) comments on skills in the harvest field. He records that there could be 160 workers in one field and these were arranged in working teams of 6 people per rig *'with one bandwind'*. The bandwind – bound *'the corn and set it up'*. He notes that women shear as much as the men. [NRO 851].

Another apprentice is observing work at Barnhill near Elgin. He again notes the skills required to organise groups of workers into working teams and numbers them as 144 shearers and 24 bindsters. He also notes three-fourths of the shearers are women and that they *'are our neatest cutters'*. [Howatson 1984].

Hastings Neville wrote in great detail about harvesting the corn. He details how the *'bindster, who followed the shearers, was supplied with bands by one of the women, who, as she reaped, would every now and then make a band, and throw it down for him. The band was quickly made, by giving the handful of corn a double twist near the head; and woe to the woman who only made one twist, and supplied "slipped" bands.'*

He also mentioned how strife could arise in the field and this struggle was called "kemping'. *'At first it looks a peaceful contest enough, the golden heads of corn make neither attack nor defence, but they fall as the reapers evenly advance, and the width of stubble gradually but surely widens. It is a wonderful scene of well-organized labour, and harmony and good nature reign throughout the field. But some young man, fond of a joke, has cast a firebrand of mischief among the workers. He has suggested to the shearers at the end of the line furthest from where he works, that the women at his rig intend to run them hard, and outstrip them in the work; and coming back to his own place, tells the women for whom he binds, that those at the other end are preparing to outdo them. Angry and suspicious looks are quickly cast across the field, and in a few moments the real battle has begun. All the shearers redouble their labour, the whole field is "on the kemp".'* [Neville 1896].

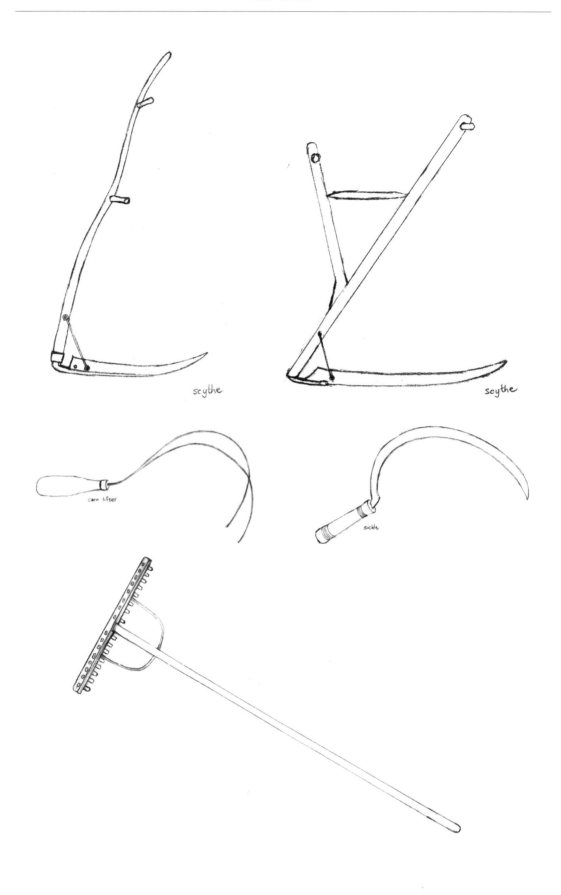

Figure 104. A Collection of Farm Tools. (Dinah Iredale)

11. Morality

Mr. James Sanderson wrote an essay about the Peasantry of the southern counties of Scotland which was published in the Transactions of the Highland Society and by W. Blackwood and Sons (price 1s.6d.). Of this essay the compiler of the Rutherfurd's Directory (1866) stated *'Of the Bondage system, which is universal in the district, Mr. Sanderson possesses a rose-coloured opinion, and passes it with a pat on the shoulder'.* This the compiler suggests is too complacent *'as the system is evidently destined, sooner or later, to be the means of trouble, and affect the present relations of farmer and hind.'* The compiler then concludes his introduction to the system by highlighting the difficulty of the name *'bondage system'* and *'bondager'.* He says *'the name to many living where the system does not exist'* implies *'a sort of serfdom'.*

William Fairbairn, who wrote the prize winning essay in 1865, comments in his essay on the way the bondage system takes *'young women from their father's house, and placing them among strangers – free from all restraint – beyond the guardian supervision and control of their parents, leaving them at liberty to act according to the best of their own inclinations, and this at years of indiscretion, and at an age when, above all others, they are apt to become the dupe and prey of the designing and the deceiver.'* He also remembers as a boy working with the bands of women in the fields. He says *'In one year in particular, there were two women hired as bondagers from neighbouring towns, the obscenity of whose language I have never since heard equalled. It is true, there are some who discountenance this kind of chat, others are prevented from joining in it by the presence of a brother or sister, but even the hearing of it must have a tendency to adulterate their minds, and lower their ideas of all that is "pure, and lovely, and of good report."* Cuthbert Bede noted, when writing about Northumberland in his novel, that because the demand for bondagers outstripped the supply *'there is not always a strict enquiry into the "bondager's" character. As with the case of hop-pickers – whom these bondagers somewhat resemble both socially and morally – they are oftentimes the inhabitants of densely populated towns, who are tempted to live a brief agricultural life, not so much from the temptation of the wages, as from the desire to pass a summer-time in the country.'* [Bede 1877]. Both writers look to the town as a major source of the problems of morality but Cuthbert Bede seems to dismiss all bondagers and hop-pickers for that matter as less than desirable workers, when the tradition of families of skilled workers, suggests otherwise. Farm workers in the Borders were noted for their hard work and sobriety which is underlined by William's dismay on hearing particularly foul language when a boy.

Mrs Williamson, an ex-bondager, who also wrote a prize-winning essay in 1865, criticised the bondage system very strongly. She wrote about the close working relationship between the hind and bondager. She says *'We are aware we are venturing on delicate ground, and had it not been that we speak from personal observation, we could not have cared for bringing forward the subject at all. This intimacy may exist without a feeling of guilty love on either side, and yet be very improper, if it excites the jealousy of the wife, whose feelings ought to be respected and held sacred. It is all the worse for her if she has a careless, thoughtless husband, and she feels her anger to be impotent, as she is not able to turn the object of her dislike and suspicion to the door; and she may think there is too much cause for her fears when she contrasts her own face, prematurely robbed of its youthful bloom by the cares and anxieties incident to the wife and mother, with that of her supposed rival, set off by the advantages of dress, which their high wages enables them to procure. At the same time, the young woman feels herself insulted by those suspicions, while it is not in her power to leave the presence of the enraged wife until the term of her servitude expires'.* Mrs Williamson is also concerned about the lack of privacy for the hind and family and comments on how their home-life is disrupted by the presence of a stranger. Under the title *'Bondagers Tell Secrets'* she says, *'We allude to the tale-bearing and gossip indulged in at the expense of the families with whom the bondagers reside. We are sorry to lay this to their charge, but it is too true, and all who have had any experience in this matter will bear us out in this, that endless are the quarrels occasioned by this dishonourable practice.'* A little later she adds *'Their bondager shares their fireside with them, sits at the same table, and what is worse, in many cases sleeps in the same apartment; and they know they are at the mercy of a thoughtless tongue, or a malicious one, perchance a lying one, and may account themselves fortunate if they meet with a discreet one.'* It is easy to imagine how embarrassing and awkward difficulties could arise for the family when the bondager was merely being thoughtless. Obviously even greater difficulties could be generated if the bondager was discontented and became malicious. The resulting problems could quite easily escalate into major feuding and falling out up and down the hind's row.

William Fairbairn had noticed that the hind's wife, who had been a bondager herself only recently was *'as much to blame as the other* (the bondager*) in making dispeace'.* Those who had complained about *'the behaviour of mistresses and their children towards them'* were *'giving their own bondagers the same causes of complaint'.* He sympathises with the bondagers in seeking out *'more agreeable companions'* but thinks that these meetings in the cottages of more congenial neighbours attract young men. He worries about these random meetings and the lack of supervision given to the young people.

Mrs Williamson also comments on how the situation can be very difficult for the bondager. She mentions how the bondager might have *'to put up with rude and ill-governed children,'* and also *'the food could be scanty and ill-prepared.'* Despite the bondager's desire for the freedom of living away from home *'young women'* she thought were *'better of, or rather that they need, a restraining care exercised over them'.*

Mrs Williamson recommended the building of more and better cottages for farm workers. She suggested that some farm workers were lost to agriculture because, if a hind died, his family was *'obliged to remove to a town'.* The reason for this move was, of course, because the cottage was needed for a hind, a replacement for the hind who had died. Mrs Williamson thought landlords, with the *'high and increased rents'*, should provide enough cottages to make *'carrying on the business of the farm'* easier and *' without wrong to any one.'* These cottages, she thought, could be let at a low rent to widows, with children old enough to work to support her, and any younger children.

Both William Fairbairn and Mrs Williamson mention that Irish workers might help the shortage of workers if the bondage system was abandoned but this raised the difficult topic of bothies which neither writers favoured. They both mention that in some areas, Peebleshire and East Lothian are named, the farm work in the busy months is carried out by the women workers that *'the hinds can turn out'* plus workers from the Highlands and from Ireland. The solution then was the family system plus migrant workers. These migrant workers sometimes lived together in a cottage if available but sometimes they occupied outbuildings and lived in a very rough and ready way.

Josephine Butler wrote in 1874 about the *'certain indefensible parts of the agricultural arrangements of that county* (Northumberland) *such as the "bondage system".'* She also quotes her father as saying, 40 years earlier, to a committee of the House of Lords, that it was important for people to *'pursue social inquiry in a just and honest spirit, and not under the direction of sentiment, prejudice, or self-interest'.* He said that *'physiologists and moralists alike have a little too hastily pronounced farm work to be unfit and unseemly for women, and have asserted that it is invariably accompanied with moral degradation'.* [Butler 1874].

The Rev. Thomas Knight may have been one of these moralists, although he is obviously writing of his own experiences and knowledge of the situation around Ford. He writes that *'There is little doubt that the employment of females in agriculture is one of the causes of the low state of morality in this district. In large gangs of from 12 to 20 there are too often some who are given to indulge in improper conversation, by which the minds of the young are corrupted. Hence the objection to field work, and their anxiety to find places for their daughters in respectable families.'* One intriguing thought that might be worth considering is that fieldwork was very visible to the casual observer, whereas the drudgery and unpleasantness of some of the household chores undertaken by servants were hidden certainly from male eyes. Giving evidence to the 1867 Royal Commission, The Vicar of Kirknewton, the Revd. P. G. McDouall, is less condemning but considered that the work for women should be *'limited, and not be constant throughout the year, so as to allow them more time for fitting themselves for domestic duties'.* [Henley 1867].

Much earlier, in1843, when writing his report Sir F. H. Doyle stated that *'It is not considered, by those whom I consulted, that the bondagers are less chaste than the other women of the county, though their occupations render them somewhat masculine. "Never take a household servant from north of Bremish (the river Till)," a saying among the Northumbrians, implies that the turnip-hoe and the scythe do not train up girls to be neat-handed in-doors.'* [Doyle 1843]. Even this criticism is refuted, in 1893, by Mrs Black, wife of the steward, when she says *'The girls who work in the fields make better wives than those in service, for they ken how to save and pinch. They cannot cook food, perhaps, for gentry, but they can do well enough for themselves and they can bake, milk a cow, and make butter.'* Also in the 1893 Mr. Cleghorn of Milfield remarks that *'Most of the women who work out are good needle women and good knitters'.* [Fox 1893].

The vicar of Norham, W. S. Gilly, had in 1841 worried about morality in connection with the poor housing and P. G. McDouall echoes this in 1867 saying – *'accommodation is sadly deficient which is prejudicial to morality'.* The Rev. McDouall also refers to *'bondage houses'* and states these are *'inhabited by single women who work on the farm; this is a great cause of immorality'.* [Henley 1867]. Single women were able to obtain a *'cote house'* in return for work as a bondager or agricultural labourer. We saw this earlier where Jane Dougharty is noted as working for David Brown at Yearle and living in the Cote House.

Jane Dougharty's conditions are set out in the farmer's pocketbook where she is listed alongside the hinds and shepherds.

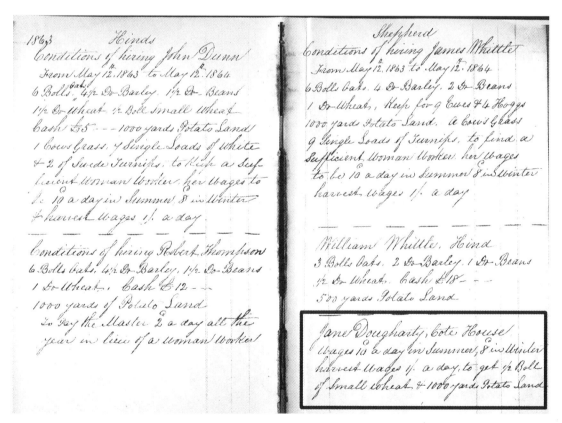

Figure 105. Mr. Brown's pocketbook – Jane Dougharty.
(Anne & Derek Fairnington, Wooler)

Why this caused the Revd. McDouall particular concern may reflect the attitude of the period when women needed the protection of a man to be respectable but he does not elaborate or explain the situation.

In the 1867 Royal Commission it is noted that *'Bell Fortune a retired bondager, in Dunse Parish, has a cot house and keeps a woman worker (same system as the hind). She pays the girl £7 summer, £4 winter and gets cottage, garden, coals, 1300 yards potatoes and barley.'* Bell Fortune also echoes Mrs Williamson's comments about dress when she says *'the girls are much better off now than they used to be, but they dress so fine; the merchants get a good deal out of them.'* [Henley 1867].

'A Farmer' writing to the Kelso Chronicle in reply to 'A Draper' chides him for encouraging bondagers to spend foolishly. He says the draper's hands *'are very little out of bondagers' pockets'*. He says, *'It is very amusing to stand behind our women workers at a happening time, and hear the conversation about the spending of their money, and reflecting how they misspend it with the drapers'. One would speak up and say, "If you go into a draper's shop with a few pounds, you will not get out till it is all gone." Another one will say, "Before I would go into So-and-so's shop I would go to the neck in Tweed, for he will sponge you of every penny." Another prudent girl will call out, "Oh! But I do not spend my money in the drapers' shops that way; I put £3 into the savings Bank last year, and I intend, if health permit, to put £4 this year." Another states, "I can tell you a fine story about Jenny This. She went into a draper's shop with £5 in her pocket, in purpose to pay an account of 10s. which she owed, not intending to spend any more, but or she wan out was more in debt than before, and the money gone.'* [Thomson 1869].

This spending power of the bondagers certainly caused jealousy and tension with the hind's wife who had to be much more frugal.

Walter White also wrote about the attitude of the hind's wife to the bondage system and says that *'if wives could have their own way, the habit* (Bondage System) *would, no doubt, soon be changed.'* He also mentions jealousy and states *'There has been at times cause for jealousy, the hind has proved himself unfaithful; but such instances as I was informed on diligent inquiry, are rare'.* [White 1859].

Wat Thomson spoke about cottars when he shared his memories in 1974. He said that *'women on their own were called "cottars". 'Women,'* he said, *'were wanted'.* The interviewer suggested this was because women were cheaper but Wat thought their value was more than that, because they *'could turn their hand to anything'.* [Thomson 1974]. Women workers continued to be highly valued.

In the Rutherfurd's Directory (1866) the perceived problem of immorality and illegitimate births in relation to the bondage system is thoroughly aired. The statistics are carefully examined and the writer states that *'Of late it has been the frequent habit to write down the agricultural counties on the score of moral laxity'* but he found that the county of Berwickshire *'strictly agricultural – where the bondage system exists in great intensity (which is universally allowed to be a cause of moral laxity) – may be reckoned as really most virtuous'.* He notes that the manufacturing areas have more illegitimate births as a proportion of births than agricultural areas. He also looked at the number of unmarried women of child - bearing age in a parish and the legitimate and illegitimate birth rate and still could not come to the *'present received opinions'* about agricultural areas and *'moral laxity'.* At the same time he acknowledges that looking at statistics and making interpretation is open to abuse saying *'that figures can be made to read both ways'.*

Another point made by the writer is that *'the mothers expectant of illegitimate children very frequently migrate from their resident parish to some distance previous to the birth of the child, for instance, in the case of servant girls, to their country homes, principally from necessity and partly from concealment; and, where ever it is at all practicable, the child will be boarded thereafter in a rural parish. Wherever this system is carried out, it may readily be observed that the rural parishes thus become libelled with the immorality which, strictly speaking, had its source in the towns'.* In the 1867 Royal Commission, Mr. Richard Huntly King, occupier, Wooperton, shared this opinion and said *'I know, however, of very many instances where the country has to bear the imputation of immorality properly belonging to the town.'* [Henley 1867].

The problem of irregular marriages is also examined in the Rutherfurd's Directory (1866). It quoted that in 1838 Dr. McCulloch wrote, *'a run-away marriage was scarcely considered a social misdemeanour; in reality it was merely an ecclesiastical offence,'.* He had noted that *'in some agricultural parishes they were almost the rule. In fact, the woman thought it a want of gallantry in the man if a "run-away" marriage was not proposed'.* It is also pointed out that not many ministers felt able to record this in the statistical accounts. The doctor *'had an honest pride in referring to a matter which all the other ministers thought best to ignore'.* By the 1860s when the Directory was produced the compiler could report *'These marriages although still frequent in some localities of the district, are now, as a rule considered disreputable by all classes.'* The penalty of 20s. to get an irregular marriage registered led to the couples rarely registering. *'Of the Border Marriages in the district for the year 1861, only one pair paid the penalty (of 20s.) and got (by authority of the Sheriff) legally registered.'*

Dr. McCulloch was also the *'only writer in the statistical accounts of the district'* who takes *'notice of the evictions of the poor from country parishes which had been going on for the last fifty years'.* This, of course, was to prevent further cost to the parish. Dr. McCulloch was obviously very concerned for the poor and was not afraid to speak out, and state honestly, facts that would be unpalatable to many.

It is recorded in 'Wooler and Glendale a Brief History' Vol I that *'James Hall, one-time minister at Branxton, writing about one hundred years ago* (in about 1886), *described a curious marriage ritual performed at the ancient fair by local priests. These priests were known by their nick-name of "Book i' bosom", because they carried, as well as the Bible, the marriage rites and responses within the bosom of their cloaks. A Young couple visiting the fair with marriage in mind, would watch the sports, purchase some small item and drink ale in one of the tents, before deciding to take each other. When this decision was made, each would take the other's hand, called "fasting" or "festing", then swear to live together for one year, and if they found each other suitable, to return the following year and be married by one of these priests. James Hall expressed the view that this clasping of hands was a Danish custom. The attitude of the church, in those days, must have been tolerant, as some of these women would be bearing a child, if not carrying one in her arms a year later. However, what happened if the lovers decided they were not suited was not mentioned.'* [Collier 1986].

Thomas Knight mentions when writing about morality in his parish that *'women who have once fallen never become utterly depraved, but generally marry and turn out good wives.'* [Henley 1867].

Actual accounts of births are few but Mr. Tait of Duns, as a boy during the time of the First World War, recalled seeing a girl have a baby by the potato clamp, wrap it in her jacket and just carry on. 'She would have got the sack if she'd taken time off,' he said.

Mrs Williamson of Galashiels recalls in her essay that she knew of one young girl who, twelve months after leaving home to become a bondager, was the mother of an illegitimate child. She sums up the situation saying *'And here let us not be mistaken; we do not aver that such are the usual consequences of the bondage system, or that it is necessarily a hotbed of vice, but such things have occurred, and evils of a similar kind have resulted from it oftener than what is generally known.'* Mrs Sybil Straughan, of Galewood, remembers hearing how a bondager gave birth to an illegitimate baby and that her family, whilst allowing her to live with them, insisted the baby went to work slung on the back of the mother.

I remember the wife of a farmer's son recalling that in the 1930s or early 1940s she took her baby to the field so that she could help with the busy times such as hay time. It was a small farm and she said everyone was expected to help. The baby in this case slept by the hedge as work proceeded.

12. Life in Service as an Alternative

Many bondagers strongly asserted that they did not wish to go into service. This was often the only other career opportunity open to country girls. The reason most often given for this antipathy towards service is summed up by Wat Thomson, when he says *'they were never done'.* [Thomson 1974].

Back in the 1970s Mrs Buglass said that she thoroughly enjoyed her work on the land but service was considered cleaner. Mary Rutherford, a bondager near Mellerstain, left service to go on the land but Mrs Cockburn did the reverse. Mrs Sally Dunn described her time as a bondager as *'a lovely life'.* Mrs Violet Smith, aged 92 in 2006, said that *'service was considered a step up'.* This was the case, even though, as she said *'you ended up scrubbing floors'.* Mrs Mona Thompson, aged 97 in 2006, said she did not want to be a bondager as she knew the life was hard. She began work as a maid at Glanton Pike and Lilburn Towers. Mona did eventually work on the land due to her husband, a gamekeeper, being severely injured in an accident involving a lorry whilst walking along a road. He looked after the children and she worked on the land.

A comment made to the 1867 Royal Commission from Fairnington, Roxburghshire was that *'Girls in service get less than they do working out, but it takes less to keep them. Some of them incline to service in the house, but I daresay most of them like field- work better. They that have them within themselves (i.e. daughters of their own) like best to keep them at home, though I think the bondagers are just as well looked after as house servants; maybe they are not subject to such strict rules, and that's why they like it better.'* [Henley 1867].

In the report of the 1893 Royal Commission, Mrs Silby, a steward's wife, said *'I like my daughters at home. I think it is often as hard work for girls in situations as in the fields, and the hours may be longer.'* [Fox 1893]. So views were polarised and girls did seem able to move from one career to another through choice as well as necessity.

Catherine Johnson, of Ladykirk, kindly lent me a copy of Mrs Winnie Sanderson's account of her life in Northumberland and later in Australia. This is extremely interesting as Mrs Sanderson, as a girl and young woman, moved between working on the land and in service. She met Mr. John William Sanderson on 12 May 1920 when the Sanderson family (John William – 19, younger brother George Edward – 11 and mother) and her family (parents, brothers and sisters) lived in the same row at Murton Farm near Berwick. Winnie began her working life at a *'model farm'* and remembered that she *'liked working there'* but went to work in a farmhouse when the *'model farm'* was sold. Her account of her work as an *'in and out'* girl gives a vivid picture of life in this kind of situation and also the attitude of some adults to the younger generation.

'The owners of this farm had worked hard all their lives and were very strict. I was engaged for six months, from May to November. I rose at 5am and had to light the kitchen fire; this was part of a big range consisting of oven, fireplace and hot water tank. I was allowed one match with which to light the fire. One morning the match went out before I got the fire alight so I went into the breakfast room and asked the mistress for another match. She said "I gave you one". I said "Yes, you did, but it went out", she grudgingly gave me another match, grumbling about "careless folk", "Wasting matches", "Matches cost money", etc.

In this job I worked from daylight to dark, milking cows, feeding calves, poultry, cats and two riding horses, and during the day I did the housework. The mistress did the cooking but I prepared the vegetables, plucked the poultry, skinned the rabbits, etc., etc.

The kitchen furniture was made of pine and had to be scrubbed weekly, this was quite a task, as first, I had to go to a nearby field to get a lump of sandstone, bring it back and champ it into a powder. This I used to scrub the furniture with, which, I am proud to say was always snow white.

For my six months work I was paid £10 .0 .0. When November came my mistress asked my mother "What are you doing with Winnie the next six months". I said "Winnie's leaving", the old lady said "I'm not talking to you, I was talking to your mother", then I said

"I'm still leaving, unless I get a lot more than £10 .0 .0. for six month's work". The old lady was almost speechless at my temerity in daring to ask for higher wages. "What" she said, "More wages". "Don't you know the days are shorter in the winter, you can't see to work outby as long, so we only pay £8 .0 .0. for the winter term", so that decided the matter as far as I was concerned.'

Later she recalls ' I collected my ten pounds wages from the mistress, and as I turned round a corner outside of the house, the old farmer was standing there leaning on his walking stick, he said "Well, you're off girl?" "Yes" I answered, "Well, I'm sorry to see you go, you've been a good girl. I've never had to ask you to clean my boots, they were already cleaned and waiting for me every morning, if you ever wanted work you can always come back here". He held out his hand to shake mine and he gave me five shillings, which was really something, coming from him. I don't think his wife would know of this gift, hence the waiting outside of the house.'

Winnie next worked 'as a general servant' at Etal for thirty-six pounds a year. This position, had been obtained for Winnie by Bill's mother. Again she describes her situation very vividly. She begins by saying she had a few days at home before setting off for Etal.

'My new situation was quite a change from my previous one; to start with I had to call the mistress "Ma'am", also wear a cap and apron which made me aware that I was only the maid, and was treated as such.'

This was not a happy situation and Winnie says that despite the uniform she soon found she was just 'a maid of all work' from lighting fires, to cooking, ironing, cleaning and helping with the children.

She was taken to task about burning her candle late. This had been because Winnie was writing a letter but the mistress said this had to be done on Winnie's "day out" and not at night. This was rather harsh as Winnie explains. 'My parents lived twelve miles away from where I worked and as my "day out" started at twelve noon, by the time I had cycled twelve miles, had a chat with my folks at home, and having to be back at the manse by nine-thirty p.m. I didn't have much time to write letters so I continued writing as usual at night; when I went to bed I hung clothes around the doorway, and put a rug at the bottom of the door to prevent anyone seeing the light, but I forgot about the keyhole so once again I was in trouble.'

Winnie stayed in this job for six months and was told 'I was the only one to stay as long as I had'. In later life she realised that the 'mistress was neurotic' and thinks if she had known this earlier she would have stayed longer but the life there was very lonely as she was forbidden to mix with people in the village. In June she left Etal to work on a farm near where her parents lived. She says 'Gone was the neat black dress and pretty lace trimmed caps and aprons of my former job. The work on the farm was all fieldwork so clothing had to be appropriate and all the women wore the same kind of outfit.' She then describes the typical bondager clothes. Her parents worried about her and she says they 'thought that farm work was too heavy for me so suggested I go back to domestic work'.

A year later the cook, at the place where her father was gardener, was leaving so he suggested Winnie apply for the job. This position required much more elaborate cooking and there would be a lot of entertaining so Winnie hesitated about applying. In the end she did apply and went for interview. She immediately liked 'the lady of the house' who spoke to her 'as an equal'. A trial period of three months was decided on with the lady saying 'Why not come for three months, and if I'm satisfied with your work, I'll tell you, and if you don't like working for me, you tell me'. Winnie stayed there for four years. She later sailed to Australia to join Bill where they married and began a successful life which would demand courage, resourcefulness and determination.

Andrew Purves also mentions life in service and how restrictive the life could be. He says 'In most mansion houses 'followers', as the swains were called, were allowed in the servants' hall, and romance flourished'. In some smaller establishments including farmhouses 'their lads' were allowed 'in the kitchen of an evening, but in some houses followers were forbidden'. He also writes of another way that employers might mistreat their servants. 'One despicable practice employed in mansion houses to test the honesty of young girls and *new servants was to leave money and valuables lying around. Farmers' wives and other persons who employed maids, including alas! some ladies of the manse, used the same method.'* He concludes by saying *'On the working folks' part, the inference to be drawn from such conduct by employers was that they themselves must be dishonest, seeing they suspected other people.'* [Purves 2001].

Alastair Orr gives an illustration of how the relationship between farmer and servant changed due to the agricultural revolution. The *'gudeman'* became the master, the farmhouse was replaced by a bigger, better farmhouse which was *'built with its back to the farmyard'.* When servants (in this case *'servants'* is referring to outdoor workers, ploughmen, etc.,) lived in the farmhouse the farmer could impose *'a patriarchal discipline'* but when few servants lived-in then farmers had less power over the servants' lives after work. Some attempts were made to *'uphold traditional relations of dependence'.* One Kelso magistrate in 1807 stated *'It is a mistake in servants, hired by the year or half-year, to suppose that, after their ordinary work hours, they are at liberty to dispose of or absent themselves as they please without their master's leave; that, on the contrary all such servants are bound to be at their master's call, at all times during their service by day or by night, when occasion requires'.* Alastair Orr goes on to say *'such edicts were powerless to prevent the breakdown of patriarchal discipline. By the 1860s, few farmers made any attempt to regulate their servants after working hours'.* [Orr 1984].

So the feeling of more freedom as a bondager was very strongly held and many comparisons are drawn when memories are shared. Minnie Bell said, *'We were as happy as larks! We were better off than those in service because we finished at 5pm.'* All her sisters (six of them) were bondagers though sadly her eldest sister died early at 15 years. Another sister did not like working on the farm and eventually went into service. *'Yes',* Minnie said, *'they had a choice.'* Their parents gave them a choice. [Bell].

Jean Kinghorn thought the work hard but was glad to do it. Of service she said *'I wouldn't have the life for nothing'.* She liked being outside and *'seeing the beasts and althing'.* *'I wearied for the next day.'* [Kinghorn 1999]. Mrs Driver, a former school teacher (92 in 2003), went to school with a girl called Jeanie who followed her two sisters into a career as a bondager (c1924). Mrs Driver remembers them as very cheerful girls. Mrs Janet Tait of Duns went into service but after a few weeks decided she preferred the outside life.

Barbara Robertson quotes two comments about working on the farm. *'There was aye some kind o'banter going on'* and *'Ye saw something for your labours.'* [Robertson 1990].

Mrs Margie Dixon of Wooler, was not a bondager herself, but remembers a worker wearing the bondager clothes. She and her sister worked outside at Kimmerston and she said it was a happy life. They worked hard but also had fun. Margie has a funny story which demonstrates how exhausting the work could be. Margie's mother made the meals for two bondagers who shared a cottage at Kimmerston. One day Margie's sister went to call the bondagers for their meal. She found them in bed with their big boots sticking out of the bottom of the bedclothes. Too tired to take their boots off before resting! So no doubt about the hard work!

The 1893 Royal Commission found that the women workers presented *'the picture of health'*, and they could be seen *'working actively and cheerfully'.* The impression gained was *'that their employment is considered no hardship, and that it has made them physically a race of which Northumberland may be proud.'* In the same report Mrs. Dumma, a hind's wife says, *"My daughter is much better since she worked out. For two winters before she did so she was quite an invalid from poverty of the blood, and her father had to lift her in and out of bed. Now she is quite strong from working in the fields. I would rather my girls stayed at home and worked than go into service. Field work is not bad for them from a moral point of view, and they hear no bad language."* [Fox 1893]. Mrs Isabel Barrie of Milfield began to work on the land, as a teenager, on the advice of the doctor who thought it would improve her health. She enjoyed the work and stayed for twenty-one years.

13. Kirns and Recreation

The harvest was obviously a significant milestone in the year and many customs have developed to celebrate this important time.

Michael Robson writes about *'the festivity marking the end of shearing and the end of leading in. The latter known as the 'Kirn'; on 12 October 1796 a farmer noted that 'The servants keeps their Harvest home tonight. Gave them 4 pints o' whiskie value 20/- and they had a Roast goose for supper. And Dance as usual.'* He also notes how the farmer was prepared to help the workers when working conditions were hard. *'The same man, a careful master, was liberal when circumstances suggested he should be. Four years earlier in 1792, the shearing was not finished until 26 October, and to mark the end of it he gave his servants six bottles of whisky to make into punch and killed a sheep – 'not a good one indeed' – which he thought would be needlessly extravagant if the corn was all cut in eight days as ideally it might be, but 'Where there is a long tedious Harvest such a Fete is quite necessary and an object to look to cheer their spirits in a damned wet Harvest as all ours are'.* [Robson 1984].

In 1893, Mr. John Robinson read a paper on Harvest Customs to the Society of Antiquaries in Newcastle. He remarks how customs have changed over the last 50 years and that *'the old traditions and familiar omens of the harvest field were out of place in this age of scientific farming and mechanical appliances'.* He then goes on to describe the kern supper which he says *'was the great carnival of the year',* as important as Christmas. The kirn *'the harvest feast was often converted into a rude masquerade. Some dressed themselves in female attire, others were encased from head to heel in straw ropes, wound round the body and limbs, and others again were attired in animal skins that masked the face and concealed the body.'* Mr. Robinson then quoted from William Mitford's song *'Harvest Home'.* (William Mitford was a well-known Tyneside songwriter and the original manuscript of Harvest Home is owned by a Mr. Thos. Allan). The song is dated 1820 and the farm described was about 3 miles west of Newcastle.

Harvest Home, or the humours of a Kern Supper
By William Mitford

Come, none of your nonsense, but let me proceed,
To sing of a kern supper, held at Hill Heed,
Where Manus and Bacchus together unite,
To Crown the mirth of a kern-supper night.
Oh! The fiddler was there with his graces,
The lasses and lads take their places;
Mirth seated on each of their faces,
At the Kern supper held at Hill Heed.
Two chaps fra Newcassel was there 'mang the rest,
Who called at West Denton and got themselves drest.
The one a fat squire, wi' reed coat, buits and spurs,
Mustachies as large as a Russian hussar's.
He had tassels to bob in jig, sir,
A monstrous cocked hat and a tie wig, sir,
With a belly as round as a pig, sir,
At the Kern supper held at Hill Heed.
The other disguised in a long lugged cap,
With a bonny silk handkerchief round it did wrap,
A bedgown, thick waist, petticoats short and airy,
And a pair of old trousers furnished his dairy;
He astonished byeth bumpkins and gawkey,
For his sex there began a long argey,
And they swore it was just Pally Fargie,

At the Kern supper held at Hill Heed.
There was double-milled Jenny fra Walbottle Dene,
The ackwardest sweathearter ever was seen,
Off a lasses knee lapt, then he gare a great curse,
At a beast they led in wiv a heed like a horse.
While they held by a chain they kept grinning,
He snatched at the men and the women,
Till they down the step ladder was running
Fra the Kern supper held at Hill Heed.
Fair nymphs were in fine regimentals equipp'd,
With their beaus dress'd in petticoats nimbly tripp'd.
The supper's announced, then they finished the play,
When byth fon and weary they toddle away.
Pally Fargie was wet to the smock, sir,
Reached town about six o' the clock, sir,
Had a pint at the sign of the cock, sir,
And told of the fun at Hill Heed.

The contents of the song Mr John Robinson suggested were links with much earlier times and he gives examples. *'The Ancients celebrated the gathering-in of the harvest by offerings to Ceres, The goddess of husbandry. Her image had the body of a woman, but the head was that of a horse.'* Also he notes that in Southern England the last cut corn was called a *'mare'*.

The custom of the *'master'* mixing and socialising with his work people, at the kern, is commented on by Alastair Orr. He says this was *'the symbol of human and class cooperation in labour'* and *'on many farms, this was now the only occasion in the year when master and servant ate together at the same table'.* [Orr 1984].

Mr. John Robinson said this custom went back to *'our Saxon Forefathers' days'* when *'bondsmen were indulged with liberty, and were on an equality with their masters for a certain time. This custom had been handed down to within memory of some still living, masters and men at the Kern Supper being placed on an equal footing, sitting at the same tables, feasting, singing, and dancing together without distinction'.*

Mr. Robinson mentions the events which cause *'excitement'* during *'the last day of harvest'* – *'preparations made for the last cut'*, *'the plaiting of the last stalks of corn'*, *'the effort to win the kern by the throwing of sickles at the plaited stalks'.* The superstition was that it was *'a lucky omen if a young woman won the kern by cutting it down with one throw of her hook(sickle). The girl who won was to be married, it was said, before the next harvest came round.'* He then said that *'The last out kern was again carefully plaited, was decorated with ribbons and was then presented to the farmer's wife and hung up in the kitchen.'* Perhaps *'the last out kern'* suggested there were a number of plaits of straw and the *'last out'* was the one that escaped the sickle longest. After this excitement the *'kern was proclaimed'* and this was done with the help of a kern dolly. *'An old dress of a woman was stuffed with straw from the last sheaf, and when the dolly had been dressed the hayfork was thrust into the figure and it was hoisted high into the air and saluted as a Kern Dolly, amid shouts and harvest cry of all in the field. All shouted at the top of their voices "A Kern! A Kern! Hee, hoo". This was repeated three times, and the Dolly was held up as high as possible. A procession was formed, a fiddler in front, and there was dancing and shouting and harvest cry throughout the village. In his youthful days the farm steward at Seaton Delaval was Mr. Barnabas Fenwick and the usual thanksgiving song chanted by the women was altered to suit the occasion to:*

"Barny Fenwick's corn is well shorn
God bless the day that he was born,
A Kern! a kern! Hee Hoo."

The Dolly was at last flung high up into the air, the neighbouring tradesmen and houses were visited, and donations were secured for the supper that followed.'

The last part of the above is interesting as it suggests that the supper was not provided by the farmer, as it was in the previous recollection of 1796, but by a collection. Joan Pringle, in more recent times during the Second World War, said the supper was provided by the farmer's wife whereas Mrs Violet Smith and Mrs Mona Thompson talked of a *'pooled supper'*.

In the Parsons and White Directory of Durham and Northumberland in 1828 the description of the *'village labourers'* is very full of praise depicting them among other attributes as resolute and enterprising. It then goes on to mention *'their days of festivity are cheered with hilarity, hospitality, and a variety of rustic amusements. Their merry-meetings are often convened for the purpose of relieving some honest neighbour in distress, to whom they give the surplus of subscriptions, after paying the host for their entertainment'*. The *'pooled suppers'*, collections for charity in connection with events such as ceilidhs, country dances and concerts using local talented entertainers still goes on today. This includes singers, choirs, musicians, storytellers and comedians.

In about 1900, Hastings Neville also writes about harvest customs. He writes that people in his parish still remember harvest customs which are no longer followed. In particular he mentions the *'kirn dolly'*: *'This (kirn dolly) was made not of the first fruits of the harvest, but of the very last sheaf, of the last field cut, upon the farm. There was much rivalry among shearers to obtain this last "grip", as it was termed, and to cut it. This sheaf was nicely rounded by the workers, and fully dressed with a skirt, and ribbons round the neck, to represent a young girl. It was raised aloft upon a fork, and carried about the field with dancing and singing to the strains of the local fiddler, his fiddle being decorated with coloured ribbons like the pipes of the Scotch pipers. It was ultimately carried in procession to the farmyard, where, as the people say, the farmer showed hospitality.'* [Neville 1909].

This was very similar to the previous account, but he does have an additional custom involving the last load to be carried home. *'There was also the procession of the last load, after the rest of the harvest was all carried. One of the women workers was mounted on the top of the load, which was accompanied by all the harvesters, from the field to the front door of the farmhouse, with music and singing. Here the farmer's wife appeared, and was expected to take the whip and drive the horse and cart to the stackyard. This done, she selected a small bunch of wheat ears from the cart, returned to the house, having provided food and drink for the hands. In a case where she showed no inclination to show hospitality, the hands would, as a penalty, make it difficult for her to drive the horse.'*

Another version of this ceremony was that *'when the last load of corn was to be taken into the stack garth, the horse was to be driven by a young girl; the farmer's daughter was sometimes asked to perform this task.'* [Balfour 1904].

Hastings Neville mentions the theory that Frazer expresses in Golden Bough Vols. II and III of the corn spirit being embodied in the last sheaf and the worship of the spirit are *'ancient rites'* to express *'thankfulness for the fruits of the earth in their season'*. He tells us that *'The term "kirn" is now only applied to the harvest home dance given by the farmer to the hands after the corn is all led and comfortably stacked for the winter. The "kirn dolly" used to be kept until the kirn dance, and was again exhibited in the barn where the dance took place'*. He then goes on to recount a more mischievous custom which occurred at the end of shearing where *'a practical joke was played on the farmer if he dared show himself in the field'*. The farmer was *'set on' 'chiefly by the women workers'* they *'pulled him off his horse, and "grip" him, and toss him in the air, not once but three or four times, catching him as he fell'*. It is easy to understand that the farmer generally made every effort not to be caught out in this way. This custom was called "putting up the master".

He then recounts a story where the farmer plays a trick on a friend. *'Once a farmer had as his visitor a friend from London, who, as may be supposed, knew nothing of this custom. He took him into the field, having previously arranged with his people that they should "put him up". The farmer, walking in amongst them with his friend, gave them as a signal a quiet nod over his shoulder. They first hesitated to do his bidding, thinking it too bad to take a stranger by surprise in so rough a manner, but another nod from their master meaning, "put him up", was taken as a command, and the poor man, who was somewhat stout, was suddenly "gripped" by a number of strong hands and tossed up and down, again and again, crying in terror, "What's the matter? Thompson, Thompson, come here! What's all this? What have I done? Oh take care of my watch," etc., until panting and trembling, he was again placed on his feet. It was, naturally, some time before his anger was appeased, and before he could receive with good grace the explanation of his friend that it was an old harvest custom. (The idea seems to be that the proprietor, like the last sheaf, is an embodiment of the Corn Spirit and is to be reaped and bound and handled as the sheaf is. And comparative folk-lore leads to the belief that in our old custom of putting up the farmer or the man who has cut the last sheaf we have traces of the practice of human sacrifices which in the ancient world and among rude races in more recent times have been offered to promote fertility of the earth. Golden Bough, vol.1, chapter3). Many a farmer now living on the Borders has undergone this sort of penance. Like the "barring out" of the schoolmaster, it was a good-natured way of showing that old scores, if there were any, could be paid off, even by the women workers. It says a great deal for the strength, nerve and dexterity of the harvest maidens of those days, that the farmer was always safely caught after his tossing, and suffered no harm.'* [Neville 1909].

Tom Arres, a dry stone dyker, says, of more recent times, that he *'remembers how "trig" the bondagers were and full of spirit. "They liked nothing better than taking the trousers off the young lads and throwing them in the horse trough.'* [Wager].

In the book *'In the Troublesome Times'*, the Cambo Women's Insititute members share their memories of country life as it used to be. Some memories stretched back to the first half of the 19th Century. The last sheaf of corn was important and it was said that *'The one who got the last sheaf would be the first married.'* The *'kern babby'* was made *'out of a sheaf with a skirt on it, and carried round the field.'* [Bosanquet 1989].

Others recorded that the kern babby was still paraded round Whalton village and Mrs Charles Trevelyan said she had seen *'the kern dolly hanging up in a sitting-room at the Robsons' farm at Sweethope'*. Rosalie E. Bosanquet records that *'Miss Richardson remembers the men coming to ask her mother to lead in the last load of corn on their farm, the Lee Moor, near Alnwick.'* So that all important last load is again brought in with ceremony.

Glen Aln recalls that the 'kern-doll, kern-baby, corney-doll, or mell-doll' was 'fixed to a pole' and 'was carried by a bondager' [Aln 1945].

The County Folk-Lore collection records how 'On the last day's shearing they had a "kern baby"' i.e. a small sheaf of corn dressed as a child, upon a fork carried by the prettiest girl, all shouting "Kerney, kerney, hoo," and when the last riggs were being cut there was "kemping" which was to finish first. When all were done the kern baby was taken from the stook in which if was placed and carried to the farmhouse with loud cries of "Kerney, kerney, hoo." The workers then had supper and sometimes a dance. This book also mentions another celebration called the 'Full Plough,' which was to mark the completion of ploughing. The hinds wore white shirts 'on which were stitched a profusion of coloured ribbons and rosettes' and 'they yoked themselves to the plough and went round the countryside preceded by a flag bearer, and accompanied by a man with a gun. At each house a fee was demanded, and when a gift was obtained the gun was fired. A refusal of the customary largess was followed by the plough being drawn in many furrows through the ground or pavement in front of the house.' [Balfour 1904]. No apparent role here for the women, but the stitching and decorating of the men's shirts would be, no doubt, undertaken by them.

In more recent memory, Mrs Mona Thompson of Wooler recalls that *'the kirn happened after harvest but before the thresher arrived as then the granary would be needed to store grain. The granary was swept, whitewashed and decorated. The floor was made, to the best of their ability, suitable for dancing.'*

The Berwick Advertiser of 15 November 1851 describes a Harvest Home given at Scremerston by Mr. and Mrs Thomson. The decorations included, *'festoons of flowers and evergreens,' and 'Speed the Plough neatly formed in bay leaves at one end of the granary,'* plus *'4 chandeliers from the ceiling ornamented with flowers.'*

Mrs Violet Smith, as previously mentioned, talked about the food at the kirn. *'It was a pooled supper and there was an element of competition in providing the best food for the supper. 'Only the best would do!' She felt that she was too young to dance much but she particularly enjoyed the food.'*

Jean Leid also remembers the *'kirn dances, at Redden, Hadden, Coshie, and the Windywa's. They held them after the hervest and a'that. Oo yaised tae gaun tae thae. Oo'd come hame aboot fower in the morning. Thae wis the days, sittin' at the kirns wi' the paraffin lamps gaun in the granaries and the bags o' corn a' roond aboot or bales o' strae, ee're sittin, or dancin' away there. Oh, ah loved the dancing.'* [MacDougall 2000].

Joan Pringle remembered that each farm had a kirn and neighbours were invited so there was *'a few weeks of jollity'*.

Wat Thomson also enjoyed the kirn supper and dance held at some farms. *'A great night'*. He said as a young man he would hang about a girl from the appropriate farm to get invited to the kirn! [Thomson 1974].

Andrew Purves mentions th*at 'each worker was allowed to bring along a couple of friends'*. He also recounts how the dancing was started. Beginning *'with the Grand March followed by the dance called the Triumph, led off by the farmer himself* with *the steward's wife for partner.* They were followed by the *'steward partnering the farmer's wife, the shepherd came next with the farmer's daughter, then the farmer's son and the shepherd's wife'*. [Purves 2001].

George Mole recounts how he and other young men from Fenton *'were invited to a kirn at Wooperton Farm, maybe some eight miles away. We set off to cycle there, but with no road signs because of the war, and very little light from our bike lights, we went first to the wrong place a few miles from where we were supposed to be. We were soon on the right road again and arrived just in time to hear a man reciting 'The Battle of Pea soup!' This was followed by dance after dance.'* [Mole 2002]. There were numerous dances throughout the year and people travelled distances to attend. The kirn at Scremerston had included people from Kelso who had arrived *'in a well laden omnibus.'*

In the Berwick Advertiser of 20 March 1841 there is a report headed *'Ball at Cockburnspath'*:

'On Thursday evening last, the "agricultural labourers" of the district held a ball in Mrs Weatherly's inn, which was numerously attended and the dance kept up with "Unflagging glee" till a late hour in the morning. Mr. Kirkwood, Dunbar gave a great satisfaction as musician, performing several good tunes at intervals, and particularly one most appropriate for the occasion "Speed the Plough" which he played on the highland bagpipes with great success.'

Evidently when fairs were held in Alnwick *'it was the custom to dance up and down the two Bondgates, Bondgate Without and Bondgate Within'*. The reporter says it has now become the custom to say, *"Will you' tramp the Bondgate' with me*? when asking for *"the pleasure of a dance"*. [Balfour 1904].

Some of the dancing was less formal. Many people recall impromptu dancing *'at the end of the row'*. According to Walter Elliot the rows could be very long. Those at Crailinghall had 16 cottages, Cessford 22 cottages and Fairnington 19 to 20 cottages *'and every house bung full of folk'*. So plenty of people attended and usually *'somebody with a melodeon or fiddle or both'*. [Elliot 2004].

Figure 106. West Fenton Cottages. Notice the boy with a concertina.
(Johnny Moore, Wooler)

In the 1930s a Mr. Ion Jamieson of Langshaw collected old dances and trained a dancing team of local people. This team dressed traditionally with the women in bondager costume and the men in brown overalls with nickie tams. Nickie tams were pieces of string or leather thongs tied under the knee to lift the bottom of the mens' trousers clear of the mud.

Jim Wilkie of Coldstream, later of Jedburgh, was one of Mr Jamieson's dancers. Some of the others were Betty Dodds (née Kerr), Jenny Riddell (née Easton), and Bessie Hermiston (née Macvicar), and Tommy Robison played the accordion. Mr. Wilkie was also a musician and played the fiddle at seventeen and later the button accordion. [Wilkie 1956]. A photograph of these dancers appears in Ian MacDougall's book 'Bondagers'. [MacDougall 2000]. A short film was also made of the team and it was about this time that they were invited to dance at the Albert Hall in London. *Mrs Riddell (née Easton), who was a farm-worker in Lauder in 1935, recalled her trip to London. "I don't really know why I was picked to dance for my country, but the folk of London must have wondered what was happening when we travelled through the city in an open-topped bus in our bondager costumes. I mind being awful tired when we got back to Lauder."* (The Southern Reporter, Thursday 10 August 2000).

Glen Aln writing in 1945 says that '*The kern is a dying custom but on 27 November 1936, the first kern to be broadcast by the BBC was from Trewhitt Steads in Coquetdale, and the kern was given by Mr. Tony White, son of Sir Archibold White of cricket fame. The kern was on the air for 45 minutes and the programme was drawn up by Mr. George Brown, of Whittingham, who acted as M.C. and compere in his native Northumbrian dialect, to the delight of all who love it.*' [Aln 1945]. Perhaps this broadcast still exists in the BBC archives.

Other recreational activities included sewing, knitting, clippie and proggy rug making, mending – darning and patching. At one time there could be candle making and soap making. Candle making was remembered as once being an illicit activity '*as it was a Government monopoly,*' said Mrs Bell of Broom House, Meldon. [Bosanquet 1989]. Mrs Robson's father (aged 81) remembers that '*the windows, were shuttered, and the doors barred, during candle making, for fear of the gaugers.*' Mrs Robson was from Broom House, Cambo. Many women when recording their lives mention knitting and sewing. Jean Kinghorn said, '*there was knitting to do at night'* and that *'we had jobs to do as children'* one being to carry water. [Kinghorn 1999].

Barbara Robertson writes that *'"Waste not, want not" would be the maxim of the efficient home-maker. Advice which doubtlessly was repeated frequently to children in the family. She would be expert not only at cooking and baking, at knitting and sewing, but in mending of all kinds and in particular the altering of children's clothes as they were "passed down the line". "Good" clothes would be kept separate for church, Sunday school, and possibly visiting. Produce from the garden would be fully utilised throughout the year and, in the summer holidays, the children would also be involved in good housekeeping practice by helping to gather wild raspberries for the making of jam'*. She also points out that *'time itself, was utilised to the full'*. Even, *"a walk"* was *'rarely undertaken without something such as sticks being brought back'*. [Robertson 2005]. I can remember taking the milk cows to pasture and bringing back kindling or with great excitement mushrooms. Mam was the arbiter of whether the mushrooms were the edible kind or not. 'Greater excitement' still when my brother Andrew found a giant puffball which was quite a delicacy! Blackberry gathering was also a happy social time.

Cobbling was done by the man of the household, but shoe cleaning was done by the women. The men looked *'after their own work boots'*. The children *'would graduate'* through simple tasks such *'as cleaning cutlery, polishing any brasses, cutting up rags for clootie rugs,'* to *'fireside tidying and black-leading of the grate, or the cleaning of boots and shoes'*. [Robertson 2005].

One woman recalls playing at washing the door-step - *'I can recall quite clearly playing at washing the doorstep: this was before I went to school, and probably it was a kind of game to keep me occupied, for our cottage was apart from the row and my older siblings were at school. Goodness knows what kind of mess I made, but it certainly was a fun occupation for me, sploshing around with a bucket of water and making designs and patterns on the stone doorstep with the whitening stone.'* [Robertson 2005].

The agricultural and industrial revolutions did bring about changes in labour requirements and this also affected the cultural aspect of life. James Hogg in 1831 lamented the *'falling off' of song-singing'*. He felt that the printing of Scott's Minstrelsy had affected the aural tradition but David Buchan feels that *'widespread education and literacy and the new media'* all played their part in changing the tradition of story-telling and song-singing. [Buchan 1984]. Tam Arres says *'I was only once at one (kirn) in the granary with my father and mother. I can always remember there was a bondager there from Rutherford Burnside, Net Balmer was her name and she sang old Scots songs, I never forgot it!'* [Elliot 2004].

David Buchan describes *'the farm kitchen on the long winter evenings, with a heaped fire crackling and men and women plying their different tasks like spinning or shoe-mending – telling stories, singing, making music, playing games, and "speeran guesses" (posing riddles). Neighbours would drop in and various itinerants – chapmen, beggars, peripatetic tailors – would also enliven proceedings. Other milieux for performance during leisure hours were the bothy and the chaumer while during working hours song or story could be heard in the field, to while away the dreary hours of hoeing for instance, or, in bad weather, the stable when men caught up on the indoor tasks. Away from the farm, performances also occurred at the smithy, the shoemaker's shop, or a local howff'*. [Buchan 1984].

David Buchan also mentions how *'itinerant fiddlers made a living in the country districts'*. He mentions *'James Stuart, based on Tweedmouth,'* who *'traversed the south-east, it was said, until he was 114 years old'*. [Buchan 1984]. James Stuart was also known locally as Jimmy Strength.

Figure 107. James Stuart (sketch by J Hartley from a print by Thomas Hogarth)

James Hogg said '*every farmer acknowledged one only as his family musician*' (from among the itinerant fiddlers) and this musician '*knew well when to make his appearances. These were at the sheep-shearing, when he got his choice fleeces; at the end of harvest, to the kirn supper; at the end of the year, for his cakes and cheese; and at the end of seed time, for his lippie of oats.*' '*On these occasions*' he notes '*it was customary for everyman to give the musician sixpence*'.

David Buchan also mentions the dancing classes and how these classes became, in the 19th century, a feature of country life. Notices were placed in newspapers to announce the venue for classes and during the winter months '*the dancing-master, besides being the recognised master of the revels, was generally the country model of elegant and polite bearing*'. [Buchan 1984].

Here are some examples of rhymes that might have been recited on dark winter evenings:

> *Far up on Lammermoor amang the heather green*
> *The earliest ha'rst that e'er was seen*
> *Was seen at Bentydod.*
> *Because, they were shearing the remainder of their crop*
> *There, on a New–year's morning.*

> *Hutton for auld wives,*
> *Broadmeadows for swine;*
> *Paxton for drunken wives,*
> *And saumon sae fine:*
> *Crossrig for lint and woo',*
> *Spittal for kail,*
> *Sunwick for cake and cheese,*
> *And lasses for sale.*

[Buchan 1984].

A Northumbrian Rhyme from '*A Northumbrian Remembers*' by Nancy Ridley is as follows:

Dorrington lands is bonny and Dorrington lads is canny,
And I'll hae a Dorrington lad, and ride a Dorrington cuddy.
Holy Island for need, and Grindon for Kye,
Of a' the towns e'er I saw, Dorrington for Rye.

('*Dorrington*' is Doddington near Wooler.)

Hastings Neville writes in 1909 about pastimes where he says '*there is a social life among the working class of wide extent, and the greatest interest to themselves'*. He thinks young people migrate to the town, not because of '*the dulness'* of rural life but due *to* '*the glamour of the city, as they hear from friends or read of it in the newspapers'*. He mentions the love of dancing but dislikes the impromptu dances '*in the open air of an evening, in any open ground there maybe adjoining the cottages'*. This is due to the dancing taking '*place generally on winter nights by candlelight, and without any supervision by elder folk'*. He also mentions travelling dancing masters who '*stay in the village for two or three months in the winter'*. The class members pay '*him a small sum'* and he holds from '*time to time'* '*a more public dance, which he called "a small occasion".'* Finally he holds '*at the close of the season "a grand ball" for his own benefit.'* Hastings Neville also mentions, among other sports, games of bowls, or bools which are '*In principal'* he says '*more akin to golf'*. [Neville 1909].

Bob Lee of Wooler, whose two sisters were bondagers, shared some memories of his long working life, from 14 until he was 80, on the farm and in forestry. He remembers quoits being played at the end of the row. Quoits is still played in Northumberland and many local shows will include a quoits competition.

Annual football matches, which still occur in a few towns today, were once a feature of many towns. In the Berwick Advertiser of 6 March 1852 there is a report of the Wooler Annual Football Match between single and married men. This was played through the town and some of the shopkeepers boarded their windows! It says '*the ball came several times through portions of the town'* and the married men won. '*The ball was hailed by the married party'*. The goal for one side was the hopper of Earl Mill and the other side aimed to get the ball over a tree, which stood at "*the crook of the Till*". The game would certainly required lots of stamina. [Balfour 1904]. The result of this game, in 1852, was disputed, so a re-match was played the next day. The married men won again! The date, 6 March, may mean this was in conjunction with the Hiring Fair.

Another important aspect of country life, which should be mentioned, was the role of the church. Besides being a place of worship and fellowship, where the agricultural year could be traced through the various religious celebrations, the church also had an important social role. The social role would include the weekly meetings, of friends and 'scattered' neighbours, which allowed news to be passed on and gossip exchanged. Then throughout the year would be the special services and events organised by the church. The biggest event would probably be the church outing, which took people by cart, omnibus and train to places far beyond their normal area of travel. For people living in the depth of the country the seaside would be an enormous change and a great treat, particularly if the weather was kind.

Margaret Moffat remembers going to Sunday School in the morning and then the church service every Sunday. She says, '*Oh, ah didnae mind that.'* Mary King as a kitchen maid, said '*The servants didnae all go tae church on a Sunday, they did not. Ah wis the only one that went tae the service. Ah yaised to ask – ah think it wis mair tae get oot than onythin.'* [MacDougall 2000].

Hastings Neville, writing about his parishioners, says how fashionably dressed the bondagers were on a Sunday. [Neville 1896].

Andrew Purves recalls attending the Cheviot Street Presbyterian Church in Wooler. He travelled there by bus or bike and joined in two of '*a whole range of activities'*. His two interests were the choir and the Literary Society. [Purves 2001].

Winnie Sanderson from Murton Farm remembers going to the Presbyterian church at Ancroft North Moor and also joined the choir. Bill Sanderson walked with her to the choir practice and talked to the Minister, Rev. Thomas Renshaw McKay, whilst waiting. The Minister and Bill walked up and down *"The Quarter Deck"*, a stretch of lawn in front of the manse.

A report in The Berwick Warder on the Dunse Hiring Fair in November 1865 is interesting. It was cold and wet but there were *'several shows, sweetie stalls, etc.,'* which *'studded the Market Place'* and *'religious services were conducted in the Town Hall as usual'*. This is the first reference to religious services I have noted, but significantly it uses the phrase *'as usual'*.

Other entertainment and interests were supplied by ploughing matches, agricultural and horticultural shows, the reading rooms, billiards, football, quoits and for the women (later) the Women's Institute and Scottish Women's Rural Institute (early 20th Century).

Although buses and trains are mentioned as the services became available, replacing walking, carrier's cart or coach, the bicycle is frequently spoken of by workers in the early part of the 20th Century. The ability to get on a bike and travel to events and to pay visits to friends and family must have been enormously liberating. The freedom and independence must have been very exhilarating. One instance of the usefulness of being able to travel by bike is given in an 'Account of Farming Life in early 20th Century Wooler'. Good Friday was a holiday and was sometimes referred to as the *'gardening day'* says the account. *'Early morning saw men on bikes (or shanks pony) with spade on their backs going to see their new garden and house. Also carrying packets of seeds and seed potatoes. The last call from the wife'* would have been, *"If they ask you in, see what the paper is like".'* [NRO 1706].

Andrew Robertson from Salcoats, tells a funny *story,* told to him by his mother, who was a bondager at Brockholes near Chirnside:

'Two young, buxom bondagers, dressed in full regalia, were on their way home from Brockholes to Chirnside, when they were overtaken by a gent in the first motor car they had seen in their lives. As the vehicle passed, the women hailed the driver and although he was a complete stranger to them, he accommodated them in the "dicky" seat up rear, and set off tearing along the Berwickshire by-ways at ten or twelve miles an hour!

Figure 108. Two Bondagers take a lift. (Dinah Iredale)

Finally, the car was brought to a standstill in the middle of Princes Street, Edinburgh, when two very crestfallen damsels found themselves well and truly lost on the first visit to a large city. However, all ended well, when the car gent suggested that he would accompany them to Waverley Station, and purchased a couple of single fares to "Chirsit". I am quite sure it was a long time before the two Berwickshire Bondagers requested a car-lift with an unknown driver!' (Border Life – October 1967).

Perhaps this story has grown a little in the telling but it still provides us with an idea of the curiosity which would be aroused by something new and the 'get up and go' of these women workers even after a hard day's work!

14. The Costume

The bondager costume continued to be worn long after the bondage system had died out. The women were still called bondagers and referred to themselves as bondagers although the term "women workers" was also used.

The costume consisted of a shady hat, often with a wimple or "heid hankie" beneath. This kind of head covering had a long history as the wimple and straw hat had been worn by country women over many centuries in Britain and Europe. The long sleeved blouse was of printed cotton and over this was worn a woollen shawl or a tweed waistcoat. The skirt, reaching to just over the knee, was made of drugget and covered by an apron. Black woollen stockings and heavy boots completed the outfit.

Figure 109. A Bondager in traditional costume. (Dinah Iredale).

In living memory there were two types of hat – the straw hat and the cotton bonnet.

The Berwickshire Hat

The Berwickshire Hat was a large shady hat made of plaited straw. Straw was a material widely used to make hats and other items in the 19th Century and earlier. Veronica Main, one of the world's leading exponents of the craft of straw plaiting, writes: *'Roughly 240 million yards of plait were produced annually in the U.K., and tens of thousands of people were employed in the trade. Straw plaiting was used to make not only hats, but also shoes, cribs, parasols, rope and many other household items.'* [Period Living, October 2004].

Hastings Neville wrote that straw hats were once made in Ford. *'Margaret Gibson used to display straw bonnets and hats to suit all tastes. They were made of rye straw, plaited in a neighbouring village. Some were of coarse texture for bonnets to wear in field work.'* [Neville 1909].

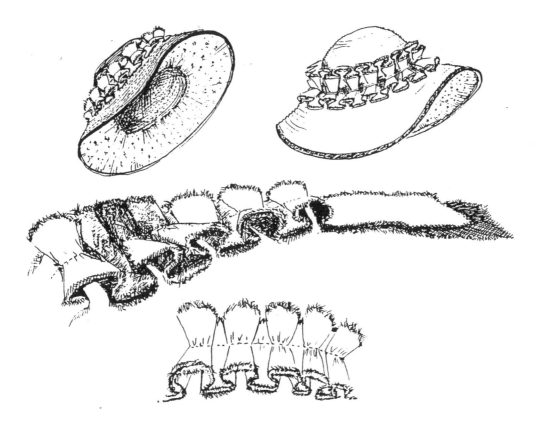

Figure 110. The Berwickshire Hat. (Detailed drawing of the straw hat by Mrs Anne Scott, Melrose.

The Berwickshire Hat was lacquered black to make it more durable. Under the extremes of weather the lacquer would fade, and would have to be re-done. This was to protect it and to keep up a smart appearance. Minnie Bell remembers that the hat was readily available. Some hats, she says, were black when you bought them. [Bell]. Margaret Moffat said the hats cost 1s.6d. (early 20th century). Mrs Winnie Sanderson said she paid 1/- for hers at about the same time. One lady said the hats looked dark blue in colour though this may have been the effect of the sheen or perhaps a sign that the hat needed to be re-lacquered. Most recollections are of a black hat.

The bondagers lined the hat with cotton material, often red - Jean Kinghorn said red Turkey [Kinghorn 1999] - but sometimes a cotton print. The edge of the brim was bound with braid for protection. The crown was decorated with ruching which was usually made from red and black material torn into strips, and the edges left to fray and become decorative. This ruching was gathered or pleated around the crown of the hat. Sometimes the ruching was worked into rosettes and these rosettes were decorated with beads, flowers and feathers. Mrs Winnie Sanderson said *'the hat was a work of art, or the trimming of it was'*. Mrs Mona Thompson of Wooler described the hats as having *'like clippy mats around the crown'*. Jean Kinghorn said she added *'silly little things from the shows to make it bonnie'*. [Kinghorn 1999]. These embellishments obviously made the hat more attractive and individual.

The hats were tied down with string when the wind was strong which made them look like a poke bonnet. Mr. Tom Wilson, of Wooler, described the hats as pulled down at the sides and looking more like an upturned boat. He also remembers, as does Mr. Bryson, that Wooler High Street could be thronging with people on a Saturday afternoon and the bondagers were very colourful.

Mary Rutherford said, *'I wore the bondager claes and a muckle big black hat wi' ruchin' round it. If the wind was high, we tied the hat beneath our chins with a bit of string. Oh, my, I likit that hat, though if we were doing heavy jobs I used to have to leave it at the hedge root.'* Mrs Cockburn said she tied her hat to her belt rather than wear it on her head and Mrs Meg Moffat's sister disliked the hat so much she wore it as little as possible. Mary King said, *'Ah wouldnae wear it. It always lay the back o'a gate in a field till ah wis feenished.'* Edith Hope said, *'Ah aleways wore ma big hat tae keep the sun off me, ah kept aye the hat on, right enough!'*

The East Lothian Ugly

The East Lothian Ugly was a cotton bonnet which was supported and held in shape by canes. The cotton was sometimes printed or quite often gingham. The canes were slotted through channels stitched into the cotton. There could be as many as 22 canes but the only examples examined have contained 14 canes.

**Figure 111. The East Lothian Ugly. East Saltoun Tythe Byre Museum.
(Photograph by A.R. Thompson)**

The bondagers interviewed in the 1970s called the cotton bonnet the East Lothian Ugly and made a strong distinction between the hats of Berwickshire and East Lothian. Over the years there has been the occasional reference to the "ugly" in different areas but the type of hat referred to has been unclear. Sometimes it seems to have been used as the name for a straw hat. Recently I have discovered two references to "uglies" in Northumberland. One reference is written and the other a painting showing recognisable uglies.

The written reference is by Mrs Hedley who recalls that *'The women workers, on the farms, used to wear large shady bonnets for their work, which were called "uglies". They were quite different from any sunbonnet worn now, for the part, which shaded the face, was held out by four or five canes. The Cambo women all used to wear them for the Haymaking, in Sir Walter's time (he inherited Wallington in 1846 and died in 1879). Then clouty bonnets – sunbonnets – came in.'* [Bosanquet 1929].

Figure 112. A Clouty Bonnet from an example made by Mary Arnot for Patsy Morton of Wooler. (Dinah Iredale).

These clouty bonnets were probably the bonnets which relied on much folding and stitching to provide the stiffness for the front of the bonnet. This type of bonnet could be opened flat for laundering and the drawstring was pulled up to bring it back into shape.

Clouty bonnets can be seen in many farming photographs in many areas.

The painted reference (see Figure 113) is a beautiful and vibrant watercolour sketch by Lady Waterford of Ford Castle which she painted in 1884. This painting shows ten bondagers working at a potato heap and the location is Heatherslaw between the villages of Ford and Etal. The bonnets are clearly uglies with the cane supports standing out very clearly in some instances. This sketch is lively and so appealing that having seen the black and white version in this book, I hope you will visit Lady Waterford Hall in Ford and enjoy the original in full colour.

Figure 113. A group of Bondagers working at Heatherslaw. (Waterclour sketch by Lady Waterford. 1884)

William Darling McKay (1844-1924) also produced a painting of bondagers at a potato pit called "Field Working in Spring". This shows some workers in small straw hats but more are wearing uglies. The location is East Lothian where William McKay was born. [National Galleries of Scotland].

These bonnets called uglies were very similar to some fashionable bonnets of the mid-19th century, and were prettily put together. For instance, where the main part of the bonnet met the curtain, a frill was formed. The name, East Lothian Ugly, arose from the fact that this bonnet, though not the only head-covering worn in East Lothian, was very popular in this area throughout the early 20th century. Photographic evidence shows this bonnet being worn exclusively in East Lothian. This was true for winter or summer work. There are photographs of bondagers wearing uglies when planting potatoes, working in the hay and harvest fields and sorting potatoes at the potato clamp.

Hastings Neville wrote about the changing fashions in the field workers hats in the following way. *'The head dress is a bonnet, large and old-fashioned, with a projecting curtain at the back and a shade encircling the front, almost concealing the face which is already partly covered by a large coloured handkerchief put under the bonnet and tied below the chin. The bonnet is now becoming more rare, and a round hat is coming into use instead.'* [Neville 1896].

Alexander Fenton also writes about the hats and states that *'no longer the plaited straw hat, but one of cloth, with a light wicker frame forming a wide hood in front, and a flap at the back, to protect the face and neck from wind and rain and sun. They were a little more pleasing in appearance than the Lothian name 'ugly' and the Lanarkshire name 'crazy' would suggest.'* [Fenton 1987]. Another article uses the term *'bongrace'* for the bonnet worn by the bondagers. (Country Life Magazine – July 1901)

The above comments, written almost one hundred years apart, demonstrate how opinion about the sequence in which the hats came into use can differ.

Figure 114. East Lothian Bondager. Drawing by A. L. Collins. [Bradley 1912].

Why "Ugly"?

In the 1850s there was a bonnet extension, made of material and canes, which could be worn on top of a lady's bonnet. This was worn as extra protection from the weather (a Victorian Rain-mate!) and was called an ugly. These Victorian uglies seem to be a reasonable source for the name.

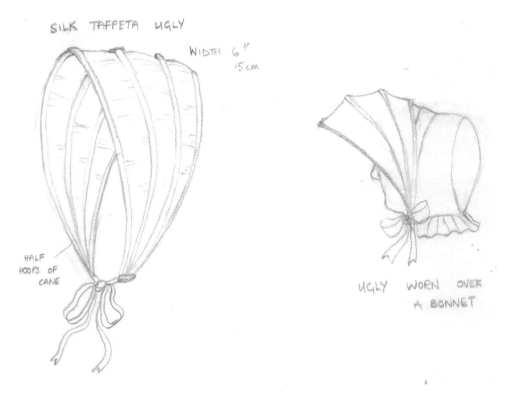

Figure 115. The ugly as originally worn in 1848-60 – Costume in Detail: Women's Dress 1730-1930 by Nancy Bradfield, 1968. (Dinah Iredale).

In her article on the East Lothian Ugly, Margaret H. Swain writes that the ugly has been adopted as the symbol for the East Lothian Federation and she traces the long history of the bonnet. She says *'it originated in the upper classes as the headgear of fashionable ladies about 1770 when it was called a calash, or Caleche in French, because the folding hood, stiffened by cane or whalebone, resembled the hood of the fast, two wheeled carriage of that name.'* The Duchess of Bedford either invented the idea or perhaps she says *'it is more likely that she was one of the first to set the fashion'*. It was *'light yet high enough to protect the piled-up hairdressing surmounted by the fantastic headdress of the period'*.

Later in *'about 1848 someone rescued the idea and made up brims, like the front of the calash, for ladies to tie over the front of their bonnets while walking in the country, or on the sea-shore which had become popular. Frith's painting of Ramsgate Sands (1854) shows several uglies being worn'*.

She then goes on to explain the name. *'The name "ugly" was given to them at that time. Thackeray refers to them in his Christmas Book for 1850, when Miss Fanny Kicklebury and her sister wore "those blue silk over-bonnets which have lately become so fashionable". "Those hoods" she said, "we call those hoods uglies"*. [Swain 1963].

Figure 116. An illustration from the "Englishwoman's Domestic Magazine" showing the ugly as worn on Margate Sands in 1852. [Swain 1963].

E. A. Walton was one of a group of artists, all of whom attended Glasgow School of Art in the late 19th Century. The group became known as the 'Glasgow Boys'. [Billcliffe 2002]. Walton's painting 'A Berwickshire Fieldworker' (1884) depicts five bondagers who appear to be working in a field of beans and are wearing Berwickshire Hats *and* uglies (see Figure 117). This is a unique image, as I have found no other evidence of bondagers dressing like this. The bondagers, most likely from Cockburnspath, are demonstrating that, although living far from the centre of fashion, they were aware of and chose to wear uglies as a fashion accessory – albeit, some years after it was at its height.

Figure 117. Bondager wearing a straw hat and an ugly. From a painting by E. A. Walton. [Billcliffe 2002]. (Dinah Iredale).

Coincidently, at the same time as E. A. Walton was painting these fieldworkers, two other Glasgow Boys, J. Guthrie and G. Henry, painted fieldworkers near Cockburnspath wearing the more usual East Lothian ugly and Lady Waterford completed her watercolour sketch of a scene at Heatherslaw (Figure 113).

Betty Mulvey of Edinburgh, who has family connections with Old Camus, near Cockburnspath, recalls a painting of fieldworkers by the artist William Scott. Though not a bondager, Betty's great aunt, Elizabeth Renton, dressed as a bondager for this painting around 1900. She later married Scott. The whereabouts of the painting is unknown.

In the conclusion to her article, Margaret H. Swain considers that *'the East Lothian ugly is a combination of the eighteenth century calash and the Victorian ugly'*. She also thinks that *'Its light yet rigid construction makes it a very practical headgear for working outdoors in the windy uplands of East Lothian'*. [Swain 1963]. I do wonder about this!

The two examples of uglies on display in the Tithe Byre at East Saltoun (1977) were made in pink checked and green checked cotton. Margaret H. Swain notes that *'the colour was traditionally blue, no doubt echoing the blue silk of Miss Fanny's ugly'*. She also notes that *'like sunbonnets in other parts of Britain, they gradually became less worn, after the First World War, when the fashion for sunburn made a shady brim undesirable.'* The ugly seems to have been worn without a wimple although it is difficult to see clearly in photographs. Hastings Neville [op. cit.] suggests wimples were worn under bonnets. Sometimes there seems to have been a kerchief which would have made sense as an alternative to a wimple.

Mr. George Hardy (Rothbury Local History Society) and Mrs Diana Sharp (formerly of The Good Life Shop, Wooler) both remember seeing bondagers working in the fields in East Lothian in the late 1940s to early 1950s. They likened the bonnets to the covered wagons in a western. Mrs Thompson (Chillingham Barns, Northumberland) remembers two bondagers wearing uglies on the family farm in Berwickshire in the 1940s/1950s. This was Redheugh Farm near Cockburnspath which is just over the border into Berwickshire.

In 1974, Bolton S.W.R.I. wrote about the *"ugly"* saying *'With the advent of scientific farming much beauty has been lost. No longer do we see flocks of women working in the fields wearing the East Lothian "Ugly" and looking in the distance like bright tropical birds. Why these bonnets were ever called Uglies is incomprehensible. Lovelies would have been a better word. Even plain girls looked pretty when wearing an Ugly. They were eminently practical, protecting the wearer against all kinds of weather.'* [Bolton 1974].

The Wimple

The wimple is a cloth covering for the head which is sometimes called a *'heid hankie'* in Scotland. The large rectangular piece of material was placed around the head, and the two front corners taken round and fastened at the back of the head. The other two corners were brought forward and fastened at the front either under or over the chin.

In Scotland, the wimple was traditionally white, whereas in North Northumberland, it was pink and white check with a definite pink border running round the edge. Possibly this is the selvedge of specially woven cloth? There are also some references to red and white checks. Often the corners pulled to the front were knotted (this can be clearly seen in many photographs) which was, perhaps, to add weight and so keep the front corners in place. Sometimes the two corners are knotted together and the wimple is pinned under the chin. Perhaps the knots enable the wimple to stay fastened even when just loosely tied.

The wimple helped the bondager retain as much pale skin as possible. This was important as in the 19th century and early 20th century it was not fashionable to be tanned and a pale skin was to be prized. Mrs Cockburn remembers one of her sisters was *'fanatical'* about protecting her skin from the sun. Sunstroke could also be avoided, as the wimple covered the back of the neck. A local doctor, in Wooler, is said to have bemoaned the dying out of the traditional costume, as he was beginning to see more cases of sunstroke. A lighthearted comment, often made, was that you could always tell a bondager, even when in her Sunday best, because she had a tanned triangle in the middle of her face!

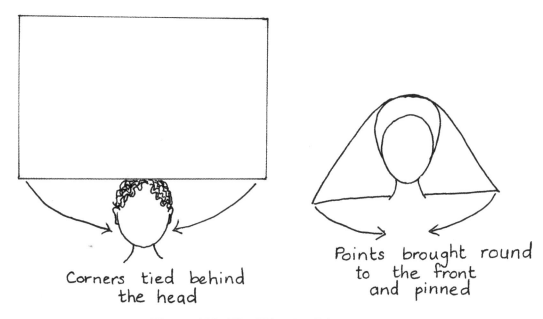

Corners tied behind
the head

Points brought round
to the front
and pinned

Figure 118. The Wimple. (Dinah Iredale)

Mary Anderson of Yetholm demonstrated how the wimple was worn and remarked on the white un-tanned areas down the side of the face. Jean Newlands talking to Fred Kennington admitted that despite great efforts not to get tanned, *'Yes, she had a bit of tanned face'*. Jean Kinghorn, when asked about getting a red face, *'No! The sun never got at you! The sun never got at you because of the hat and headsquare. It was pink and white or blue and white checks'*. [Kinghorn 1999]. Minnie Bell said *'We were never sunburnt despite working outside and we also kept our hands nice'*. [Bell].

The 1893 Royal Commission includes an account of a strange custom among the bondagers. *'The women eat raw rice at odd intervals when working'*. Sucking starch is also mentioned. [Fox 1893]. One suggestion is that this is related to the desire to maintain or retain a pale skin although, when George Grey, of Milfield, put this to the women, he found them *'ignorant of that effect'*. It was thought that these habits cause indigestion and eventually ulceration of the stomach which then led to anaemia. Dr Walker of Wooler testifies to the existence of this habit and says it is *'an exceedingly bad one'*. The Commissioner comments that *'it is difficult to ascertain the reason why the women do this. Some say that it is purely a habit, others that the girls think it makes their complexions white, but if this is really the reason, the whiteness doubtless arises from a continuance of indigestion.'* Mary and Agnes Black said *'Girls get a craving for it'*. Mary Logan, byrewoman, Akeld, *said 'I have seen the girls eat rice for the last ten years; they do it to pass the time away.'* [Fox 1893].

The wimple was also a great protection in bad weather or when the work in hand was particularly dirty or dusty. It could be pulled higher to cover the mouth and even higher to cover the nose and mouth. Mrs Violet Smith of Wooler who wore the wimple but not the hat (the hat was too old-fashioned for her and her friend and they rebelled!) says the wimple prevented straw and chaff getting down the neck of her blouse.

In a number of photographs a large safety pin is clearly seen pinned into the bondager's blouse. Obviously this was there for a purpose. Pins were used throughout the costume for fastening the wimple, the shawl and breeking the petticoats. Mrs Dorothy Hall of New Haggerston has kindly allowed me to photograph a brooch which had been passed down through her family as a bondager brooch or pin. It is a large 2" (5cm) strong safety pin made, we thought probably, of brass with a very attractive front rather like plaited straw - a very suitable brooch to pin a wimple.

Figure 119. A Bondager Pin. (Mrs Dorothy Hall, New Haggerston).

Mr. Jim Mallen of Yetholm remembers a similar pin used by a bondager who had come from Northumberland. Derek Fairnington, when metal detecting, often uncovers safety pins but these are the plain utilitarian safety pins. He also discovers many thimbles, small, medium and large. What were they used for in the field? Obviously, they were used to protect the finger tips but from what? Were they used during stooking? However, this does not seem entirely practical. Perhaps, they were used when shearing corn with a heuk.

Finally, Hastings Neville expresses his opinion about hats, bonnets and wimples. He writes: '*All this covering up of the head and face which renders these our sisters in the field hardly recognizable even to their Pastor who knows them well enough on Sunday at church, where they appear dressed in very good taste and even fashionably, arises not from any such idea as the concealment of their features like the women of the East, although the effect is somewhat similar. There is indeed in these toilers when at work a manner which seems to say, "Yes, this is our costume, our uniform when we are doing this work, it is not beautiful, and we prefer being recognized at some other time when we are dressed according to our taste". The idea, of course, is to preserve the complexion from injury by sun and wind, but whilst admiring and respecting this womanly instinct of care for the appearance, one cannot but think that all this covering up of the face and head is the cause of much of the neuralgia from which these young women suffer, and that their bright complexion is actually due to the climate in which they work and live.*' [Neville 1896].

The Blouse

Another attractive element of the costume was the '*print blouse*'. The ladies who gave me information in the 1970s always referred to their '*print blouses*'. These can be seen very clearly in many of the photographs. Sometimes striped, spotted or flower sprigged but always with long sleeves!

Generally, in the early 20th century, the blouses were bought '*ready-made*' although Minnie Bell said, '*Mother made my blouses*'. [Bell]. Jean Kinghorn said she made her own blouses. [Kinghorn 1999]. In earlier times they would all have been 'home-made'. The blouses were lined with calico, often 're-cycled' flour bags. This was to make the blouses last longer and for added warmth. Minnie Bell recalled they were '*lined for winter*'. [Bell]. Mr.

Tait of Duns described the blouse as being padded, but when asked why this was, he admitted his wife Janet had never told him.

Some bondagers are shown wearing a checked dress over their blouse and skirt. They also appear like this in a photograph in *'A Corner in the North'* [Neville 1909], and in *'Under a Border Tower'* [Neville 1896]. Hastings Neville describes this cotton dress as *'a cotton dress, always looped up'*. [Neville 1909]. Could this be a remnant from a previous era when skirts were looped up to show the petticoat underneath? The bondagers in Cuthbert Bede's drawing have looped up skirts revealing a striped petticoat. The 1867 Royal Commission also describes this dress as a *'washing pinafore with sleeves (called a slip), which preserves the dress from dirt.'* [Henley 1867]. Few photographs after 1900 show this cotton dress.

Figure 120. Farm Staff, Northumberland. Notice the straw ropes and the cotton over dresses. An early photograph. 1870? (John Lackenby – the 4th figure from the left in the back row is John's great grandfather).

The Shawl and the Swaffie

Traditionally the bondagers wore a shawl for added warmth, and this was fastened in a particular way to enable the bondager to work without any hindrance from the shawl. The shawl was pinned at each shoulder, and the loose ends thrown over to the back and tied. A belt was fastened round the waist trapping the bottom corner of the shawl, and so ensuring it was snug against the worker's back and out of the way.

The shawl generally appears to be made of a woollen woven material usually in a broad check, sometimes tartan. Hastings Neville did mention *'a little knitted shawl over the shoulders'*. Many photographs show bondagers wearing the shawl fastened in this special way with just a small amount of shawl showing on each shoulder.

Figure 121. The Shawl – notice how it is fastened at the back to allow the bondager to work freely. (Mrs Anne Scott, Melrose).

When I was researching the costume, in the 1970s, another garment was mentioned. This was the *'swaffie'* which was a waistcoat or bolero. One lady said, *'I wore the swaffie but mother wore the shawl'*. It is thought the name *'swaffie'* came from the name *'zouave'*, which was a fashionable open jacket or waistcoat in the 1830/60s. This fashionable garment was based on the uniform jacket of a *'French-Algerian Infantry Regiment'*.

The *'swaffie'* was a short sleeveless tweed jacket, sometimes with lapels. The bondagers decorated it with studs, buttons and ric-rac braid. The buttons and studs can be clearly seen in some photographs as straight or curved lines of white dots.

Figure 122. Bondagers wearing swaffies (tweed waistcoats) whilst shawing turnips.

Additional Protection from the Weather

Additional warmth was also provided by the cut-off legs of stockings which were pulled on over the sleeves of the blouse. Mr. Bill Davidson of Duddo called these pokies. Sometimes these pokies were worn pulled over the hand for warmth with fingers left free for work. Bill also thought this was an attempt by the bondagers to keep their hands white. Mr. William Tait of Duns mentioned the bondagers wearing more layers when it was cold, and in wet weather they would wear a sack. They made a hood out of the two bottom corners (one corner tucked inside the other) and the rest of the sack draped over the shoulders and back. It was tied down with a belt.

Ada Mary Howarth remembers seeing farm workers in 1920s and 1930s using sacks in this way. She says of clothing *'The men wore heavy leather ankle boots studded with nails called tickerty-tacks, with leather laces, and rough tweed jackets and trousers. They had mackintoshes or oilskins for wet days, or, lacking these, a thick hemp potato sack tied round the shoulders with string or binder twine. The sight of a farm worker thus clad, slouching up the back road from the cottages to the steading at Gatehousecote struck pity in my heart'.* [Howarth 1998].

Mrs Scott, of Melrose, mentions *'glazy scougies'* which were *'home-made oilskins of unbleached calico dipped and re-dipped in boiled linseed oil'.* She says they seemed to have come in about 1910. Linseed oil was also used on the skirts.

Mr. Mallen and his wife, Betty, of Yetholm, also talked about clothing. They said that the men all wore good tweed jackets, waistcoats and trousers. These were bought ready-made from the travelling tailor who called every six months. The system was that the suit or whatever was needed was obtained immediately and paid for when the tailor visited again in six months. Betty said that, *'It was six months credit!'* The shoemaker operated a similar system – calling once every six months and giving credit.

Working in all weathers could be a *'bone of contention'.* Mr Tait of Duns mentions that ropes were made and dung cleared on wet days. He says *'Work was done in bad weather. You could lose your job if you didn't.'* Jean Willis of Alnwick mentions that there was plenty to do even on wet days. There was *'no skiving on a farm'.* She also includes the following piece of dialogue in dialect. *"I'll had away hym"* (hym meaning home) as a gaffer used to say. Also *"Have ye no gan an dun it yet?"* If not *"git away and git cracking a'for ye git run doon the road". (Run down the road meant getting the sack).'*

Mrs Nancy Clark, speaking to Fred Kennington, said *'We just had to get on and work'*. She only lost half a day in all her working life. On this occasion she had really sore hands through harvesting work and she was absent one Saturday morning. [Clark].

Dr. R. Shirra Gibb of the Lauder area mentions time away from work for women workers. He says *'The women were generally allowed a day off except when special work was going on; the time of their "holiday" was then deducted at pay-time, so that they practically had holidays when ever they wanted them'*. He also states that whilst a woman might be *'promised constant work, except in the wild weather, they had neither the full-time nor full pay of the men. He did try to honour his promises of work and says 'On two occasions only, during the whole fifty years of my farming life, had I to tell the steward to send the women home as there was nothing for them to do; both times were during deep-lying snowstorms'*. [Gibb 1927].

So working in all weathers was difficult and *'protective clothing'* had to be ingeniously improvised. On the other hand, to be sent home for whatever reason, impossible weather conditions or no suitable tasks available, meant loss of earnings.

The Skirt or Petticoat

The skirt was often referred to, in the old fashioned way, as a petticoat. It reached to just over the knee (much shorter than skirts were usually worn at the end of the 19th century) and was made of a material called *'drugget'*. This was a woollen /cotton or woollen/linen mixture. The warp was cotton or linen and the weft was wool. *'Drugget'* was made locally and sold by travelling salesmen. The material was sometimes plain, but very often striped. Striped skirts are part of many traditional costumes, and most people will have seen photographs of fishwives and Welsh women wearing striped skirts.

The skirts were made of a length of *'drugget'* with the cut edges sewn together, leaving a back opening, which was closed by a one button fastening or tapes at the waist. There were two and a half to three yards of material in each skirt. The SWRI questionnaire revealed a reason for this, which was that there had to be enough room to ride astride a carthorse. This is interesting as it was said by some men that the bondagers did not get to ride anywhere whereas the hinds did.

Figure 123. A skirt made of striped drugget with a waistband made of braid. The Gladstone Court Museum, Biggar. (Photograph by A.R. Thompson)

Glen Aln's memories differ in that he says *'It was not uncommon when the men and women were working in the same field for the women to mount the horse behind the man, sitting sideways, that is both legs on one side and clinging to the arm or shoulder of the hind.'* Notice in this case they are not riding astride. He also says *'The braver spirits, instead of jumping down, would slide over the hind quarters of the animal.'* [Aln 1945].

The material was pleated not gathered. There was a large box pleat at the front and pleats were continued round to left and right to the centre back seam. Mrs. Scott said *'some women specified nineteen pleats on each side.'* Jean Kinghorn, said the skirts were pleated all round so they could be *'breeked'*. Some skirts were tucked just above the hem and these tucks were decorated with black or red braid. [Kinghorn 1999]. One bondager skirt I examined had braid at the hem making a false hem or binding, possibly to protect the *'drugget'* from wear at the bottom edge of the skirt.

The skirts were sometimes worn one on top of another – sometimes as many as three, but more often two. Mr. William Tait of Duns, whose wife Janet was a bondager, commented that the outer skirt was plain and rather dull in colour, but underneath was worn a brighter coloured or striped skirt. Mary Rutherford of Mellerstain said – *'The skirts were a sort of stripey material and we wore two or three, one on top of the other.'*

A final process, to make the skirts waterproof, was to oil them with linseed oil. *'When the skirts had been made, they were spread out and oil rubbed into the cloth, then they were hung out to let the oil dry or harden'* (Mrs Sybil Straughan recounting the memories of Mrs Bella Moffat of Ewart). Mr. William Tait of Duns also mentioned this method of waterproofing material. The linseed oil treatment also made it easier to remove mud from the skirt.

Although the ladies, ex-bondagers, whom I spoke to in 1976 considered the costume to be practical for most of the work they undertook, for the dirtiest work they pinned the skirt to keep it out of the way. This was called *'breeking'* the petticoat and could involve the use of one or three pins – regretfully, this was not demonstrated in 1976. One method was to pin the front and the back of the skirt together using one pin. The other method was to pin the skirt together round each leg and another pin in the centre at the bottom.

Figure 124. Bondagers with breeked petticoats and straw rope leggings.

Mrs. Sally Dunn of Seton Hall remembered '*breeking*' her skirt and was amused to see a photograph of bondagers with '*breeked*' skirts.

Aprons

Aprons were worn over the skirt and these varied depending on the work being undertaken. White or pink cotton aprons were used for the cleanest work such as hay-time and harvest. Hastings Neville writes in '*Under a Border Tower*' that '*a gay pinafore often of a light pink colour, which certainly is a redeeming point, because it lights up well in the sunshine, and is seen afar in the fields*'. [Neville 1896].

Glen Aln mentions print pinafores, '*of blue and white or pink and white*' which is unusual. The only photographic record, of patterned pinafores or aprons, are those worn by Ion Jamieson's dancing group in the 1930s.

Nancie Foster, a well-known artist from Wooler, painted an attractive painting of bondagers in a harvest field wearing white aprons. She called it '*Yesterdays Harvest*'. In contrast, Beatrix Potter noted in her diary that aprons were blue and skirts short. [Potter 1986].

Sometimes, '*drugget*' aprons to match the skirt were chosen and these were considered smart. A linsey/woolsey apron was mentioned by Mrs Scott, of Melrose. '*Another material used for aprons was "brat" which was a kind of linsey/woolsey in hopsack weave and in a brown and black mixture. The apron itself was called a "brat".*' A hessian or sacking apron also seems to have been known as a '*brat*' or '*brattie*' and was worn for the dirtiest work. Mrs Sally Dunn of Seton Hall mentioned how they used the '*brattie*' to carry potatoes when planting them and to carry stones when clearing a field. Sometimes the '*brat*' was worn over the cotton or '*drugget*' apron for extra protection.

Jean Newlands, speaking to Fred Kennington, recalls that the apron was a plain strong material. She said, '*It was not called a 'brat' – a ' brat' was for housework*'. [Newlands].

Many women do recall the word *'brat'* and in their memory this was a hessian apron for the *'rough'* housework.

Lesley Bentham, a researcher into traditional dress, mentioned that a 'kick-tape' was often attached to the aprons. This was low down on each side of the skirt of the apron and, when it was tied at the back, it prevented the apron from flying up. This kept the apron in place, therefore making it more efficient, and at the same time it was kept out of the way of the worker.

Mr. Bill Davidson, of Duddo, remembered that the aprons were sometimes a full pinafore with a bib rather than just a waist apron. An illustration in *'The Old Halls and Houses and Inns of Northumberland' by* Frank Graham shows a bondager with a full-length pinafore rather than a waist apron. Mrs Anne Telfer, of Milfield, discovered this illustration.

Stocking, Stays and Drawers

Bondagers wore hand-knitted black stockings which, according to one account, were knitted by the bondagers on their way to and from the fields. This *'knitting on the hoof'*, was commonly undertaken by country people, and they had specially adapted belts to help with this process.

Jean Kinghorn said she learnt sewing and knitting at home and school. The black stockings were knitted in 5 ply for work and others were knitted in 2 ply for Sunday. Knitting was something to do at night. [Kinghorn 1999].

Mrs Scott, of Melrose, mentions that *'machine made stockings gradually replaced the hand knitted ones as at 2s. 11d. per pair they were cheaper'.*

A useful tip to rid stockings of rough bits of straw or particularly barley horns, was to place the stockings in the oven beside the fire overnight. Once the barley horns were crisp and dry they could be rubbed out of the stockings.

Strong boots called *'tackety boots'* were worn and are visible in many photographs. Clogs were also worn, and these can be seen in the painting, previously mentioned, by E. A. Walton, who painted some fieldworkers near Cockburnspath in 1884.

Mr William Tait of Duns also mentioned clogs, saying *'Those who could not afford boots had clogs.'* The clogs were made locally. Boots were made in Coldstream and they cost a man's wage for a month. Strong footwear was very necessary to protect feet from the hazards of tools, machinery and animals' feet, particularly 'iron-clad' carthorses. These boots were cared for carefully and polished for a good *'turn-out'* each morning. Comments about Wellingtons, which came in about the 1940s, were that they never looked as smart as boots and they did not give the feet the same amount of protection.

Gaiters or leggings were worn to protect the legs from cold and dirt. These were made of leather, leatherette, canvas, cut down trousers and army puttees (Army puttees after World War I). Mr. William Tait, of Duns said that linen leggings were oiled to make them waterproof. In the very dirtiest conditions, perhaps shawing turnips during a wet spell of weather, straw ropes were wound around the legs on top of the leggings for extra protection.

Figure 125. A bondager dressed for winter work. (Dinah Iredale)

Mrs Scott of Melrose records that straw ropes were *'also used round the forearm when shawing turnips'*. These ropes could be made using a thraw crook or thrack hook but Mr. William Tait, of Duns, said his wife made wopies or ropies for her legs by twisting the straw round her thumb. One hand pulled the straw tight and the thumb twisted the straw into a fine, light rope. In *'The Chambers Scots Dictionary'* – *'wap or wop mean wrap, fold, bind, tie, join, especially by splicing;'*

Thraw crooks were used to make ropes for many purposes around the farm including ropes for tying down stacks once they were thatched. Nancy Clark, speaking to Fred Kennington, said, *'Piles of ropes were needed for harvest'*. [Clark].

Mrs Joan Pringle remembers various straw rope makers. She found some easier to use than others. One had three hooks to make a stronger, thicker rope. Mr. Jim Mallen of Yetholm, recalled that the thraw crook with three hooks was used with binder twine to make reins where three strands or three double strands were twisted together.

**Figure 126. A Thraw Crook, a straw rope maker. Tythe Byre, East Saltoun.
(Photograph by A.R. Thompson)**

Mrs Maisie Campbell of Wooler recalled that some visitors to a fairly remote area of Russia in 2001 noticed workers in the fields wearing straw ropes round their legs.

Divided drawers were worn by bondagers. These were really two separate legs held together by a waistband which had a one-button fastening at the back. Divided drawers were commonly worn by women in all walks of life in the 1900s and were very practical. Mary Rutherford, of Mellerstain, mentions divided drawers, and Mr. William Tait, of Duns, described them as *'long knickers - white, with a frill at the knee'*. Mrs Mary Whittle, of Milfield, has very kindly given me a pair of divided drawers which were found amongst the belongings of an elderly relative. They are beautifully hand-stitched with hand-made lace trimmings.

Mr. John Dixon, of Wooler, tells a funny story about knickers! John's brother worked for a threshing firm and the custom was that the two men with the threshing machine were fed by the farmer. On this particular day the first course of the meal was fine, but the pudding, a cloutie dumpling, was served up in what were obviously pink bloomers and it itself was pink from the dye, which rather took away his appetite!

Stays were also worn and can be clearly seen in some photographs. Again, stays would be commonly worn by most women but for the bondagers it was stated by many that the stays helped them lift heavy items. The bondagers felt that stays supported their back. A good strong leather belt was also considered to be a support for the back.

Figure 127. Two older bondagers who have done a lot of hard work. Notice the horse, man and bogie behind them which shows they are working in a hay field. (Mrs Craigie, Wooler).

In 'The World is Ill Divided' Barbara Robertson quotes from Hansel Craig by Allan Fraser. '*Mrs Graham was a dignified old lady with small hands. She spoke the Border dialect. She had extraordinary grace and poise. They said she was seventy at that time, yet except for her furrowed face and her white hair she looked quite young. Her waist was gimp (slender) as a maiden's although she had borne three children, her step was firm and very light, her blue eyes set in her brown face looked proud and unafraid.*' [Robertson 1990].

Mrs Scott of Melrose mentions that '*Most girls had a watch on a string around their necks, tucked into a pocket in the skirt waistband.* (Earlier, Sally Dunn said that it was the first woman who had the watch, and this was probably the case in some groups of workers.) '*Another pocket of black sateen was worn under the skirt on a tape round the waist.*'

The Costume Declines

The costume, although basically remaining the same for many, many years, did clearly change in small ways. The waistcoat or swaffie increasingly replaced the shawl, for instance. Furthermore, the Berwickshire Hat, the East Lothian Ugly and the clootie bonnet were worn at different times. One change, which played a big part in the decline of the bondager costume, was the difficulty in obtaining *'drugget'* which had once been a locally made material. Also wimples and large shady hats were no longer needed when it became fashionable to be tanned!

The introduction of the Women's Land Army during the First World War and the Second World War had a big influence on the work undertaken by the bondagers, as well as on the clothes they wore. After the First World War puttees were worn by bondagers but trousers were still not an accepted part of female dress, although attitudes were changing. Land Army girls in the First World War did dress in trousers (breeches) but with a long knee-length smock over the top. Mrs Cockburn, who worked as a bondager in the 1920s, stated when asked about trousers, that she did not remember any objections to trousers, but they did not *'take on'* like the petticoats! Mrs Sally Dunn, of Seton Hall, said she never wore trousers. *'You'd have been thought a fool to wear trousers.'*

In the Second World War the Land Army girls wore breeches (without the smocks) or dungarees. Working as they did to produce food, whilst the men were away fighting, perhaps made dressing like a man more acceptable. From the 1940s, trousers did become acceptable wear for women, although they were generally confined to leisurewear.

The bondager costume had, in effect, been replaced by another uniform, which was more practical in many ways. Women could now, through their war work, wear trousers without threatening the position of men or demeaning their own femininity.

15. Conclusion

Women have always made a big contribution to the work carried out in any agricultural area, particularly at hay and harvest times. This work could be labouring in the fields alongside the men, or at home providing refreshments for the harvesters. Perhaps one reason for the prominence of women workers in this border area was due to the very low population. Another reason, suggested by Mr Donald Scott of Caistron, was that since historically the men were away dealing with the '*raids and other warlike activities*', women had to shoulder the burden of keeping the farming processes going and it became a tradition.

'*A French traveller in the area' (towards the end of the 16th century) Dr. Perlin, recorded that "the people are all armed; the labourers, when they till the ground, leave their swords and their bows in a corner of the field".* [Collier 1986].

Recently, although the bondage system no longer existed, farm workers with a wife who was willing to help with harvesting, particularly (latterly) with the potato harvest, were sought after. Mrs Isabel Barrie, of Milfield, remembers her father saying that a common question a farmer would ask a man waiting to be hired was, 'Have you a bondager?' Those who could answer yes were hired first. This was well into the Twentieth Century, around 1930. Mrs Anne Telfer, of Milfield, recalled that her mother was not a bondager, but part of the agreement her father made with the farmer, whose cottage they rented, was that she (Anne's mother) would single turnips and also work on the potatoes. This was during the Second World War. Anne's father worked for a drainage contractor and not on the farm.

H. Cecil Pawson in '*A Survey of the Agriculture of Northumberland*' says, when discussing women workers, '*as recently as 1953 the County Rural Community Council stated that "this form of bondage has not as far as we are aware ceased to operate'.* [Pawson 1961]. No further detail, other than historical, is given.

The bondagers' major role in the agriculture of Northumberland, the Scottish Borders and the Lothians should be remembered. Their eye-catching and distinctive costume, which ensured they were noticed, was eminently practical and adaptable but at the same time allowed the women, through various embellishments, to express their femininity. Working as they did, alongside the men, we should remember them as strong, independent women who knew their own worth. Maureen Brook discovered a letter, written by some bondagers, which demonstrates this strength of purpose. It is undated but was probably written in the late 19th century because of the money amounts demanded. They wrote '*Notice hereby given – That we women workers wishes to inform the farmers in this neighbourhood that we intend to struch for more wages after this week beginning on May 5th when we want eighteen pence a day and in haytime eighteen pence and our tea in corn harvest three shillings and our tea and if you think it tow much you must take into consideration the price of your beef and mutton eggs butter and chease and consider we have them to bye it is to be hoped that there will be no blacklegs amongst us good night..* ' [Brook 2005].

The bondagers were not downtrodden menials but through their wide-ranging skills were equal contributors to the rural economy in a pre-mechanised age.

Figure 128. My sister Dorothy dressed as a bondager in 2006.
(Photograph by Dinah Iredale)

<u>Acknowledgements</u>

It is a pleasure to end this book by thanking the kind and special people, many named in the text, who have so generously shared with me their memories, photographs and artefacts. Each piece of information, large or small, has been invaluable in building up a picture of the women workers and their lives. I have endeavoured to accurately record these memories and apologise for any inaccuracies.

Many thanks to Roger Miket for encouraging my research, and for his subsequent advice. Special thanks to Linda Bankier, Brian and Dorothy Sharpe and Hilary Briggs for unstinting help, guidance and encouragement and Rena Telfer for, in particular, some invaluable books. Very special thanks to Kevin Malloy for giving so much time and his technical expertise so that the document could be produced in an excellent format. Thanks to Derek and Anne Fairnington for providing some wonderful photographs and their interest in the developing project, Lesley Bentham of 'Yes! We Have National Costumes' for her enthusiasm for the bondagers and their dress and Susan Veitch for helping in a number of ways, but particularly for her artistic knowledge, Helen Astley for her interest and encouragement and for a lovely description of women wearing the East Lothian ugly. Meg and David Thompson for their encouragement with this project, and David for taking the time to show and explain the workings of many tools and machines in his wonderful collection at Chillingham Barns. Also for allowing me to make drawings of the tools included in this book.

Many grateful thanks to my family and friends who through their interest, in some cases over many years, have inspired and encouraged me.

Very special thanks to the Glendale Local History Society for their interest and enthusiasm about the bondagers but most of all for undertaking the publication of my book; and to The North Northumberland Leader Gold Small Grants Scheme administered by Community Action Northumberland for awarding a grant towards publication costs.

Sincere thanks for the expert, professional and friendly help from members of staff at the Berwick-upon-Tweed Record Office; Kelso Library; Hawick Library; Jedburgh Library; Selkirk Library; Woodhorn Museum, Northumberland County Record Office; School of Scottish Studies; National Library of Scotland; National Museums of Scotland; Hawick Hub, Scottish Borders Archive and Local History Centre; Scotsman Publications; Scottish Women's Rural Institute; Berwick Library; Wooler Library; Morpeth Library; Museum of English Rural Life, University of Reading; Edinburgh University Library; Newcastle-upon-Tyne Libraries and Information Service.

Finally, for anyone or institute who has not received appropriate thanks in the above I express my appreciation and thanks.

Photographs which are privately owned are acknowledged individually throughout the text. Many, many thanks once again for those.

Document, newspaper extracts and photographs, which are held by institutions, are reproduced by kind permission of:

Viscount Allendale
Figure 6.

Berwick Records Office
Figures 5, 9, 64, 66-69, 72, 89, 91, 107.
Figures 17-19,21-24, 26, 27, 31, 32, 45, 52-58, 65, 70, 71, 101, 102. (Berwick Advertiser)
Figures 46, 47, 59, 61. (Alnwick Mercury)
Figures 20, 25, 29, 30. (Berwick and Kelso Warder)

The Carmichael family
Figure 87.

National Library of Scotland
Figures. 33-44, 48-51, 60, 62, 63

Trustees of the National Museums of Scotland
Figures 97, 110, 121-124.

Newcastle Libraries and Information Service
Figure 28.

Northumberland Collections Service (formerly Northumberland Record Office).
Figures 7, 10-15, 93.

Ford and Etal Estates (Lord and Lady Joicey).
Figure 113.

Bibliography

Age Concern. *I mind the time!* Kelso Graphics, 1984

Aln, Glen. *Around and about Northumberland.* 2nd Edition. Richard Logan, Amble, 1944

Aln, Glen. *People and Places of Northumberland.* Richard Logan, Amble, 1945

Bailey, J. and **Culley**, G. *General View of the Agriculture of Northumberland, Cumberland and Westmorland, 1805*. Facsimile of third edition. (Introduction by D. J. Rowe). Frank Graham, 1972. ISBN 902833-46-4

Bailey, Mark. *The English Manor c.1200–c.1500*. Selected sources translated and annotated by Mark Bailey. Manchester University Press, 2002. ISBN 07190-5229-7.

Balfour, M.C. Examples of *Printed Folklore concerning Northumberland*. (Edited by Thomas, Northcote W.). County Folklore. Vol IV. Printed Extracts No. 6. David Nutt, London, 1904

Bede, Cuthbert B.A. *The Adventures of Mr. Verdant Green.* James Blackwood and Co., 1877

Bell, Minnie. SLH Bell M J07.011.01. School of Scottish Studies. University of Edinburgh.

Billcliffe, Roger. *The Glasgow Boys. The Glasgow School of Painting 1875-1895.* John Murray (Publishers) Ltd., 2002. ISBN 0-7195-6033-0

Bolton Parish description. Scottish Women's Rural Institute, 1974. http://www.ndhm.org.uk/page_22.htm

Bosanquet, Rosalie E. (Editor). *In the Troublesome Times.* 1929. Reprinted by The Spredden Press, 1989. ISBN 1-871739-03-9

Bradley, A. G. *The Gateway of Scotland.* Constable & Company Ltd., London, 1912.

Brook, Maureen. *Herring Girls and Hiring Fairs.* Tyne Bridge Publishing, 2005. ISBN 1-85795-147-6

Buchan, David. *The Expressive Culture of Nineteenth Century Scottish Farm Servants*. Chap 12 of *Farm Servants and Labour in Lowland Scotland 1770-1914.* (Edited by **Devine**, T. M.). John Donald Publishers Ltd., 1984. ISBN 0-85976-439-7

Butler, Josephine. *Memoir of John Grey of Dilston.* Henry S. King and Co., 1874

Christie, The Rev. Jas., B.A.Lond. *Northumberland. Its History, Features and People.* Thurman, 1904

Clark, Nancy. Recorded by **Kennington**, Fred. Berwick Record Office 608-28 & 608-29.

Colbeck, T. L. *On the Agriculture of Northumberland.* Journal of the Royal Agricultural Society Vol. VIII, 1847.

Collier, C and **Stewart**, L. A. *Wooler and Glendale. A Brief History.* Vol. I and II. Published by The Glendale Local History Society, Wooler, 1986

Crosbie, Jim. *Grantshouse.* 2002.

Davidson, W. G. *Letter to The Border Magazine.* Vol. 27, 1922. W. G. Davidson, Lyne, Peebles.

Devine, T. M. *Introduction: Scottish Farm Service in the Agricultural Revolution*. Chap 1 of *Farm Servants and Labour in Lowland Scotland 1770-1914.* (Edited by **Devine**, T. M.). John Donald Publishers Ltd., 1984. ISBN 0-85976-439-7

Devine, T. M. *Women Workers, 1850-1914.* Chap 6 of *Farm Servants and Labour in Lowland Scotland 1770-1914.* (Edited by **Devine**, T. M.). John Donald Publishers Ltd., 1984. ISBN 0-85976-439-7

Doyle, Sir Francis, Hastings. *Reports of Special Assistant Poor Law Commissioners on the Employment of Women and Childeren in Agriculture.* HMSO. 1843

Dunmore, Richard. *Hiring Fairs and Wakes Weeks*.
http://www.applebymagna.org.uk/appleby_history/in_focus24.htm

Ellingham Women's Institute. **Collectanea. Scraps of English Folklore.** XI, 1904.
http://links.jstor.org.uk

Elliot, Walter. *Working the Land, Harvesting the Forest.* Scottish Borders Council, 2004.
ISBN 0-9545052-3-9

Entwhistle, Mark. *Tied to Their Work*. Interviews with Nessie Burns. Southern Reporter,
Thurs. 17 December, 1998

Fairbairn, William (shepherd, Bartlehill, Coldstream). *Evils of the Bondage System and the Best Mode of Removing Them*. Prize Essay. Andrew Elliot, Edinburgh; James Dalgleish & R. Black, Hawick; 1865.

Fairnington, Derek and **Miket**, Roger. *Views of Wooler and Glendale District, 1850–1950*. Maclean Press, 2004

Fenton, Alexander. *The Housing of Agricultural Workers in the Nineteenth Century*. Chap 10 of *Farm Servants and Labour in Lowland Scotland 1770-1914*. (Edited by **Devine**, T. M.). John Donald Publishers Ltd., 1984. ISBN 0-85976-439-7

Fenton, Alexander. *Country Life in Scotland. Our Rural Past.* John Donald Publishers Ltd., 1987. ISBN-10: 0859761886

Fenton, Alexander. *Farm Servant Life in the 17th–19th Centuries.* The Scottish Country Life Museums Trust, Edinburgh, 1975

Flinn, Michael W. *An Economic and Social History of Britain Since 1700.* MacMillan and Company Ltd., 1966

Foster, Joan. *Diaries of a Northumbrian Farmer. William Brewis 1778-1850*. Northumbrian Magazine, October/November 2004

Fox, Mr Arthur Wilson. *The Agricultural Labourer: Report upon The Poor Law Union of Glendale (Northumberland)*. Royal Commission on Labour, HMSO, 1893.

Fuller, John. *The History of Berwick-upon-Tweed.* M.D. Berwick, 1799

Gard, Robin (Editor). *Northumberland at the Turn of the Century.* Northumberland Local History Society. Oriel Press Ltd., 1970. ISBN 0-85362-100-4

Gard, Robin (Editor). *Northumberland Yesteryear.* Northumberland Local History Society. Frank Graham, 1978. ISBN 0-85983-107-8

Gibb, Dr. R. Shirra. *A Farmer's Fifty Years in Lauderdale.* Oliver & Boyd, Edinburgh & London, 1927

Gilly, Rev. W. S. *The Peasantry of the Border. An Appeal on their Behalf. 1841.* Square Edge Books, 2001. Original publication by the Warder Office, Berwick-upon-Tweed, 1841.

Hawthorne, Rosemary. *Knickers. An Intimate Appraisal.* Souvenir Press Ltd., 1991. ISBN 0-285-63061 X

Henley, Mr. *Employment of Children, Young persons and Women in Agriculture*. 1st Report. Royal Commission on Labour, HMSO, 1867.

Howarth, Ada Mary. *Life in a Scottish Border Farmhouse in the Twenties and Thirties. A Social Chronicle*. The Chapter House, Berkshire, 1998

Howatson, William. *Grain Harvesting and Harvesters*. Chap 7 of *Farm Servants and Labour in Lowland Scotland 1770-1914*. (Edited by **Devine**, T. M.). John Donald Publishers Ltd., 1984. ISBN 0-85976-439-7

Howitt, William. *Visits to Remarkable Places: Old Halls, Battlefields and Scenes Illustrative of Striking Passages in History and Poetry. Durham and Northumberland*. Vol II. Longman, Brown, Green, Longmans & Roberts, London, 1856

Hughes, Edward. *North Country Life in the Eighteenth Century. The North East 1700–1750.* University of Durham Publications, Oxford University Press, 1952

Hunter, Dr. *Inquiry on the State of the Dwellings of Rural Labourers. Northumberland and Durham.* Seventh Report of the Medical Officer, with appendix. Privy Council, 1864

Ions, Adrian. *As She is Spoke. Alnwick and North Northumbrian Language.* Aln Printers, 2006

Johnson, Cuthbert W. Esq., F.R.S. *Prompt Payment. Labour and the Poor in The Rural Districts of Devon, Somerset, Cornwall and Dorset.* Farmer's Magazine, 1850.

Kermack, W.R. *The Scottish Borders (with Galloway) to 1603.* Johnston and Bacon, 1967

Kinghorn, Jean. Recorded by **Kennington**, Fred. Berwick Record Office 608-69 & 608-70. 1999.

Lang, Jean. *North and South of Tweed.* Thomas Nelson, 1913

Leishman, James Fleming. *Linton Leaves.* Oliver & Boyd, Edinburgh, 1937.

Levitt, Ian and **Smout**, Christopher. *Farm Workers Incomes in 1843.* Chap 9 of *Farm Servants and Labour in Lowland Scotland 1770-1914.* (Edited by **Devine**, T. M.). John Donald Publishers Ltd., 1984. ISBN 0-85976-439-7

MacDougall, Ian. *Bondagers. Eight Scots Women Farm workers.* Flashbacks series. Tuckwell Press, 2000. ISBN 1-86232-122-1

Marshall, William. *The Review and Abstract of the County Reports to the Board of Agricultural Departments of England.* 1808

Mole, George. *A Man of North Northumberland, 1923–1988.* Glen Graphics. 2002.

Neville, Rev. Hastings. *A Corner in the North.* Andrew Reid and Sons, 1909. Reprinted by Frank Graham, 1980. ISBN 0-85983-131-0

Neville, Rev. Hastings. *Under a Border Tower.* Mawson, 1896

Newlands, Jean. Recorded by **Kennington**, Fred. Berwick Record Office 608-31.

Northumberland, A History of . Vol. III, 1896. Issued under the direction of The Northumberland History Committee

Northumberland, A History of . Vol. V, 1899. Issued under the direction of The Northumberland History Committee

Northumberland, A History of. Vol. XI, 1922. Issued under the direction of The Northumberland History Committee

NRO. *An Account of Farming Life in early 20th Century Wooler.* Northumberland Collections Service (formerly Northumberland Record Office). NRO 1706.

NRO. *Farm Apprentice Diary 1842.* Northumberland Collections Service (formerly Northumberland Record Office). NRO 851.

Orr, Alastair. *Farm Servants and Farm labour in the Forth Valley and South-East Lowlands.* Chap 3 of *Farm Servants and Labour in Lowland Scotland 1770-1914.* (Edited by **Devine**, T. M.). John Donald Publishers Ltd., 1984. ISBN 0-85976-439-7

Oxford English Dictionary of Historical Principles, The Shorter. 1988 Edition. ISBN 0198611269

Parsons and **White** Directories. Vol. I, 1827 & Vol. II, 1828

Pattison's Pictures, Mr. Bowes Museum, Co. Durham, 1976

Pawson, H. C., D.Sc. F.R.S.I. *A Survey of The Agriculture of Northumberland.* Royal Agricultural Society of England, 1961

Period Living, *Traditional Homes.* Ascent Publishing Ltd., October 2004.

Porteous, Katrina (Editor). *The Bonny Fisher Lad.* People's History Series Ltd, 2004.

Porter, Valerie. *English Villagers. Life in the Countryside.* Bounty Books, 2004. ISBN 0-7537-0892-2

Potter, Beatrix and **Cavaliero**, Glen (Editor). *Beatrix Potter's Journal.* Frederick Warne Publishers Ltd; Abridged edition, 1986. ISBN-10: 0723233349

Pritchard, R. E. (Editor). *Shakespeare's England.* Life in Elizabethan and Jacobean Times. Sutton Publishing Ltd, 2003. ISBN 0 7509 3211 2

Purves, Andrew. *A Shepherd Remembers.* Flashbacks series. Tuckwell Press, 2001. ISBN 1-86232-157-4

Ramage, Walter A.. *An Auld Herd's Memories*

Ridley, Nancy. *A Northumbrian Remembers.* Robert Hale, 1970.
ISBN 0-7091-1830-9

Robertson, Barbara W. *Family life: Border Farm Workers in the Early Decades of the Twentieth Century.* Chap 25 of Scottish Life and Society. The Individual and Community Life. John Donald, Edinburgh, 2005. ISBN 10:085976-6322

Robertson, Barbara W. *In Bondage. The Female Farm Worker in South-East Scotland* from T*he World is Ill Divided. Women's work in Scotland in the 19th and Early 20th Centuries.* (Edited by Gordon, Eleanor and Breittenbach, Esther). Edinburgh University Press, 1990. ISBN-10: 0748602127

Robinson, Mr. John. *Harvest Customs, Northumberland.* A paper given to the Society of Antiquaries, September 1893

Robson, Michael. *The Border Farm Worker.* Chap 5 of *Farm Servants and Labour in Lowland Scotland 1770-1914.* (Edited by **Devine**, T. M.). John Donald Publishers Ltd., 1984. ISBN 0-85976-439-7

Robson's Directory for Northumberland, 1841

Russell, Sir John. *English Farming.* Britain in Pictures series. (Introduction by Henry Williamson). William Collins, London, 1943

Rutherfurd's Southern Counties' Register and Directory. 1866. Reprinted for Borders Regional Library, Selkirk. Cedric Chivers Ltd, Bristol, 1990. ISBN 0-9516756-0-5

Sanderson, Mrs William. *Memories of Mrs William Sanderson of Cannington, Western Australia.* Unpublished.

Scott, Anne M. *Women's Working Dress on the Farms of the East Borders.* Costume periodical. Vol. 10, 1976

Scott, Donald (of Caistron). *Agriculture.* Chap 8 of The Three Northern Counties of England. (Edited by Headlam, Sir Cuthbert, Bart., D.S.O.). Northumberland Press Ltd., 1939

Sharpe, Dorothy (née Thompson). *Children of the Outbye. A Social History Of Rural Northumberland From c 1800 As Revealed In the History Of Kirknewton School With Additional Notes On The Schools At Howtel, Milfield and Southernknowe.* Glen Graphics 2007

Southern Reporter. Reel to reels celebrates '*Bondagers*'. Thurs. 10 August, 2000

Stephens, Henry F.R.S.E. *The Book of the Farm. Detailing the Labours of the Farmer, Farm-Steward, Ploughman, Shepherd, Hedger, Farm-Labourer, Fieldworker and Cattle-Man.* Revised by James MacDonald. Blackwoods, 1891

Strang, Charles Alexander. *Borders and Berwick.* Rutland Press, 1994.
ISBN 1873190-107

Swain, Margaret H., *The East Lothian Ugly.* Scottish Home and Country' (S.W.R.I.). April 1963.

Taylor, Liz. T*he Days of the Bondager*. Interviews with Mary Rutherford. The Scotsman, Wed. 5 July 1978

Taylor, Liz. *To Be a Farmer's Girl. Bondagers of the Border Counties*. Country Life Magazine, 12 October, 1978

Thompson, Dinah M. (now Dinah Iredale). *Female Agricultural Workers' Costume in the Borders from 1890 to 1939*. Unpublished essay, 1977

Thomson, Rev. John (Editor). *Voices from the Plough.* Robert Black bookseller, Hawick, 1869

Thomson, Rev. John. *Address at the Great Meeting of Ploughmen held at Lauder on 30th Jan., 1866*. Printed by Neill & Co., Edinburgh, 1866

Thomson, Wat. SA 1974-195-A3; SA 1974-195-B. School of Scottish Studies Archive, University of Edinburgh.

Trevelyan, G M. *English Social History.* Longmans, Green & Co., 1944

Wager, Hazel. *The Bondagers of South East Scotland.* Unpublished

Whellan's Directory for Northumberland, 1855

White, Walter. *Northumberland and the Border.* Chapman and Hall, 1859. cited by **Bridges**, Mike. *Records & Recollections*. Aln & Breamish Local History Society, 2006

Whyte, Jan & Kathleen. *The Changing Scottish Landscape 1500-1800*. Routledge, 1991

Williamson, Mrs of Galashiels. *The Bondage System.* Essay from *Voices from the Plough*. (Edited by Thomson, Rev. John). Robert Black bookseller, Hawick, 1869

Willis, Jean. *A Bondager's Year in Northumberland.* Unpublished

Willis, Jean. *The Other side of a Bondager's Life.* Unpublished

Wilkie, Jim. SA 1956-108-A5. School of Scottish Studies Archive University of Edinburgh.

Wood, Christopher. *Paradise Lost. Paintings of English Country Life and Landscape. 1850–1914.* Barrie and Jenkins Ltd., 1988. ISBN 0-7126-2085-0

Yetholm History Society. *Bygone Yetholm. Portrait of a Border Village 2006*. Meigle Colour Printers, Tweedbank. ISBN 0-9554149-0-3.

Index

A

Aberlady, 102
accidents, xiii, 90, 119, 130, 132, 133, 142
Aitchison, Robert, 130
Akeld, 104, 165
Aln, Glen, 112, 134, 148, 150, 171, 172
Alnwick, xi, xii, 19, 21, 33, 49, 60, 61, 62, 73, 74, 76, 77, 78, 83, 96, 97, 105, 114, 116, 130, 148, 149, 169, 181, 184
Amos, Walter of Hawick, 49
Ancroft, 153
Ancrum, xi, 51, 52
Anderson, Mary of Yetholm, 132, 134, 165
Angerton Mill, 104
Angus, John, x, 27
apprentice, Lilburn farm, 12, 45, 46, 92, 114, 135
apron, 115, 143, 156, 172, 173
Aprons, 172
Arch, Joseph, 47
arles, 62, 89, 91
Armstrong, Mr of North Charlton, 24
army puttees, 173
Arnot, Mary, 159
Arres, Tam, 151
Arres, Tom, 148
Aynsley, Robert, x
Ayton, x, 33, 34, 72

B

back rope, xii, 109, 110
Bailey, John, 8, 98, 104, 109, 119, 121, 122, 129
Bailey, Mark, 4, 182
Bainbridge, R S of Woodhorn, 106
Baker, Patrick of Lowick, 103
Bakewell, Robert, 8
baking, 64, 151
Balmer, Net, 151
Bamburgh, ix, 48
Bamburghshire, xi, 56, 57, 58, 62, 63, 64, 72
Banks of the Blackadder, xi, 35, 36
Barrasford, Nr Hexham, x, 4, 5
Barrie, Mrs Isabel of Milfield, 96, 123, 144, 178
Bartlehill, ix, 183
Bede, Cuthbert, x, 2, 112, 137, 167
Bedford, Duchess of, 162
Belford, xi, 68, 130
Bell, Emma of Mindrum, 117
Bell, Minnie, 81, 106, 126, 133, 144, 157, 165, 166

Bell, Mrs of Meldon, 150
Bellshiel, 96
belt, leather, 175
bennells, 106
Bentham, Lesley, 173, 180
Berwick Advertiser, x, xi, xii, xiii, 9, 14, 19, 31, 32, 33, 34, 35, 36, 37, 38, 39, 40, 41, 43, 44, 45, 59, 68, 69, 70, 71, 72, 84, 88, 89, 91, 92, 130, 131, 148, 149, 153, 181
Berwick and Kelso Warder, 33
Berwick Hill, Nr Morpeth, 103
Berwick Warder, xi, xii, 10, 49, 50, 51, 52, 53, 54, 55, 56, 57, 58, 62, 63, 64, 65, 66, 73, 75, 76, 78, 79, 154
Berwickshire, xii, xiii, 1, 8, 47, 54, 68, 100, 102, 113, 140, 154, 155, 157, 158, 164, 177
Berwickshire Fieldworker, A, 163
Berwickshire News, The, 85, 89
Bewick, 102
bicycles, 154
Biggar, xiv, 1, 171
binder, 109, 119, 124, 135, 169, 174
binder twine, 169, 174
bindster, 135
Bird, Alexander of Fogorig, 89
births, 140, 141
Birtley, Northumberland, 90
Black, Mary, 125
Black, Mary and Agnes of Ilderton, 84, 165
Blackden, J C, 12
blouse, 156, 165, 167, 169
bogie, xiii, xiv, 122, 124, 132, 176
bolero, 168
Bolton S.W.R.I, 164
Bolton, Nr East Saltoun, East Lothian, 97, 164, 182
bondager brooch, 165
Bondgate, Alnwick, 149
book i' bosom, 141
bookkeeping, 85
Boon, Nr Lauder, 80, 107
boots, 2, 117, 132, 143, 144, 151, 156, 169, 173
Bosanquet, R E, 121, 148
Bosanquet, R W of Rock, 96
bothy system, 36, 53
Bovine tuberculosis, 92
Bowmont Church, x
box bed, 107
box pleat, 171
Branxton, 117, 141
brat, 172
brattie, 172

Breamish Valley, Northumberland, 117
breeked, breeking, xiv, 165, 171, 172
Brewis, William of Throphill, 33, 183
Broadwood, Andrew of Drinkstone, 62
Brockholes, Nr Chirnside, 154
brooch, 165
Brook, Maureen, 122, 178
Broughton, Peebleshire, 16
Brown, David of Yearle, x, xiii, 27, 28, 139
Brown, George of Whittingham, 150
Brown, Mrs Violet, 133
Bruce, Hetha of Lowick, x, xiv, 10, 108, 110, 122, 197
Bryson, Mr, 158
Buccleuch, Duke of, 15, 102
Buchan, David, 151, 152
Buglass, Mrs, 142
Bulmers Directory, 98
Burns, Nessie, 114, 183
Butler, Josephine, 12, 138
buttons, 15, 168

C

calico, 166, 169
Cambo, 88, 104, 150, 159
Cambo Women's Insititute, 148
Campbell, Mrs Maisie of Wooler, xiii, 126, 175
Campbell, William, 73, 75
candle making, 150
canes, 158, 159, 162
Capheaton, 111
capons, 6
Carham, 117
Castle Heaton, ix, 1
cattlemen, 110, 133
Cessford, 149
Charterhall, Nr Duns, 106
Chatton Moor, 95
Chatton Sandyford, 95
Cheviot, 104, 117, 153
chickens, 6, 127
Children, 47, 54, 95, 116, 183, 185
Chillingham Barns, Northumberland, 114, 164, 180
Chillingham Castle, ix, 8
Chirnside, 89, 154
Chrinklaw, Isable, xii, 85, 86
Christon Bank, 76
church, 141, 151, 153, 166
Clark, Nancy, 111, 170, 174
Clay, John of Winfield, xi, 53, 54
cleaning, 96, 111, 143, 151
Cleghorn, Mr of Milfield, 139

38, 40, 41, 43, 44, 50, 71,
81, 100, 101, 110, 111, 116,
118, 120, 121, 123, 126,
127, 128, 129, 132, 133,
134, 139, 141, 144, 148,
150, 153, 154, 157, 158,
159, 164, 165, 172, 175,
176, 180, 182, 183, 184,
197

Wooler and District Advertiser,
  85
woollen, 156, 167, 170
Wooperton, Nr Wooler, 140,
  149
wopies, 174
Working Hours, 112

Y

Yearle, Nr Wooler, 27, 139
Yetholm, 9, 95, 122, 124, 125,
  132, 134, 165, 166, 169,
  174, 186

Z

zouave, 168

Dinah Iredale first became aware of Bondagers when she started her teaching career in Coldingham in 1972. Her first interest was with the distinctive costumes that Bondagers wore when working in the fields. In 1976, she wrote a short essay on the costume. Her interest grew into a fascination with their work, lives and social context throughout the 19th and into the early 20th centuries. She and her husband Alec moved to Doddington near Wooler in 1995 and this gave a new momentum to her research. She has amassed a large collection of books, press cuttings and photographs and by talking to former bondagers, Land Army girls and farm workers in the area she has gathered an unrivalled record of their memories.

The Glendale Local History Society was founded in 1977. It aims to bring together those interested in the history of the Glendale area of North Northumberland and to promote and encourage the study and recording of local history by means of lectures, field trips and publications.

Figure 129. Farm Staff, North Northumberland (Mrs Hetha Bruce, Lowick)